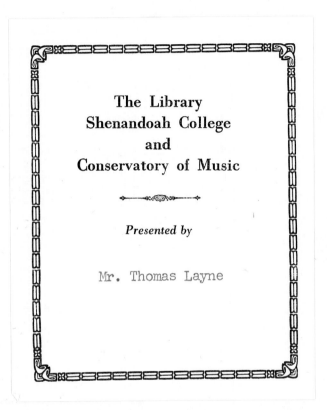

MATHEMATICS
FOR
ELEMENTARY
TEACHERS

MERRILL MATHEMATICS SERIES
Erwin Kleinfeld, Editor

MATHEMATICS
FOR
ELEMENTARY
TEACHERS

Lyle J. Dixon
Kansas State University

Charles E. Merrill Publishing Company
A Bell & Howell Company
Columbus, Ohio

Published by
Charles E. Merrill Publishing Company
A Bell & Howell Company
Columbus, Ohio 43216

ISBN: 0–675–08830–5

Library of Congress Catalog Card Number: 73–91306

1 2 3 4 5 6 7 8 9—80 79 78 77 76 75 74

Printed in the United States of America

To
C³DFG²M

Preface

This text was written primarily for pre- and in-service elementary teachers. It covers nearly all of the content found in most elementary textbook series, and some beyond. The emphasis is upon helping teachers understand the mathematics that they need in order to be better teachers of mathematics. The material is presented in an intuitive, yet somewhat rigorous, approach and is based upon a minimum background in mathematics.

The mathematical content covers most of that recommended for the training of elementary teachers. Particular attention is given to the algorithmic processes which teachers must understand before they can effectively teach these processes to their students. Emphasis is directed to geometry and the decimal representation of numbers. A short chapter (12) is devoted to the metric system and its relationship with the positional number system.

The first five chapters cover the basic material of sets, numeration, exponents, the whole numbers and the algorithmic processes for computing with whole numbers. Chapter 6 gives the student an opportunity to apply this knowledge to bases other than base ten. Following these chapters, a teacher might select the sequence of the text which parallels the sequence of elementary school arithmetic by going next to fractions and then on to decimals, followed by integers, rationals in general and real numbers. On the other hand, a teacher may choose the mathematical sequence of whole numbers, followed by integers, followed by rationals (including the chapter on fractions) and then the real numbers. Chapters 7 through 13 can be arranged in almost any sequence (except chapters 9 and 10 on geometry which must be taken in sequence) that the teacher might like to follow. The time needed to cover this material is one term.

I am grateful to Charles E. Merrill Publishing Company for giving me the opportunity to contribute to the literature and for their assistance in preparing the text; to my family for their encouragement; and to Mrs. Lynn Caldwell and Mrs. Phyllis Pickel for typing the manuscript.

Lyle J. Dixon

Contents

3   Set Theory   19

4   The Set W   41

MATHEMATICS
FOR
ELEMENTARY
TEACHERS

1

SYSTEMS OF
NUMERATION

1.1   Introduction

Man's first recognition of the need for numbers probably arose from his need to count; in order to count, he needed to name the numbers that he wanted to use. By naming the numbers, he was able to distinguish one from another and could communicate the quantity involved to others around him. Thus, the names came to have general acceptance within given corners of civilization. We continue this practice today by assigning specific meanings to words like *one, two, ten* or *million*. A system of naming numbers, for example, the counting numbers, is called a *system of numeration*.

In order to understand a system of numeration, we must distinguish clearly the difference between a number and a numeral. A *number* is an abstraction; it cannot be written. A *numeral* is the written symbol which represents a number. For example, we can use the numeral 2 to represent the numbers which tells us how many items are in the box ⬚*△⬚. We can also use two, II, dos, 1 + 1 or any other symbols or words. However, these are merely names and are distinct from the *concept* of the number itself. In this chapter we are concerned with different ways to name numbers, i.e., with numerals.

If numeration is done in a systematic way (as we do in our Hindu-Arabic system), we can continue to create names for any new or larger numbers by a manner spelled out within the system of numeration. For illustration, we will examine two systems which are quite old and will compare these with the system we now use.

1.2   The Egyptian System of Numeration

The Egyptian system is not the oldest one known, but the Egyptians kept records as early as 5000 B.C., so we know as much about their system as any other. At some time they probably had names for all numbers, but quite early in their written history we find the use of symbols in naming numbers. For example, they used a single vertical mark for *one*, two vertical marks for *two* and so on until they had nine vertical marks for *nine*. These could have been written as follows:

Number Represented	one	two	three	four	five	six	seven	eight	nine
Egyptian Numeral				||	||	|||	|||	||| |||	||| |||
	|	||	|||	||	|||	|||	|||	|||	|||

These are called *tally marks* and are often used in modern day practices, for example, votes at election time are tallied to determine the winner.

If one were to continue indefinitely this procedure of using tally marks, the system would become quite burdensome to write and equally difficult to read. The Egyptians recognized this and used a new symbol ∩ for *ten*. Combining this symbol with tally marks enabled the Egyptians to extend their system to larger numbers. Thus they had the following table:

Number Represented	ten	eleven	twelve	thirteen	...	eighteen	nineteen
Egyptian Numeral	∩	∩|	∩||	∩|||		∩ || |||	∩ ||| |||

The value of the number in our system is the sum of the numbers represented by each Egyptian symbol. For example, ∩||| represents one ten and three ones, which we call thirteen. For twenty, the Egyptians used two ∩'s, or ∩∩; for twenty-one, ∩∩|; twenty-five, ∩∩|||, and so on. With this kind of system for writing numerals, one could write numerals as large as 99. The following table presents some comparisons of the Egyptian system with our Hindu-Arabic way of writing numerals.

Hindu-Arabic	28	43	61	86	99
Egyptian	∩∩ || ||| |||	∩∩∩∩ |||	∩∩∩ ∩∩∩ |	∩∩∩∩ ∩∩∩∩ |||	∩∩∩∩∩ ∩∩∩∩ |||| |||||

One interesting observation might be made at this point: Could eleven be written as |∩? If the number represented in our system is equal to the sum of the values represented by each Egyptian symbol, then the answer could be yes, for |∩ means one one and one ten, which is eleven. Although the Egyptians did not write numerals this way, it could be done. The placing of the symbols is not important in determining the value of the number represented.

Other symbols which the Egyptians used are presented in the following table.

Number Represented	Symbol Used	
10	∩	(heel bone)
100	ϙ	(scroll)
1,000	⚇	(lotus flower)
10,000	⌐	(pointing finger)
100,000	⌒⌒	(burbot fish)
1,000,000	⍦	(astonished man)

The Egyptians used no larger representations, as they apparently needed no larger numbers.

Exercises

1. What numbers do the following Egyptian numerals represent?

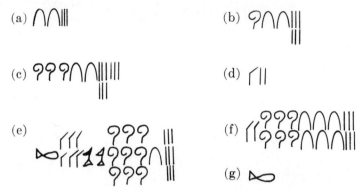

(a) (b)

(c) (d)

(e) (f)

(g)

2. Write the following numerals as Egyptian numerals:
(a) 43   (b) 138
(c) 392   (d) 2,003
(e) 24,982   (f) 999
(g) 121,407   (h) 10,000

3. Which system of writing numerals, ours or the Egyptians', is the most efficient as far as writing is concerned?

1.3 The Roman System of Numeration

The Roman system is not quite as old as but is somewhat similar in structure to the Egyptian system. However, the Roman system contains features which the Egyptian lacks, so we will examine it briefly.

Like the Egyptian system, the Roman system begins by using I's in combination to represent certain numbers, for example,

Number	one	two	three	four	five
Roman Numeral	I	II	III	IV	V

Two important differences exist between this table and the Egyptian table for the same numbers. A new symbol V is first introduced for five; in the Egyptian system, a new symbol first is introduced for ten. The second and more significant difference is noted for four. The symbol IV means one less than five; no corresponding type of symbol exists in the Egyptian system of numeration. The technique of using IV as a symbol makes use of what is called the *subtractive principle* in writing numerals.

The symbol IV must be read as "one less than five"; IX is read as "one less than ten." Other similar symbols are used for certain numbers, for example, XL, XC, CM, etc. The use of the subtractive principle in writing these symbols implies that we must be very careful how we write symbols. For example, IV and VI are clearly different and are used to represent different numbers. In contrast, $\bigwedge$ and $\bigwedge|$ in the Egyptian system are different in writing but represent the same number. The Roman system is the only historical system which uses this principle.

The use of VII for seven continues the idea that the number represented is the sum of the values of all symbols involved, that is, VII represents the sum of one five and two ones. This principle is called the *additive principle* in writing numerals. Thus the Roman system of numeration uses the same principle as the Egyptian system, *in addition to* using the subtractive principle at selected places.

Other symbols used by the Romans are as follows:

Arabic Numeral	Roman Symbol
10	X
50	L
100	C
500	D
1000	M

Some typical representations in Roman numerals follow.

Arabic Numeral	14	29	46	98	369
Roman Numeral	XIV	XXIX	XLVI	XCVIII	CCCLXIX

Exercises

1.   Write the following Roman numerals in our system of numeration:
(a) XVI   (b) XXXIX
(c) XLIV   (d) LXXIX
(e) CCXL   (f) DC
(g) MMCDXLIV   (h) MCMXLIX

2.　　Write the following as Roman numerals:

(a)　9　　　　　　　　　　　　(b)　49
(c)　167　　　　　　　　　　　(d)　599
(e)　1,004　　　　　　　　　　(f)　3,041
(g)　1,971　　　　　　　　　　(h)　444

3.　　Is the Roman system of numeration more efficient in writing than the Egyptian system?

4.　　Which system, Roman or Egyptian, requires more symbols to write all numerals up to 9,999? How many Egyptian symbols are needed? How many Roman?

1.4　　The Hindu-Arabic System of Numeration

If the question were asked, How many women presidents of the United States have there been before 1970? how would the answer be written in Egyptian and Roman numerals? The Egyptians and Romans apparently did not recognize the need for a symbol for zero, or found that the verbal word was sufficient, because a symbol for zero is nonexistent in their systems. Since zero has special properties in adding and multiplying, it is probable that neither civilization found it necessary to invent a symbol.

However, a segment of another civilization in India found it convenient to adopt a symbol for zero and to use this symbol with nine others to develop a new system of numeration which has proven to be superior to all others created. The Hindus began to use our present system of writing numerals sometime before A.D 600–800. Exactly how long before is not known because historical records were destroyed by periodic invasions of other peoples, and hence we can only speculate when this system was actually developed. After Arabic tribes invaded India, the Arabic world adopted the Hindu system themselves. Still another invasion, the Crusades, resulted in the dissemination of the Hindu-Arabic system throughout the rest of the civilized world in Europe. Thus the name used today to describe the system is the Hindu-Arabic system of numeration.

The system begins with ten independent symbols used to name ten numbers. The following table shows the meaning for the symbols:

Number Represented	zero	one	two	three	four	five	six	seven	eight	nine
Numeral Used	0	1	2	3	4	5	6	7	8	9

The symbols are interpretations of the Hindu symbols which were used for centuries and constitute the basis for all symbols to represent all other numbers. We say this is a base ten system, for we use ten basic symbols, 0 through 9, to construct a system of numeration. After we have reached the number nine we must create a new number, since we have used all of the independent symbols. This new number must be made from combinations of the first ten numerals. Thus we write ten as 10 and read this symbol as "one zero" or use the word *ten*. The symbol 10 indicates that we have exhausted one group of symbols (0, 1, 2, . . ., 9) and are now starting on the next group. This implies that 10 means one base of ten ones and zero more ones. In similar fashion, 11 means one base of ten ones and one more one. Since the base of this system is ten, 10 means one ten and zero ones. The term *ones* refers to one of the ten basic symbols, 0 through 9. Although it is composed of two different symbols, 10 must be considered as a *single* symbol. Likewise, 23 means two tens and three ones and is a single symbol. This pattern of development is used to create further symbols representing larger numbers.

A system of numeration in which the position of the various parts in a given symbol is important is called a *positional system of numeration*. Since 154 and 541 represent different numbers, it is evident that the order or arrangement of symbols is important in the Hindu-Arabic system. Neither the Egyptian nor the Roman system is a positional system of numeration, although the Roman system makes limited use of the subtractive principle for certain individual symbols such as IV or IX.

Numbers larger than ten are represented by other arrangements of these ten independent symbols (0, 1, 2, . . ., 9). For example,

Number	eleven	twelve	thirteen . . . eighteen	nineteen
Numeral	11	12	13 . . . 18	19

In each numeral we find a 1 in a certain position (called the *tens* position), followed by each of the different independent symbols. For twenty we must select a different grouping of symbols, for we have used all possible two-symbol representations (also called two-digit representations) with 1 in the tens position. Thus we start over at twenty with the symbol 20. Then we repeat the pattern: 21, 22, 23, 24, . . ., 29; after 29 comes 30 and the pattern continues. In fact, we continue this sequence of symbols until we come to 99. At this point, there are no more two-digit representations, for we have used all possible arrangements of two symbols. Hence, we go to using three symbols, i.e., after 99 comes 100. We repeat the same technique at 100 that we did for 10 and we can, therefore, use the same patterns to write other numerals after 100. For example, 101, 102, 103, 104, . . ., 108, 109, 110, 111, 112, 113, 114, ... This continues until 999, and we repeat the pattern for the next number by writing 1,000.

The Hindu-Arabic technique of writing numerals is quite ingenious. It requires only ten symbols and the use of a systematic pattern. Extremely large numbers can be written with relative ease, a condition not found in the Roman or the Egyptian system of numeration. There are other advantanges which will become obvious as we continue working with the Hindu-Arabic positional system of numeration.

One other comment about this system is also in order here. That there are ten independent symbols (0, 1, 2, . . ., 9) is probably due to the fact that we are equipped, via nature, with ten fingers (also called *digits*). However, it is possible to use more or fewer than ten symbols and to create other positional systems with the same ease as the Hindu-Arabic base ten system. For example, if we were to use only five symbols, we would be using a *base five* system. We will explore more about the other base systems in chapter 6.

1.5   Expanded Numeral Form

In writng a numeral such as 20, we can observe that there is a second meaning for the numeral. Since we know that 20 is 10 + 10, or two tens, we could write 20 as $2 \cdot 10$. Thus the 2 in the tens position means two tens. Similarly, 35 means three tens and five, and since five means five ones, 35 means three tens and five ones. Furthermore, 247 can mean two hundreds, four tens and seven ones, with 2 in the hundreds position. If we apply this meaning to every symbol in the Hindu-Arabic system, we can write a corresponding statement. For example,

$$20 = \text{two tens and zero ones}$$
$$35 = \text{three tens and five ones}$$
(A) $$247 = \text{two hundreds, four tens and seven ones}$$
$$4,392 = \text{four thousands, three hundreds, nine tens and two ones}$$
$$309 = \text{three hundreds, zero tens and nine ones}$$

The words can be replaced by symbols:

$$20 = 2 \cdot 10 + 0 \cdot 1$$
$$35 = 3 \cdot 10 + 5 \cdot 1$$
(B) $$247 = 2 \cdot 100 + 4 \cdot 10 + 7 \cdot 1$$
$$4,392 = 4 \cdot 1,000 + 3 \cdot 100 + 9 \cdot 10 + 2 \cdot 1$$
$$309 = 3 \cdot 100 + 0 \cdot 10 + 9 \cdot 1$$

A numeral written in this last form is written in *expanded numeral form*.

Expanded numeral form has at least two distinct advantages. First, it clearly indicates that the 2 of 20, 247 and 4,392 are in different positions and hence have different values in each position, which further illustrates that the Hindu-Arabic system is a positional system. Second, the numeral form of (B) demonstrates that each position has some relation to the base of the system, i.e., base ten. (In chapter 2, we shall see a slightly different form of the tens when we use an exponent to write each positional value.) The word form of (A) gives us a convenient way to read (in words) the various numerals, once we assign a word name for each position, and it allows us to read any numeral and provides a means of communicating to others around us. For example, we often see in newspaper articles that government expects to spend 15 million dollars or 7 billion dollars. These are, of course, large numerals which require zeros in certain positions, i.e., 15 million = 15,000,000. The actual size or amount of some of these enormous numbers is probably beyond our comprehension, but we are able to understand the numerical representations.

Exercises

1.   Write the following numerals in expanded numeral form (A) and in expanded numeral form (B).
(a) 13   (b) 48
(c) 363   (d) 4,002
(e) 56,789   (f) 123,456
(g) 0   (h) 6

2.   Write the following expanded numeral forms as positional numerals.
(a) $3 \cdot 10 + 4 \cdot 1$ (b) $4 \cdot 100 + 0 \cdot 10 + 6 \cdot 1$
(c) $2 \cdot 1,000 + 2 \cdot 100 + 2 \cdot 10 + 2 \cdot 1$ (d) $6 \cdot 1$

3.   What is the positional numeral which represents $3 \cdot 100 + 17 \cdot 10 + 14 \cdot 1$? How is this written correctly in expanded numeral form?

4.   Suppose we wish to have a positional system of numeration in which there are only five independent symbols (0, 1, 2, 3, 4). Write the first 27 numerals in this base five system of numeration.

5.   If in the base five system of Exercise 4 we have "34," what are its expanded numeral forms (A) and (B)?

6.   Given 213 in base five system, what is the (B) form for its expanded numeral?

7.   The following chart is used to name the positions of base ten

numerals:

4	9	8	7	6	5	3	2	3	4
billions	hundred millions	ten millions	millions	hundred thousands	ten thousands	thousands	hundreds	tens	ones

(a) What position is 4 in 342,956?
(b) What position is 6 in 27,693?
(c) What position is 7 in 72,000,000?
(d) What position is 1 in 342,591?

References

Smith, David E. *History of Mathematics*, Vol. 2. Boston: Ginn and Company, 1925.

Smith, David E. *Number Stories of Long Ago*. Washington, D.C.: National Council of Teachers of Mathematics, 1969.

Smith, David E., and Ginsburg, I. *Numbers and Numerals*. Washington, D.C.: National Council of Teachers of Mathematics, 1937.

2

NUMERALS IN EXPONENTIAL FORM

2.1 Introduction

In this chapter we will develop an exponential form for the expanded numeral. In order to do so, we need to define and develop some properties of exponents for natural numbers.* Exponents are useful in many ways, as we will see as we progress through our study of number systems.

2.2 The Natural Numbers as Exponents

Numbers such as 100, 1,000 or 10,000 can be written as multiplication problems; for example,

$$100 = 10 \cdot 10$$
$$1,000 = 10 \cdot 10 \cdot 10$$
$$10,000 = 10 \cdot 10 \cdot 10 \cdot 10$$

---

* A natural number is a counting number $(1, 2, 3, 4, 5, \ldots)$.

Since 100 can be written as the product of two factors, with each factor being ten, it is possible to use what is called *exponential notation* as another means of representation. For example,

$$100 = 10 \cdot 10 = 10^2 \quad \text{where } 10^2 \text{ means } 10 \cdot 10$$

Also,

$$1,000 = 10 \cdot 10 \cdot 10 = 10^3$$

$$10,000 = 10 \cdot 10 \cdot 10 \cdot 10 = 10^4$$

The numerals 2, 3 and 4 of these examples are called *exponents* and the numeral 10 is called the *base*.

The use of exponents provides a convenient way of writing very large numbers. For example,

$$100,000 = 10^5$$

$$10,000,000 = 10^7$$

$$1,000,000,000 = 10^9$$

These equations can be verified; for example,

$$10^5 = 10 \cdot 10 \cdot 10 \cdot 10 \cdot 10$$

which yields 100,000 when multiplied.

From these examples it is possible to formulate a definition.

DEFINITION 2.1 If n is a natural number, 10^n equals the product of 10 multiplied times itself n number of times, or 10 used as a factor n number of times. If $n = 1$, there is only one factor of 10, and $10^1 = 10$. If $n = 5$, there are five factors, and $10^5 = 100,000$.

2.3   Use of Exponents in Expanded Numeral Form

In Sec. 1.7 the following examples of expanded numeral forms were presented:

$$20 = 2 \cdot 10 + 0 \cdot 1$$

$$35 = 3 \cdot 10 + 5 \cdot 1$$

$$247 = 2 \cdot 100 + 4 \cdot 10 + 7 \cdot 1$$

$$4,392 = 4 \cdot 1,000 + 3 \cdot 100 + 9 \cdot 10 + 2 \cdot 1$$

$$309 = 3 \cdot 100 + 0 \cdot 10 + 9 \cdot 1$$

Since each expanded numeral contains the base 10 and products of tens, we can write these in exponential form. For example,

$$20 = 2 \cdot 10 + 0 \cdot 1 = 2 \cdot 10^1 + 0 \cdot 1$$

$$35 = 3 \cdot 10 + 5 \cdot 1 = 3 \cdot 10^1 + 5 \cdot 1$$

$$247 = 2 \cdot 100 + 4 \cdot 10 + 7 \cdot 1 = 2 \cdot 10^2 + 4 \cdot 10^1 + 7 \cdot 1$$

$$4{,}392 = 4 \cdot 1{,}000 + 3 \cdot 100 + 9 \cdot 10 + 2 \cdot 1$$

$$= 4 \cdot 10^3 + 3 \cdot 10^2 + 9 \cdot 10 + 2 \cdot 1$$

$$309 = 3 \cdot 100 + 0 \cdot 10 + 9 \cdot 1 = 3 \cdot 10^2 + 0 \cdot 10^1 + 9 \cdot 1$$

Thus it is possible to use exponents to write expanded numeral forms in the Hindu-Arabic system of numeration.

Exercises

1.　Using Definition 2.1, write the following in exponential form:
(a) $10 \cdot 10 \cdot 10$ (b) $10 \cdot 10 \cdot 10 \cdot 10 \cdot 10 \cdot 10$
(c) 10 (d) 1 trillion
(e) 10 million

2.　Express as products of 10's:
(a) 10^2 (b) 10^4
(c) 10^8 (d) 10

3.　Using exponents, write the following in expanded numeral form:
(a) 348 (b) 6,999
(c) 72 (d) 46,521
(e) 10,003 (f) 327,723
(g) 4,927,869

4.　Although it is easier and more efficient to write 1 million as 10^6, it is never expressed in this form in newspapers. Why?

2.4　Properties of Exponents

We will develop some properties of exponents which are useful in applications of expanded numerals and other mathematical expressions.

Suppose we wish to find the value of the expression $10^2 \cdot 10^3$. By using the definition of 10^2 and 10^3, we can write

$$10^2 \cdot 10^3 = (10 \cdot 10)(10 \cdot 10 \cdot 10)$$

Computing, we obtain

$$10^2 \cdot 10^3 = (10 \cdot 10)(10 \cdot 10 \cdot 10) = 100,000$$

If we write 100,000 in exponential form, we obtain 10^5. Thus

$$10^2 \cdot 10^3 = 10^5$$

Suppose the problem were $10^4 \cdot 10^5$. If we repeat the above steps, we obtain

$$10^4 \cdot 10^5 = 10^9$$

This suggests that there may be a shorter way of finding the product.

THEOREM 2.1   If p and q are natural numbers, then $10^p \cdot 10^q = 10^{p+q}$.

We can prove Theorem 2.1 by applying the definition of the exponent and finding the corresponding product. The steps are similar to those used in the above examples; it is left to the student to do the actual computing. (Every student of mathematics should have pencil and paper at hand to work out problems. Learning mathematics requires participation.)

We have been discussing exponents for those cases where the exponents are natural numbers, i.e., 1, 2, 3, 4, ... Now we wish to extend this concept to include 0, which is not a natural number. The definition of an exponent suggests that we would have zero factors of 10, but this is not exactly clear since zero factors of 10 is no multiplication problem at all. If the zero exponent is to behave like other exponents, it should also satisfy Theorem 2.1. Consider the following:

$$10^p \cdot 10^0 = 10^{p+0}$$

We know $p + 0$ equals p, so we have

$$10^p \cdot 10^0 = 10^p$$

What number multiplied by 10^p yields 10^p? What number is multiplied by 5 to get 5? If 10^0 is to satisfy Theorem 2.1, 10^0 must equal 1. Hence we define the zero exponent with base 10 as $10^0 = 1$. Once this is defined, it is possible to return to the expanded numeral form by using exponents and by writing every position as a power of 10. For example,

$$234 = 2 \cdot 100 + 3 \cdot 10 + 4 \cdot 1$$
$$= 2 \cdot 10^2 + 3 \cdot 10^1 + 4 \cdot 10^0$$
$$4{,}567 = 4 \cdot 1{,}000 + 5 \cdot 100 + 6 \cdot 10 + 7 \cdot 1$$
$$= 4 \cdot 10^3 + 5 \cdot 10^2 + 6 \cdot 10^1 + 7 \cdot 10^0$$

The pattern of exponents in these examples is evident; the exponents decrease by 1 from left to right. The zero exponent fits this pattern, so the definition of 10^0 holds true here also.

The introduction of parentheses or other grouping symbols can change the value of an expression and require a different method of computation to be used. For example,

$$(10 \cdot 10)^3 = (10 \cdot 10)(10 \cdot 10)(10 \cdot 10)$$

The product can be rearranged:

$$(10 \cdot 10)(10 \cdot 10)(10 \cdot 10) = (10 \cdot 10 \cdot 10)(10 \cdot 10 \cdot 10)$$
$$(10 \cdot 10 \cdot 10)(10 \cdot 10 \cdot 10) = 10^3 \cdot 10^3$$

Hence,

$$(10 \cdot 10)^3 = 10^3 \cdot 10^3$$

which suggests the following theorem.

THEOREM 2.2 $(10 \cdot 10)^p = 10^p \cdot 10^p.$

If $10 \cdot 10$ were written as 10^2, then we would have

$$(10^2)^3 = 10^2 \cdot 10^2 \cdot 10^2$$

and further

$$(10^2)^3 = 10^6$$

This suggests another theorem.

THEOREM 2.3 $(10^p)^q = 10^{p \cdot q}.$

Exercises

1. Using exponents for all positions, write the following in expanded numeral form.
(a) 37
(b) 69
(c) 345
(d) 3,456
(e) 20,905
(f) 109,872
(g) 1,000,027
(h) 0

2. Using Theorem 2.1, find the following products.
(a) $10^3 \cdot 10^7$
(b) $10 \cdot 10^4$
(c) $10^2 \cdot 10^0$
(d) $10^4 \cdot 10^3$
(e) $10^1 \cdot 10^1$
(f) $10 \cdot 10 \cdot 10^6$
(g) $10^0 \cdot 10^0$
(h) $10^2 \cdot 10^3 \cdot 10^0$

3. Write the answers for the following problems in exponential form:
(a) $(10 \cdot 10)^3$
(b) $10^3 \cdot 10^2$
(c) $(10^3)^2$
(d) $(10^3)^2$
(e) $(10^4 \cdot 10^3)^2$
(f) $(10^4)^3 \cdot (10^2)^5$
(g) $(10^2 \cdot 10^3 \cdot 10^4)^0$
(h) $10^0 \cdot (10^6)^3$

2.5 Bases Other than Ten for Use with Exponents

In all problems and discussions of exponents we have used only 10 as the base in exponential expressions. However, it is not necessary to limit exponents only to powers of ten; and if we use other natural numbers, we need the following definition.

DEFINITION 2.2 If a and n are natural numbers, a^n equals the product of a multiplied times itself n number of times, or a used as a factor n number of times.

For example,

$$2^3 = 2 \cdot 2 \cdot 2 \quad \text{where } a = 2, n = 3$$

$$3^4 = 3 \cdot 3 \cdot 3 \cdot 3 \quad \text{where } a = 3, n = 4$$

$$11^2 = 11 \cdot 11 \quad \text{where } a = 11, n = 2$$

Definition 2.2 extends the application of exponents to many possibilities and requires us to re-examine the theorems and definitions to verify that they still hold true for factors having bases other than 10.

> **THEOREM 2.1'** $a^p \cdot a^q = a^{p+q}$.

The proof of Theorem 2.1' is the same as the proof of Theorem 2.1, except that the variable a replaces 10. For example,

$$3^2 \cdot 3^4 = 3^6$$

$$7^4 \cdot 7^{11} = 7^{15}$$

$$11^2 \cdot 11^3 = 11^5$$

We also can verify that the zero exponent can be generalized to base a and we have the following definition.

> **DEFINITION 2.3** $a^0 = 1$, where a is a natural number.

In a like manner, the other theorems can be generalized to base a.

> **THEOREM 2.2'** $(a \cdot a)^p = a^p \cdot a^p$.

> **THEOREM 2.3'** $(a^p)^q = a^{p \cdot q}$.

Theorem 2.2' is also true if the factors are not equal, i.e., if both factors are not a. Thus the following theorem is true.

> **THEOREM 2.4** $(a \cdot b)^p = a^p \cdot b^p$.

Exercises

1.   Write the following in exponential form:

(a) $2 \cdot 2 \cdot 2$ (b) $4 \cdot 4 \cdot 4 \cdot 4 \cdot 4$ (c) 8   (d) 9

2.   Express each of the following as a product:
(a) 3^2 (b) 6^3 (c) 12^2 (d) 11^4

3.   Using the theorems, find the following; use exponential notation to write your answers.

(a) $2^7 \cdot 2^1$ (b) $3^2 \cdot 3^4$
(c) $8^2 \cdot 8^3$ (d) $(2 \cdot 3)^4$
(e) $(2^4)^5$ (f) $(6^2 \cdot 9^2)^3$
(g) $(4^2 \cdot 5^3)^4$ (h) $(3^0 \cdot 4^2)^0$

4.   Using only four 1's in each expression, write exponential expressions equal to each of the numbers one through ten. You may use any of the operations from arithmetic, for example,

$$(1 + 1)^{1+1} = 4$$

5.   Verify that Theorems 2.1', 2.2' and 2.3' hold when they include zero as an exponent.

3

SET THEORY

3.1   Introduction

In chapters 1 and 2 we examined some ways in which numbers are
represented by numerals, i.e., we examined the naming of numbers. In
order to make our study of numbers meaningful, it is necessary not
only to name numbers but also to define them. In this chapter we will
study ways of defining number through the use of sets, to provide for
a better understanding of mathematics.

3.2   Definition of a Set

In the ordinary process of everyday affairs we often organize collections
or groups of individuals, for example, the class of students in college to

which you belong, the group of students enrolled in a mathematics course or the group of faculty members at a college or university. In addition, animals and objects can be organized into groups or collections, for example, vertebrate and invertebrate animals, fiction and nonfiction books. In mathematics, such collections or groups of objects are called *sets*, and the objects are called *elements* of that set.

In each of the sets mentioned above, the elements have a common characteristic or collection of common characteristics. However, this is not a prerequisite or criterion for organizing a set. It is possible for us to arbitrarily bring together items to form a set, and these items need not have something in common, other than the fact that they are members of our set. In other words, a set is defined by its elements, not by what the elements have in common. For example, we could choose to group the following and call it set X:

$$X = \{\text{dog, car, king, window, Tom}\}$$

Sets having elements *without* common characteristics are generally described by listing the elements in the set, as in the above example. Sets having elements *with* common characteristics are generally described by their properties; these will be discussed further in the following section on set notation.

3.3   Set Notation and Membership

A set is generally symbolized by a capital letter, for example, the set A, B or C. The members, or elements, of a set are enclosed by curly brackets, or braces. For example, the set of even prime numbers* is written in set notation as

$$A = \{\text{even primes}\}$$

In set notation an equal sign means that the quantities on the left and right are both names for the same thing, and since 2 is the only even prime number, set A can be expressed also as

$$A = \{2\}$$

To express membership in set notation, the symbol $\in$ is used, meaning "is an element of" or "belongs to." For example, we could

---

* A prime number is a natural number, other than 1, whose only factors are 1 and itself, e.g., $5 = 5 \cdot 1$, $29 = 29 \cdot 1$.

say, "2 is a member of the set of even primes," or "2 is an element of set A." In set notation this becomes

$$2 \in \{\text{even primes}\} \quad \text{or} \quad 2 \in A$$

If we wish to indicate that an element is *not* a member of a certain set, we use the symbol $\notin$, for example, $3 \notin A$. Some additional examples of membership notation are

$1 \in \{\text{natural numbers}\}$ and $0 \notin \{\text{natural numbers}\}$

$2/3 \in \{\text{all fractions}\}$ and $23 \notin \{\text{all fractions}\}$

Kansas $\in \{\text{all states}\}$ and Brazil $\notin \{\text{all states}\}$

$5 \in \{1, 5, 9, 19\}$ and $6 \notin \{1, 5, 9, 19\}$

square $\in \{\text{all quadrilaterals}\}$ and circle $\notin \{\text{all quadrilaterals}\}$

It is possible to have a set which contains no members, called an *empty* set and symbolized by $\varnothing$. For example, the set of all students who are 20 feet tall is an empty set because it has no members.

The membership of a set can be described in two ways, one by listing and the other by describing what common characteristics the members possess. For example, the set of all states in the United States could be described by a listing of the names of each state, and the roster of the students in your class describes the set of students enrolled in a course at a particular time of day. On the other hand, if we wish to describe the set of even natural numbers, we would not be able to list all of them, for there are an infinite number and to list them is impossible. Hence we can use the technique of describing common characteristics and describe the set of numbers by this characteristic, i.e., even natural numbers, called set E. Suppose we wish to know if 198 is a member of this set. One hundred ninety-eight is even (by definition an even natural number is exactly divisible by 2) and is a natural number. Therefore 198 belongs to the set.

The set of even numbers can be written as a description:

$$E = \{x \mid x \text{ is an even natural number}\}$$

which is read "E is the set of all x such that x is an even natural number." The set E can also be written as a list:

$$E = \{2, 4, 6, 8, 10, 12, \ldots\}$$

where the three dots means to continue in the manner indicated by the first members listed.

3.4   Intersection of Sets

A particular element or a set of elements can belong to more than one set. For example, let

$$A = \{1, 2, 3, 4, 5, 6, 7, 8, 9, 10\}$$

and

$$B = \{2, 4, 6, 8, 10, 12, 14, 16, 18, 20\}$$

Set A contains the natural numbers from 1 through 10, and set B contains the even natural numbers from 2 through 20. The elements 2, 4, 6, 8 and 10 belong to *both* sets and form their own new set, called, for example, set C. Set C, containing the elements found in both sets A and B, is called the *intersection* of sets A and B. In set notation the symbol ∩ is used to denote intersection, or membership in two or more sets. Thus,

$$C = A \cap B$$

or

$$C = A \cap B = \{x \mid x \in A \text{ and } x \in B\}$$

The condition for membership in $A \cap B$ is determined by specifying that $x \in A \cap B$ if and only if $x \in A$ and $x \in B$. We may observe as a consequence of this definition that the "intersection of" is a binary operation, operating on two sets and producing another set.

Exercises

1.   Define the membership rules which describe all those students who are enrolled in your mathematics class.

2.   Given the following description, list the members of each set:
(a) all multiples of 3 which are less than 19 and greater than 3 itself
(b) all even natural numbers which are greater than 7 but less than 11
(c) all odd natural numbers which are greater than 198 and less than 189

3.   Describe the set obtained by the intersection of the following pairs of sets:
(a) $\{1, 3, 5, 7, 9,\} \cap \{7, 9, 3, 11, 0\}$
(b) $\{*, \triangle, \square, \wedge\} \cap \{;, \square, \wedge, ?, !, -\}$
(c) $\{0, 1, 2, 3,\} \cap \{4, 5, 6, 7\}$

4.   Determine the set formed by each of the following:
(a) $\{0, 1, 2, 3, 4, 5,\} \cap \{0, 1, 3, 5\} \cap \{0, 3, 6, 9\}$

(b) $\{2, 4, 6, 8\} \cap \{2, 4, 6\} \cap \{4, 6, 8, 10\}$
(c) $\{1, 3, 5, 7, 9\} \cap \{2, 4, 6, 8, 10\} \cap \{1, 2, 3, 4, 5, 6, 7, 8\}$
(d) $A \cap \varnothing$, where A is any given set
(e) $A \cap A$, where A is any given set

5. Using the form $\{x \mid x$ is an even number$\}$, write in set notation:
(a) the set of all multiples of 5
(b) the set of all odd numbers
(c) the set of all states in the United States

6. Two sets are said to be *disjoint* if and only if $A \cap B = \varnothing$. Give an example of this definition.

3.5   Union of Sets

Consider the following problem: Given sets A and B where $A = \{0, 1, 2\}$ and $B = \{2, 4, 5\}$, determine the set which contains the elements of set A *or* the elements of set B, *or* both. If we call the new set C, then the membership of C consists of those elements which belong either to A or to set B, or to both. Thus, $C = \{0, 1, 2, 4, 5\}$. Here the memberships of set A and set B are included in the membership of set C; i.e., set C contains the elements of set A as well as the elements of set B and no elements other than those in set A or in set B. When this condition is satisfied, set C is called the *union* of sets A and B. This notion of the union of two sets can be formalized precisely as follows:

$$C = A \cup B = \{x \mid x \in A \text{ or } x \in B\}$$

A word of caution about the word *or*: This is the *inclusive* or, meaning one or the other or both, not the *exclusive* or, meaning one or the other but not both. The next example should help clarify this definition.

What is the union of $\{0, 1, 2, 3, 4\}$ and $\{2, 4, 6, 7\}$? The union of these two sets is a set whose members are

$$\{0, 1, 2, 3, 4, 6, 7\}$$

Notice that the elements 2 and 4 are listed only once, instead of as follows:

$$\{0, 1, 2, 2, 3, 4, 4, 6, 7\}$$

The 2's represent the same number and need to be listed only once to be included in the union. The same holds true for the element 4.

Symbolically we write

$$\{0, 1, 2, 3, 4,\} \cup \{2, 4, 6, 7\} = \{0, 1, 2, 3, 4, 6, 7\}$$

where the $\cup$ represents the union of the sets in question. Determine

$$C = A \cup B \quad \text{where } A = \{*, \triangle, \square\} \quad \text{and} \quad B = \{1, 2, \nabla\}$$

The elements of set C are the members of set A and members of set B. Hence,

$$C = \{*, \triangle, \square, 1, 2, \nabla\}$$

Exercises

1.   Define the membership rule which describes all those students who are enrolled in your mathematics class and all students who are sophomores in college.

2.   Describe in words the set obtained by taking the union of the set of even integers and the set of odd integers. Write in set notation.

3.   If $C = A \cup B$, determine set C if
(a) $A = \{0, 2, 4, 6\}$ and $B = \{1, 3, 5, 7\}$.
(b) $A = \{1, 3, 5, 7, 9\}$ and $B = \{3, 5, 7, 9, 11\}$.
(c) $A = \{x \mid x \text{ is a horse}\}$ and $B = \{y \mid y \text{ is a cow}\}$.
(d) $A = \{x \mid x \text{ is a vertebrate}\}$ and $B = \{y \mid y \text{ is a human being}\}$.

4.   Determine the set described by the following:
(a) $\{2, 3\} \cup \{3, 4, 5\} \cup \{2, 5, 6\}$ (b) $\{1, 2, 3\} \cup \{2, 4, 6\} \cup \varnothing$
(c) $[\{2, 3\} \cup \{3, 4\}] \cap \{3\}$ (d) $\{2, 3\} \cup [\{3, 4\} \cap \{3\}]$

5.   Determine the following sets:
(a) $A \cup \varnothing$ where A is any given set
(b) $A \cup A$ where A is any given set
(c) $A \cup B$ where the members of B are also members of A

3.6   Equality of Sets

Two sets are said to be equal if each of the sets contains exactly the same elements or members. Thus A and B are names or symbols for the same set if $A = B$. This is precisely the same concept as the one noted earlier when V and 5 represented the same number. An alternate definition is presented in the following section.

3.7   Subsets

Set A is a *subset* of set B if and only if every element of A is a member of B; if A is a subset of B and $x \in A$, then $x \in B$. The symbol $\subseteq$ denotes "is a subset of." For example, $A \subseteq B$ if

$$A = \{1, 2, 3, 4\} \quad \text{and} \quad B = \{1, 2, 3, 4, 5\}$$

On the other hand, B is *not* a subset of A, because B contains an element which is not an element of A, namely, 5. In addition, C is not a subset of D if

$$C = \{1, 2, 3\} \quad \text{and} \quad D = \{1, 2, 4, 7\}$$

for there is an element in C which is not in D, namely, 3.

We can now make the following definition for equality of sets:

$$A = B \quad \text{if and only if } A \subseteq B \text{ and } B \subseteq A$$

This definition says that every element of set A is an element of set B, *and* every element of set B is an element of set A. This can occur *only* when A and B are describing the same set. In the first example above, sets A and B are *not* equal, because B is not a subset of A.

3.8   Properties of Equality

Set equality is an equivalence relationship, i.e., it satisfies the following three properties.

1. Reflexive property: $A = A$ for any set A.
2. Symmetric property: if $A = B$, then $B = A$.
3. Transitive property: If $A = B$, and $B = C$, then $A = C$.

That set equality satisfies these three properties can be proved. First, for the reflexive property to hold we must show that $A = A$. The equality $A = A$ is true if and only if $A \subseteq A$ and $A \subseteq A$ (by definition of set equality). A is always a subset of A, because every $x \in A$ means $x \in A$. Thus $A = A$, and the property is satisfied.

Second, for the symmetric property, if $A = B$ then $A \subseteq B$ and $B \subseteq A$. If $B \subseteq A$ and $A \subseteq B$ (note the change in order), then $B = A$, and the symmetric property is satisfied.

Third, for the transitive property, if $A = B$ then $A \subseteq B$ and $B \subseteq A$. If $B = C$ then $B \subseteq C$ and $C \subseteq B$. Given $A \subseteq B$ and $B \subseteq C$, we have if $x \in A$, then $x \in B$ (by definition of subset), and if $x \in B$, then

$x \in C$, since $B \subseteq C$. If $x \in A$ and $x \in C$, then $A \subseteq C$. Likewise, if $C \subseteq B$ and $B \subseteq A$, then $C \subseteq A$. Hence, if $A \subseteq C$ and $C \subseteq A$, then by definition of equality, $A = C$ and the transitive property is proved for set equality.

3.9 Proper Subsets

If $A \subseteq B$ and B is not a subset of A, then we say that A is a *proper subset* of B. For example, if

$$A = \{1, 2, 3, 4\} \quad \text{and} \quad B = \{1, 2, 3, 4, 5\}$$

then $A \subseteq B$ and B is not a subset of A. The elements of A also have membership in set B, but there is one element of B, namely, 5, which does not have membership in A. Hence, A is a proper subset of B. We denote this by $A \subset B$. There are numerous other subsets of B:

$$\{1, 2, 3, 5\}, \quad \{1, 2, 4, 5\}, \quad \{1, 3, 4, 5\}, \quad \{1, 3, 4, 5\},$$

$$\{1, 2, 3, 4\}, \quad \{1, 4, 5\}, \quad \{2, 4, 5\}, \quad \{1, 2, 3\}, \quad \{1, 2, 4\},$$

$$\{1, 2, 5\}, \quad \{2, 3, 4\}, \quad \{2, 3, 5\}, \quad \{3, 4, 5\}, \quad \{1, 3, 4\},$$

$$\{1, 3, 5\}, \quad \{1, 2\}, \quad \{1, 3\}, \quad \{1, 4\}, \quad \{1, 5\}, \quad \{2, 3\}, \quad \{2, 4\},$$

$$\{2, 5\}, \quad \{3, 4\}, \quad \{3, 5\}, \quad \{4, 5\}, \quad \{1\}, \quad \{2\}, \quad \{3\}, \quad \{4\}, \quad \{5\}$$

The null set $\emptyset$ (see Section 3.3) is also a subset of B and of any other set.

Exercises

1. If $A = \{1, 2, 3, 4\}$ and $B = \{2, 1, 4, 3\}$, does $A = B$?

2. If A is the set of natural numbers and zero, describe a set B which is equal to A.

3. If $C = \{1, 0, 3\}$, list the proper subsets of C.

4. Prove that a given set A is not a proper subset of a given set B.

5. If $A \subseteq B$ and $B \subseteq C$, then is it true that $A \subseteq C$?

6. If $A \subseteq B$ and $C \subseteq B$, does $A = C$ for every set A, B and C? Justify your answer by giving an example.

7. If $A = \{1, 2, 3\}$, $B = \{0, 1, 2\}$, $C = \{1, 2, 3, 4\}$, which of the following are true?
(a) $2 \in A$ (b) $2 \in B$

(c) $2 \in C$ (d) $3 \in A$

(c) $2 \in C$
(d) $3 \in A$
(e) $A \subset A$
(f) $A \subset C$
(g) $2 \subset A$
(h) $2 \subset C$
(i) $A \cap B \subseteq C$
(j) $A \cup B \subset C$
(k) $A \cap C = C$
(l) $(A \cap B) \cap C = \emptyset$
(m) $B \subset A \cup C$
(n) $A = C$

8.   Given any three sets P, Q and R, which of the following are true?

(a) $\emptyset \subset Q$
(b) $P \subseteq P \cup R$
(c) $P \cup R \subseteq P$
(d) $P \cap Q \subset Q$
(e) $P \cap Q \subseteq Q$
(f) $(P \cap Q) \cap R \subset R$
(g) $P \cap Q \subset P \cup Q$
(h) $P \cap R \subseteq P \cup Q$

9.   Prove that $A \subset A$ is false. (Hint: To prove that a statement is false, find an example which shows that $A \subset A$ cannot be true.)

10.   Prove that if $A \subset B$, then $B \subset A$ is false.

3.10   Further Comments

In our discussion of sets we have been interested in the operations on and relations between sets, but in no instance have we indicated any interest in the number of elements in a given set. Set theory is independent of the number of elements in a given set. Rules of membership were examined not to determine *how many* belong, but rather to determine *what* belongs.

It is also important to note that subsets are not members of the given set, but rather are distinct sets whose members belong to both. For example, the set $\{1, 2, 3\}$ is a subset of $\{1, 2, 3, 4\}$ but is not a member of $\{1, 2, 3, 4\}$. The set $\{1\}$ is a subset of A where $A = \{1, 2, 3, 4\}$, but $\{1\}$ is not a member of A. $1 \in A$ and $1 \in \{1\}$. Also, $\{1\} \subset A$, but $\{1\} \notin A$.

3.11   Number of Elements

The number of elements in a given set can be determined by a counting process, provided, of course, that the number of elements is finite. For example, if $A = \{1, 2, 3, 4\}$, there are four elements in set A. There are three elements in a largest (in terms of number of elements) proper subset of A. In fact, there are four subsets which contain three elements each: $\{1, 2, 3\}$, $\{1, 2, 4\}$, $\{1, 3, 4\}$ and $\{2, 3, 4\}$. Each of these sets contains three elements, but not the same three elements.

The number of elements n in a set A is denoted by $n(A)$; we will examine examples of the various relationships between sets and the number of their elements.

Example 3.1 Find $n(C)$, if $C = A \cap B$, $A = \{1, 3, 4, 5\}$ and $B = \{3, 4, 6, 8, 10\}$. First we must determine the membership of C. We have $C = \{3, 4\}$; hence, $n(C) = n\{3, 4\} = 2$. Note: We write $n\{3, 4\}$ as a short form of $n(\{3, 4\})$ and will continue to use this short form in the future.

Example 3.2 Find $n(C)$, if $C = A \cup B$ and where $A = \{1, 3, 5\}$ and $B = \{3, 5, 7, 9\}$. Again, find C. We have $C = \{1, 3, 5, 7, 9\}$ and, as a result of our definition, $n(C) = 5$.

Example 3.3 Find $n(C)$, if $C = A \cap A$ and where $A = \{\square, *, \triangle\}$. From a problem of our exercises we know that $A \cap A = A$. Hence, $C = A$. Therefore $n(C) = n\{\square, *, \triangle\} = 3$. We might also note that $n(C) = n(A)$ since A and C name the same set.

Example 3.4 Find $n(C)$, if $C = (A \cup B) \cap D$ and where $A = \{1, 2\}$, $B = \{3, 4, 5\}$ and $D = \{2, 3, 4\}$. Again we find set C first.

$$C = (\{1, 2\} \cup \{3, 4, 5\}) \cap \{2, 3, 4\}$$

$$= \{1, 2, 3, 4, 5\} \cap \{2, 3, 4\}$$

$$= \{2, 3, 4\}$$

Therefore, $n(C) = 3$.

Exercises

For Exercises 1–9, we are given

$$
\begin{array}{ll}
A = \{1, 2, 3\} & D = \{3\} \\
B = \{3, 4, 5\} & \varnothing = \{\ \} \\
C = \{3, 5, 6\} &
\end{array}
$$

1. Find E if $E = (A \cup B) \cap (C \cup D)$. Also find $n(E)$.

2. Find E if $E = A \cup (B \cap C) \cup D$. Also find $n(E)$.

3. Find $n(E)$ if $E = (A \cap B) \cap (C \cap D)$.

4. Find $n(E)$ if $E = A \cap (B \cap C) \cap D$.

5. Find $(n)E$ if $E = A \cup D$.

6. Find $n(E)$ if $E = A \cap D$.

7. Find $n(\emptyset)$.

8. Is $n(A \cup B) = n(A) + n(B)$ true for all sets A and B?

9. Is $n(A \cap B) = n(A) \cdot n(B)$ true for all sets A and B?

10. Is it possible to describe two sets X and Y such that $n(X \cup Y) = n(X) + n(Y)$? What relationship must always exist between sets X and Y for this statement to be valid?

11. Is it possible to describe two sets X and Y such that $n(X \cap Y) = n(X) \cdot x(Y)$? Is this statement true in general?

12. Is $n(X \cap Y) = n(X) \cdot n(Y)$ true, if either X or Y is $\emptyset$?

3.12 Properties of Union and Intersection

In our consideration of the union of two sets A and B, we have considered them only in one order, $A \cup B$; but does $B \cup A$ describe the same set as $A \cup B$? Consider the following example; let

$$A = \{1, 2, 3\} \quad \text{and} \quad B = \{4, 5, 6, 7\}$$

If $C = A \cup B$,

$$C = \{1, 2, 3, 4, 5, 6, 7\}$$

If $D = B \cup A$,

$$D = \{4, 5, 6, 7, 1, 2, 3\}$$

Both C and D contain the same members, although the members are not listed in the same order in both sets. From the definition of equal sets, we conclude that $C = D$. Hence, we further conclude that

$$A \cup B = B \cup A \qquad (1)$$

Generalizing, we see intuitively that no matter what the elements of A and B are, Equation (1) holds for any sets A and B. This generalization is the *commutative* property, and, in this case, the commutative property for union.

In a similar manner, if the definition of intersection is applied to two sets A and B, $A \cap B$ and $B \cap A$ describe the same set. Consequently,

$$A \cap B = B \cap A \qquad (2)$$

which is the commutative property for intersection.

A word of caution is in order here. We have not actually proved these two commutative properties; we have merely examined examples and from them have intuitively generalized. This can be a dangerous line of thought. For example, if the first horse that we saw were black with pink and purple spots, then we might be tempted to conclude that all horses are this color. However, even if we had seen thousands of horses this color, then we could not expect all horses to be this color. Similarly, we have no logical right to generalize beyond the examples we have seen. In this case we examined examples in order to see what pattern develops; then we actually *assumed* that the two commutative properties are valid properties for union and intersection. Although the commutative properties for ∩ and ∪ can be proved, to do so goes beyond the scope and depth of this text.

In addition to the commutative properties for ∪ and ∩, there are the *associative* properties, written symbolically as

$$(A \cup B) \cup C = A \cup (B \cup C) \tag{3}$$

and

$$(A \cap B) \cap C = A \cap (B \cap C) \tag{4}$$

Consider first Equation (4), the associative property for ∩, $(A \cap B) \cap C$. $A \cap B$ consists of those elements which have membership in both A and B, which forms a set which is then intersected with C. This last intersection produces elements which had membership in A and B (via $A \cap B$) and which now also have membership in C. Hence, we see that $(A \cap B) \cap C$ produces a set which consists only of elements which belong to all three sets A, B and C at the same time.

Consider next $A \cap (B \cap C)$. Again we follow a similar procedure and arrive at the conclusion that $A \cap (B \cap C)$ produces a set which consists only of elements which belong to A, B and C at the same time. From the definition of equality of sets we can write

$$(A \cap B) \cap C = A \cap (B \cap C)$$

It is left to the student to prove Equation (3), the associative property of ∪.

The two remaining properties are called *distributive* laws: the distributive law for ∩ over ∪; and the distributive law for ∪ over ∩. The distributive law for ∩ over ∪ is

$$A \cap (B \cup C) = (A \cap B) \cup (A \cap C) \tag{5}$$

and the distributive law for ∪ over ∩ is

$$A \cup (B \cap C) = (A \cup B) \cap (A \cup C) \tag{6}$$

One of the most convenient ways to illustrate whether a property of operations for sets holds or not is to use *Venn diagrams*. Venn diagrams are pictorial ways of identifying sets, unions and intersections. Figure 3.1 shows two sets (identified by closed curves) containing elements of A and B respectively. Note that $x \in A$ and $y \in B$ and that $z \in A$ and $z \in B$. If z belongs to both sets at the same time, then z belongs to the intersection of A and B. Therefore $A \cap B$ is the set where the two sets A and B overlap or intersect and is represented by the shaded area in figure 3.2. In a similar manner, x, y and z all belong to either A or B. Hence, $A \cup B$ must be the region covered by both sets as indicated by the shaded area in figure 3.3. With this information, we now return to the problem of showing that the distributive law for $\cap$ over $\cup$ is valid for set theory.

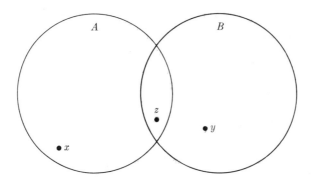

FIGURE 3.1

The shaded area is $A \cap B$.

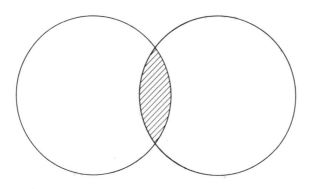

FIGURE 3.2

The shaded area is $A \cup B$.

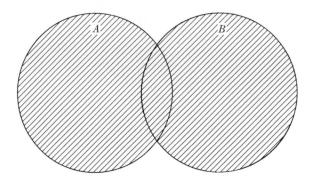

FIGURE 3.3

Since the distributive law involves three sets, figure 3.4 gives a pictorial view of their relationsips to help clarify the law. The left-hand side of the law involves $A \cap (B \cup C)$. In figure 3.5, the shaded area represents $B \cup C$, and figure 3.6 shows the intersection of $(B \cup C)$ with set A. The right-hand side of the equality involves $(A \cap B) \cup (A \cap C)$. Figure 3.7 shows $(A \cap B)$ and $(A \cap C)$, and figure 3.8 shows the union or intersections of these two sets. The shaded regions of figure 3.8 and the double-shaded region of figure 3.6 are the same. Hence, in terms of

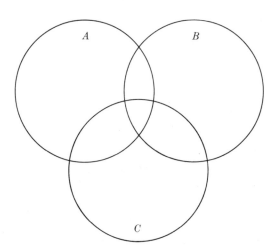

FIGURE 3.4

Venn diagrams,

$$A \cap (B \cup C) = (A \cap B) \cup (A \cap C)$$

In much the same manner we could verify the distributive law for $\cup$ over $\cap$, but this is left for the student to do. In fact, the student should verify that Venn diagrams also may be used to illustrate all the previously presented properties of sets.

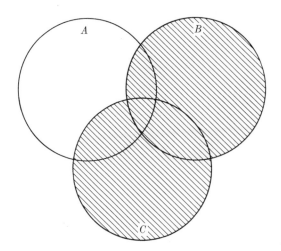

The shaded area is $(B \cup C)$.

FIGURE 3.5

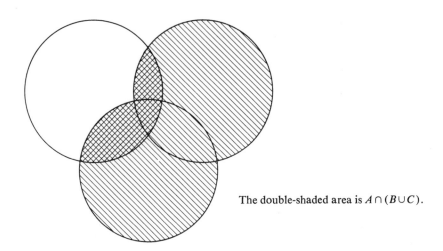

The double-shaded area is $A \cap (B \cup C)$.

FIGURE 3.6

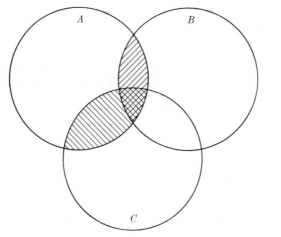

$A \cap B$ is shaded ///.

$A \cap C$ is shaded \\\.

FIGURE 3.7

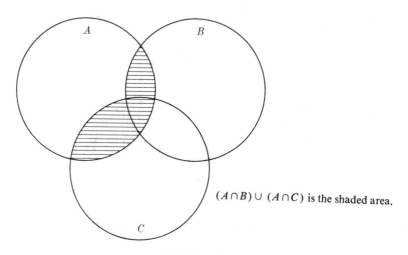

$(A \cap B) \cup (A \cap C)$ is the shaded area.

FIGURE 3.8

Exercises

1.   Using Venn diagrams, prove that the following statements are true:

(a) $(A \cup B) \cup (C \cup D) = (C \cup D) \cup (A \cup B)$
(b) $(A \cup B) \cap (C \cup D) = (C \cup D) \cap (A \cup B)$
(c) $(A \cup B) \cup C = A \cup (B \cup C)$
(d) $A \cup (B \cap C) = (A \cup B) \cap (A \cup C)$

2.   Show the following on Venn diagrams:
(a) $(A \cap B) \cap C$
(b) $A \cap (B \cap C)$
(c) $A \cup (B \cap C) = (A \cup B) \cap (A \cup C)$
(d) If $A \subset B$ and $B \subset C$, then $A \subset C$.
(e) $(A \cap B) \subseteq B$
(f) $A \subseteq (B \cup A)$

3.   Using Venn diagrams, prove: $(B \cup C) \cap A = (B \cap A) \cup (C \cap A)$.

4.   Using Venn diagrams, prove: $(B \cap C) \cup A = (B \cup A) \cap (C \cup A)$.

3.13   The Cartesian Product of Sets

Before we define the Cartesian product, we first need to define an *ordered pair*. If we take two objects, ideas, events, etc., and put them in order, one first and the other second, we have what is called an orderd pair. If x is the first and y is the second, the ordered pair is written as (x, y). We have many examples of ordered pairs. For example, taking a shower and taking off one's clothes can be represented in ordered pair form as follows:

(taking a shower, taking off one's clothes)

or as

(taking off one's clothes, taking a shower)

One can easily observe that different results are obtained from these ordered pairs; the second describes the usual order.

We are now ready to define a new operation called the *Cartesian product*, denoted by $\times$. Given the set $C = A \times B$, C is a set whose elements are ordered pairs with the first member of the pair belonging to A and the second member of the pair belonging to B. Thus C is a set of ordered pairs (x, y) where $x \in A$ and $y \in B$. For example, if

$$A = \{1, 2, 3\} \quad \text{and} \quad B = \{4, 5\}$$

then

$$C = A \times B = \{(1, 4), (1, 5), (2, 4), (2, 5), (3, 4), (3, 5)\}$$

For another example, find $A \times B$ where

$$A = \{2, 4\} \quad \text{and} \quad B = \{2, 5, 7\}$$

We can write the ordered pairs if we take an element from set A and form all ordered pairs possible using this element as the first member of the ordered pair. Take the numeral 4 in set A and put 2, 5 and 7 with it to form $(4, 2)$, $(4, 5)$ and $(4, 7)$. Then form the ordered pairs using 2 from set A as the first element:

$$(2, 2), (2,5) \quad \text{and} \quad (2, 7)$$

Hence,

$$A \times B = \{(2, 2), (2, 5), (2, 7), (4, 2), (4, 5), (4, 7)\}$$

If B in $A \times B$ is the empty set, then $A \times B = \varnothing$, because we cannot form ordered pairs (x, y) where $x \in A$ and $y \in B$ if there are no elements in B. If there are no elements in B, there can be no elements (x, y) in $A \times B$. Hence, $A \times B$ is empty. The same is true if $A = \varnothing$ or if both B and A are equal to $\varnothing$.

It is possible to prove properties of the Cartesian product. For example, we can show that $A \times B$ does not produce the same set as $B \times A$. Consider the following example: Let $A = \{1, 2, 3\}$ and $B = \{4, 5\}$. Then

$$A \times B = \{(1, 4), (1, 5), (2, 4), (2, 5), (3, 4), (3, 5)\}$$

and

$$B \times A = \{(4, 1), (4, 2), (4, 3), (5, 1), (5, 2), (5, 3)\}$$

It is obvious that the two sets are not equal, for $(1, 4) \in A \times B$ and does not belong to $B \times A$. Remember the definition of ordered pair. Hence, the Cartesian product is not commutative.

Certain other properties are true. For example,

$$A \times (B \cup C) = (A \times B) \cup (A \times C)$$

This is a statement of the distributive law for $\times$ over $\cup$. It is not our intent to prove this property. The student should take three sets and verify that the statement holds for the sets selected. .

Exercises

Given $\quad A = \{2, 3, 9\}$
$\qquad\quad B = \{4, 6\}$
$\qquad\quad C = \{7\}$
$\qquad\quad \varnothing = \{ \ \}$

1. find $A \times B$.

2. find $A \times C$.

3. find $B \times A$.

4. find $C \times A$.

5. find $(B \times C) \times A$.

6. find $B \times (C \times A)$.

7. find $A \times (B \cup C)$.

8. find $(A \times B) \cup (A \times C)$. Is this the same answer as found in Exercise 7?

3.14 Equivalent Sets

In order to define equivalent sets we first need to define the concept of a one-to-one correspondence.

DEFINITION 3.1 Two sets A and B are said to be in a one-to-one correspondence if each element of A can be paired with only one element of B and each element of B can be paired with only one element of A.

If $A = \{1, 2, 3\}$ and $B = \{x, y, z\}$, sets A and B can be shown to be in a one-to-one correspondence in one of several ways. For example, we can pair elements in the following way:

1 is paired with x

2 is paired with y

3 is paired with z

Another way of writing this is

$$A = \{1, 2, 3\}$$
$$\updownarrow \ \updownarrow \ \updownarrow$$
$$B = \{x, y, z\}$$

where the arrows indicate the pairing of elements. Another way of pairing is as follows:

$$A = \{1, 2, 3\}$$
$$\updownarrow \ \updownarrow \ \updownarrow$$
$$B = \{y, x, z\}$$

Still other pairings can be indicated. Can you find them?

DEFINITION 3.2   If two sets can be put in a one-to-one correspondence, then the two sets are equivalent.

The two sets A and B of the above example have been shown to be in a one-to-one correspondence and thus equivalent. The fact that more than one one-to-one correspondence was found has no effect upon their equivalence, as all that is necessary is to find *one* such correspondence.

Note that equivalent sets are not necessarily equal sets, as this example clearly shows. On the other hand, equal sets are equivalent sets, for if we define the one-to-one correspondence as the pairing of each element with itself, then a set is equivalent to itself.

The purpose in defining equivalent sets can be clarified by re-examining the preceding example. If $A = \{1, 2, 3\}$ and $B = \{x, y, z\}$, then A is equivalent to set B. But $n(A) = 3$ and $n(B) = 3$. The two sets have the same number of elements even if the sets are not equal. This leads to a significant definition. (Here we have an example of generalizing an idea into a mathematical statement. This example, as well as others we might cite, prompts this definition.)

DEFINITION 3.3   If two sets A and B are equivalent, then $n(A) = n(B)$ where sets A and B are finite sets.

As a consequence of Definition 3.3, we can establish certain properties which we need in order to develop properties of our number system. For example, we know from a previous example that $A \times B$ is not equal to $B \times A$. Let's look at the example again: If $A = \{1, 2, 3\}$ and $B = \{4, 5\}$ then

$$A \times B = \{(1, 4), (1, 5), (2, 4), (2, 5), (3, 4), (3, 4)\}$$

and

$$B \times A = \{(4, 1), (4, 2), (4, 3), (5, 1), (5, 2), (5, 3)\}$$

We noted that $A \times B \neq B \times A$, but look again at these two sets. Are they equivalent? Is there a one-to-one correspondence between $A \times B$ and $B \times A$? If we can find one such correspondence, then the sets are equivalent. Suppose we define the correspondence to be the pairing of (x, y) from set $A \times B$ to (y, x) or $B \times A$. Thus we would have the following pairings:

$$(1, 4) \leftrightarrow (4, 1)$$

$$(1, 5) \leftrightarrow (5, 1)$$

$$(2, 4) \leftrightarrow (4, 2)$$

$$(2, 5) \leftrightarrow (5, 2)$$

$$(3, 4) \leftrightarrow (4, 3)$$

$$(3, 5) \leftrightarrow (5, 3)$$

Hence, there is a one-to-one correspondence between $A \times B$ and $B \times A$ and, therefore, $A \times B$ and $B \times A$ are equivalent. Now, by Definition 3.3,

$$n(A \times B) = n(B \times A)$$

Thus while the sets are not equal, they do have the same number of elements. The property is true in general for any sets A and B, but we will not prove it; we shall assume it to be true.

Exercises

1.   If $A = \{2, 3, 9\}$ and $B = \{4, 6\}$, describe $A \times B$ and $B \times A$. Is $n(A \times B)$ equal to $n(B \times A)$?

2.   If $A = \{2, 3, 4\}$, $B = \{7, 9\}$ and $C = \{6\}$, find $A \times (B \cup C)$. Also find $(A \times B) \cup (A \times C)$. Next determine $n[(A \times B) \cup (A \times C)]$ and $n[A \times (B \cup C)]$. Are they equal?

3.   Pick three sets D, E and F with certain elements in the sets. (Make each set have a finite number of elements.) Is $n[A \times (B \times C)]$ the same as $n[(A \times B) \times C]$?

4.   If $A = \{2, 3\}$, $B = \{4, 5\}$ and $C = \{2, 5\}$, find $A \cap B$, $A \cap C$, $B \cap C$. Does $n(A \cap B) = n(A \cap C)$?

5.   If $A \cup B = B \cup A$, is it true that $n(A \cup B) = n(B \cup A)$?

3.15   Summary

The structure of set theory is found in the following six principles:

1. $A \cup B = B \cup A$ Commutative property for $\cup$

2. $A \cap B = B \cap A$ Commutative property for $\cap$

3. $(A \cup B) \cup C = A \cup (B \cup C)$ Associative property for $\cup$

4. $(A \cap B) \cap C = A \cap (B \cap C)$ Commutative property for $\cap$

5. $A \cap (B \cup C) = (A \cap B) \cup (A \cap C)$ Distributive property for $\cap$ over $\cup$

6. $A \cup (B \cap C) = (A \cup B) \cap (A \cup C)$ Distributive property for $\cup$ over $\cap$

We assumed three properties for $n(A)$:

7. $n(A \times B) = n(B \times A)$

8. $n[(A \times B) \times C] = n[A \times (B \times C)]$

9. $n[A \times (B \cup C)] = n[(A \times B) \cup (A \times C)]$

We also noted certain special instances involving $\emptyset$:

10. $A \cup \emptyset = A$

11. $A \cap \emptyset = \emptyset$

All of this information is preliminary to the introduction of, in chapter 4, the set composed of all $n(A)$ and the properties associated with the set, and the operations of addition and multiplication. This will lead to the development of the system of whole numbers, and, in turn, the system of integers, rationals and real numbers.

4

THE SET W

4.1   Contents of Set W

The set W consists of all n, where $n = n(A)$ for some finite set A, and where n is the number of elements in the set. The elements of set W are, in reality, the numbers used to describe how many elements are in a given set. Thus $n(C) = 4$, if $C = \{1, 2, 3, 4\}$, and $n(E) = 4$, if $E = \{\triangle, \nabla, \square, *\}$. Here we note that 4 is the n of two different sets and that the sets share only one common characteristic: They both contain four elements. Since two sets are equivalent if a one-to-one correspondence exists between them, and since sets C and E can be put in a one-to-one correspondence, they consequently have the same number of elements, that is, $n(C) = n(E) = 4$. Furthermore, any set which is equivalent to either set C or set E has four elements in it. Thus this collection of equivalent sets has a characteristic which we call "fourness."

Each collection of equivalent sets has a number associated with the collection. Since we are considering only sets with finite numbers of elements, then each collection of sets can be used to define what is called a *cardinal* number. For example,

$$n(A) = 2 \quad \text{where } A = \{\triangle, \square\}$$

$$n(B) = 1 \quad \text{where } B = \{\triangle\}$$

$$n(\varnothing) = 0 \quad \text{where } \varnothing = \{\quad\}$$

$$n(C) = 4 \quad \text{where } C = \{1, 2, 3, 4\}$$

Then if W is the set of all n, where $n = n(A)$ and where A is a finite set, W consists of all numbers which represent the number of elements in all possible sets. Thus, 0 is a member of W, as is 1, 2, 3, 4, 5, 6, etc. However, neither negative numbers nor fractions are members of W. Hence, W contains those numbers called *natural* numbers (sometimes called the *counting* numbers), i.e., 1, 2, 3, 4, . . ., and the number 0. Another name for the numbers in set W is the *whole* numbers.

4.2   Addition of Elements of W

Since set W has been defined, we are now ready to develop the properties of a mathematical system in which the elements belong to W. The first step toward this development is to define the operation or operations which are used with the set of elements.

The first operation to be defined is called *addition*. We are already aware of many facets of addition, but we define it such that its concepts develop from our previous discussions and, at the same time, we preserve those characteristics which we previously recognized. The operation of addition is symbolized by $+$ and is defined as follows.

DEFINITION 4.1   If a and b are whole numbers, then $a + b = n(A \cup B)$, where $a = n(A)$, $b = n(B)$ and $A \cap B = \varnothing$.

Thus, if $A = \{\triangle, \square, *\}$ and $B = \{\triangledown, !\}$, then

$$n(A) = 3 \quad \text{and} \quad n(B) = 2$$

Furthermore,

$$n(A) + n(B) = n(A \cup B)$$
$$= n\{\triangle, \square, *, \nabla, !\}$$
$$= 5$$

Hence, $3 + 2 = 5$.

Why the definition requires that $A \cap B = \varnothing$ needs clarification. If $A = \{\triangle, \square, *\}$ and $B = \{*, !\}$, then

$$n(A \cup B) = n\{\triangle, \square, *, !\}$$

and, therefore,

$$n(A \cup B) = 4$$

However,

$$n(A) + n(B) = 3 + 2$$

These two expressions are not equal, $A \cap B \neq \varnothing$, so the definition is defective. There is another reason why we normally consider only disjoint sets. When man first began to keep track of his possessions by counting them, he normally considered only collections of items which had no common elements. For instance, if he found two apples in the morning and three apples in the afternoon, he counted the apples together and came up with a total of five apples. The collections were automatically disjoint, and we make our definition conform to this idea.

The operation of addition is also a binary operation, that is, it "combines" two elements of W into another element also belonging to W. It is also obvious that the addition of two elements of W will produce, each and every time, another element of W. This can be used as the basis for a definition of closure of a set with respect to an operation. The formal definition follows.

DEFINITION 4.2   A set Y is closed for an operation $*$, if when $a \in Y$ and $b \in Y$, then $a * b \in Y$.

In the case of set W and the operation $+$, set is closed for the operation $+$ because if $a \in W$ and $b \in W$, then $(a + b) \in W$. In slightly different language, the closure of W with respect to $+$ simply means that the addition of two numbers of W produces another number of W, and the addition of two whole numbers produces another whole number.

4.3 The Commutative Property for Addition

In the preceding section we defined addition:

$$n(A) + n(B) = n(A \cup B) \quad \text{where } A \cap B = \varnothing \qquad (1)$$

Is it also true that $n(A \cup B) = n(B) + n(A)$? If it were, we could write

$$n(A) + n(B) = n(B) + n(A) \quad \text{where } A \cap B = \varnothing \qquad (2)$$

which is a statement of the commutative property for addition. To prove this last statement, consider the following: We know from the definition of addition that

$$n(A) + n(B) = n(A \cup B) \quad \text{where } A \cap B = \varnothing$$

We also know that $A \cup B = B \cup A$, so

$$
\begin{aligned}
n(A) + n(B) &= n(A \cup B) && \text{Definition of Addition} \\
&= n(B \cup A) && A \cup B = B \cup A \\
&= n(B) + n(A) && \text{Definition of Addition}
\end{aligned}
$$

Thus,

$$n(A) + n(B) = n(B) + n(A)$$

or, if $n(A) = a$ and $n(B) = b$,

$$a + b = b + a \qquad (3)$$

Thus we have shown that the commutative property holds for the operation of addition.

4.4 The Additive Identity

If there exists a number x such that

$$a + x = a \quad \text{for all } a \in N$$

then x is said to be the *additive identity element*, i.e., $x = 0$. To prove that zero does satisfy this statement, let $a = n(A)$ and $0 = n(\varnothing)$.

Then

$$a + 0 = n(A) + n(\varnothing) \quad A \cap \varnothing = \varnothing$$
$$= n(A \cup \varnothing) \quad\quad \text{Definition of Addition}$$
$$= n(A) \quad\quad\quad A \cup \varnothing = A$$
$$= a$$

Zero is the only number which satisfies the definition. If b ($b \neq 0$) is assumed to be an identity, then

$$a + b = n(A) + n(B) \quad \text{where } b = n(B)$$
$$= n(A \cup B) \quad\quad \text{where } A \cap B = \varnothing$$

However, $A \cup B \neq A$ because B must have at least one element since $b \neq 0$ (and hence $B \neq \varnothing$). Therefore,

$$n(A \cup B) \neq n(A) \quad \text{and} \quad a + b \neq a$$

Since b does not satisfy the definition of an identity and hence is not an additive identity element, zero is unique, that is, the only element such that $a + 0 = a$.

Exercises

1.   Using Venn diagrams, prove that for every set A and B, $A \cup B = B \cup A$.

2.   Is set A, where $A = \{0, 1\}$, closed for the operation of addition? Is it closed for the operation of multiplication?

3.   Is the set of even integers* closed for the operation of addition? Show why or why not. (By definition, an even integer is an integer exactly divisible by 2.)

4.   Is the set of odd integers closed for the operation of addition? Show why or why not. (By definition, an odd integer is an integer which is not even.)

5.   Prove that $a = 0 + a$.

6.   Which of the following are examples of the commutative property for addition?

(a) $2 + 3 = 3 + 2$ (b) $4 + 7 = 10 + 1$
(c) $x + y = x + y$ (d) $(x + y) + z = z + (x + y)$
(e) $x + (y + z) = y + (z + x)$

---

* The integers include the numbers 0, 1, 2, 3, 4, ..., and $-1, -2, -3, -4, \ldots$.

7.   Find the sum of 3 and 4 by using the definition of addition. (Hint: Find a set A such that $n(A) = 3$ and a set B such that $n(B) = 4$ and $A \cap B = \varnothing$.)

8.   Find the sum of 4 and 5 by using the definition of addition.

9.   If $C = \{2, 4, 6\}$ and $D = \{9\}$, find $3 + 1$.

4.5   The Associative Property for Addition

The associative property for addition may be stated as follows:

$$(a + b) + c = a + (b + c) \quad \text{where } a, b \text{ and } c \in W \qquad \textbf{(4)}$$

If $a = n(A)$, $b = n(B)$ and $c = n(C)$, then the associative property for addition also can be expressed in the following form:

$$[n(A) + n(B)] + n(C) = n(A) + [n(B) + n(C)]$$

$$\text{where } A \cap B = \varnothing, \quad A \cap C = \varnothing \quad \text{and} \quad B \cap C = \varnothing$$

To prove that this property holds, we need to return to the definition of addition. Note first that we have satisfied the requirements of the definition by making all sets disjoint. First,

$$n(A) + n(B) = n(A \cup B) \qquad \text{Definition of Addition}$$

and

$$[n(A) + n(B)] + n(C) = n(A \cup B) + n(C)$$

$$= n[(A \cup B) \cup C] \qquad \text{Definition of Addition}$$

But

$$n[(A \cup B) \cup C] = n[A \cup (B \cup C)]$$

because the union of sets is associative. So

$$[n(A) + n(B)] + n(C) = n[A \cup (B \cup C)]$$

$$= n(A) + n(B \cup C) \qquad \text{Definition of Addition}$$

$$= n(A) + [n(B) + n(C)] \qquad \text{Definition of Addition}$$

Hence, the operation of addition defined on set W satisfies the associative property. We may now add three elements of set W in either manner described by the associative property and obtain the same result.

An example of the usefulness of the associative property for addition can be seen in the following example. Suppose we wish to find $(4 + 3) + 7$ and do not know how to add $7 + 7$. If we know how to add $4 + 10$, then the problem can be worked as follows:

$$(4 + 3) + 7 = 4 + (3 + 7)$$
$$= 4 + 10$$
$$= 14$$

This problem may seem trivial, but adding numbers like 4 and 10 depends upon the place value system, and much of the instructional techniques for teaching addition stems from the place value notation. This will become more obvious in the next chapter.

Since we know that addition is commutative and associative, we can prove some additional properties. The most significant and extensively used property in arithmetic is the statement that the sum of three numbers can be obtained by adding these three numbers in any order. Although the proof of this statement requires the consideration of many cases, we will prove only one such case; three more are included in Exercise 4.

THEOREM 4.1 $(a + b) + c = (b + c) + a$, where a, b, $c \in W$.

Proof $(a + b) + c = a + (b + c)$ (associative property for addition) $= (b + c) + a$ (commutative property for addition).

Note that we have used the two basic properties for addition; we did not need to use sets or the definition of addition. After looking at Exercise 4, the student should write down all possible combinations of the sum of three numbers. If he proves that all his combinations give the same results as $(a + b) + c$, then he knows that the property is valid for all sums.

Exercises

1.   Which of the following are examples of the associative property for addition?

(a) $(2 + 3) + 4 = 2 + (3 + 4)$
(b) $x + (y + z) = (x + y) + z$
(c) $(2 + 3) + 4 = 5 + 4$
(d) $(4 + 7) + 11 = 11 + (4 + 7)$
(e) $[(9 + x) + y] + z = (9 + x) + (y + z)$

2.   Find each of the following sums in two ways by using the associative property for addition:

(a) $(11 + 9) + 1$ (b) $(120 + 7) + 3$
(c) $(83 + 17) + 13$ (d) $(100 + 10) + 4$

3.   Show that $B = \{1, 2, 3, 0\}$ is not closed for the operation of addition.

4.   Prove the following; be sure to include every step in the proof. a, b and $c \in W$. (Use the properties of addition.)

(a) $(a + b) + c = (a + c) + b$ (b) $a + (b + c) = (c + b) + a$
(c) $(a + b) + c = c + (b + a)$

5.   We frequently write the sum of three numbers as $a + b + c$. What does this expression mean? Is it possible to add more than two numbers at one time?

4.6   Definition of Multiplication

Sometimes multiplication is defined as "repeated addition." For example,

$$3 \cdot 5 = 5 + 5 + 5$$

This definition has some mathematical difficulties which can be corrected by giving a definition in terms of sets. For example, how do we write $0 \cdot 0$ as "repeated addition"? Since it is not possible to employ this definition for $0 \cdot 0$, we prefer to formulate a definition which includes all possible problems.

Suppose that we have two boys and three girls and we wish to know how many ways there are for the boys to date the girls. Let the set of boys be {John, Jim} and the set of girls be {Mary, Carol, Ann}. John could date Mary, Carol or Ann, and Jim could date Mary, Carol or Ann. Thus six arrangements of dates are possible. We could formalize this by using ordered pair notation and the Cartesian product to find all possible dates. Find {John, Jim} × {Mary, Carol, Ann}. The Cartesian product is

$$\left\{ \begin{matrix} \text{(John, Mary), (John, Carol), (John, Ann)} \\ \text{(Jim, Mary), (Jim, Carol), (Jim, Ann)} \end{matrix} \right\}$$

There are six ordered pairs. Hence, there are six possible dates. We formalize this into a definition of multiplication.

DEFINITION 4.3   The operation of multiplication is denoted by $\cdot$ (sometimes we might use $\times$, although the latter as a symbol has some disadvantages). The operation is defined as follows: $n(A) \cdot n(B) = n(A \times B)$.

Definition 4.3 relates a property of set theory, the Cartesian product, to multiplication. Consider the following example: Let

$$A = \{1, 2, 3\} \quad \text{and} \quad B = \{4, 5\}$$

Then $n(A) = 3$ and $n(B) = 2$. Also, $n(A \times B)$ can be determined only if we know what set $A \times B$ is. Therefore, we find $A \times B$ to be the set

$$\{(1, 5), (1, 4), (2, 4), (3, 4), (2, 5), (3, 5)\}$$

We now know that $n(A \times B) = 6$, and $n(A) \cdot n(B) = 3 \cdot 2$. Hence, $3 \cdot 2 = 6$.

4.7   The Commutative Property for Multiplication

We have already noted that the operation of addition is commutative; now we shall determine if multiplication is also commutative. We must prove that

$$n(A) \cdot n(B) = n(B) \cdot n(A) \tag{5}$$

But $n(A) \cdot n(B) = n(A \times B)$ and $n(A \times B) = n(B \times A)$. (Why?) Therefore

$$\begin{aligned} n(A) \cdot n(B) &= n(A \times B) \\ &= n(B \times A) \\ &= n(B) \cdot n(A) \end{aligned}$$

Thus, $n(A) \cdot n(B) = n(B) \cdot n(A)$ or

$$a \cdot b = b \cdot a \quad \text{where } a, b \in W$$

Hence, the commutative property for multiplication holds for elements of set W. In particular, if either A or B is the empty set, then

$$0 \cdot b = n(\emptyset) \cdot n(B) = n(\emptyset \times B) = n(\emptyset) = 0$$

This is the familiar property of multiplication involving multiplication by zero. We have

$$0 \cdot b = 0 \quad \text{where } b \in W \tag{6}$$

Since the commutative property holds for the operation of multiplication, it is possible to prove that $b \cdot 0 = 0$. This exercise is left for the student.

If both A and B are the empty set, then

$$n(A) \cdot n(B) = n(\emptyset) \cdot n(\emptyset) = n(\emptyset \times \emptyset) = n(\emptyset) = 0$$

Thus,

$$0 \cdot 0 = 0 \tag{7}$$

4.8 The Associative Property for Multiplication

To prove that multiplication is associative, we must prove the following equation:

$$[n(A) \cdot n(B)] \cdot n(C) = n(A) \cdot [n(B) \cdot n(C)]$$

The proof is as follows:

$$
\begin{aligned}
[n(A) \cdot n(B)] \cdot n(C) &= [n(A \times B)] \cdot n(C) & \text{Why?} \\
&= n[(A \times B) \times C] & \text{Why?} \\
&= n[A \times (B \times C)] & \text{Why?} \\
&= n(A) \cdot [n(B \times C)] & \text{Why?} \\
&= n(A) \cdot [n(B) \cdot n(C)] & \text{Why?}
\end{aligned}
$$

Hence, the associative property holds for the operation of multiplication, and

$$(a \cdot b) \cdot c = a \cdot (b \cdot c) \quad \text{for } a, b, c \in W \tag{8}$$

The associative property still holds if one or more of the elements are the number zero. If $a = 0$, we have $(0 \cdot b) \cdot c = 0 \cdot (b \cdot c)$, and both parts of the equality are equal to 0.

4.9   The Multiplicative Identity

We earlier defined the additive identity to be a number x such that

$$a + x = a \quad \text{for all } a \in W$$

We found that 0 is the *additive identity* element. In a similar fashion we define the *multiplicative identity* element to be a number y such that

$$a \cdot y = a \quad \text{for all } a \in W$$

Again we know that y must be 1, but we prove that 1 satisfies the definition. Let

$$a = n(A) \quad \text{where } A = \{k_1, k_2, k_3, k_4, \ldots k_a\}$$

Let

$$1 = n(B) \quad \text{where } B = \{b\}$$

Then

$$a \cdot 1 = n(A) \cdot n(B) = n(A \times B)$$

But $A \times B$ is the set of ordered pairs

$$(k_1, b), (k_2, b), (k_3, b), \ldots$$

If we define a one-to-one correspondence between set A and set $A \times B$ to be pairings

$$k_1 \leftrightarrow (k_1, b)$$
$$k_2 \leftrightarrow (k_2, b)$$
$$k_3 \leftrightarrow (k_3, b)$$
$$\vdots \qquad \vdots$$
$$k_a \leftrightarrow (k_a, b)$$

then clearly there is a one-to-one correspondence between A and $A \times B$. Hence, the sets are equivalent. Thus,

$$n(A \times B) = n(A) \quad \text{and} \quad a \cdot 1 = a$$

Thus 1 is the multiplicative identity element for set W. The proof that 1 is the only number which satisfies the definition is left for an exercise in a later section.

Exercises

1. Is the set of even integers closed for the operation of multiplication?

2. Is the set of odd integers closed for the operation of multiplication?

3. Find the following products by using the definition of multiplication:
(a) $1 \cdot 2$ (b) $2 \cdot 2$ (c) $4 \cdot 5$ (d) $3 \cdot 0$ (e) $1 \cdot 1$

4. Which of the following are examples of the commutative property for multiplication?
(a) $2 \cdot 3 = 3 \cdot 2$ (b) $4 \cdot 7 = 14 \cdot 2$
(c) $x \cdot y = y \cdot x$ (d) $(x \cdot y) \cdot z = z \cdot (x \cdot y)$
(e) $x \cdot (z \cdot y) = (y \cdot z) \cdot x$

5. Which of the following are examples of the associative property for multiplication?
(a) $x \cdot y = y \cdot x$ (b) $(x \cdot y) \cdot z = x \cdot (y \cdot z)$
(c) $(2 \cdot 3) \cdot 4 = 6 \cdot 4$ (d) $(2 \cdot 2) \cdot 7 = 2 \cdot 14$

6. Find each product in two ways by using the associative property for multiplication:
(a) $2 \cdot 3 \cdot 4$ (b) $4 \cdot 6 \cdot 10$ (c) $10 \cdot 100 \cdot 4$

7. Using properties developed in this section, prove the following:
(a) $(a \cdot b) \cdot c = (a \cdot c) \cdot b$ (b) $a \cdot (b \cdot c) = (c \cdot b) \cdot a$
(c) $(a \cdot b) \cdot c = c \cdot (b \cdot a)$

8. Prove that if $x \cdot y = 0$, then $x = 0$ or $y = 0$.

4.10 The Distributive Property for Multiplication over Addition

In our discussion of set theory, we described two distributive laws involving intersection and union. We wish to determine if corresponding laws will also hold when the elements involved are elements of set W and the operations are addition and multiplication. We shall consider first the distributive property for multiplication over addition, of which the symbolic statement is

$$a(b + c) = a \cdot b + a \cdot c \quad \text{where } a, b, c \in W \quad \quad (9)$$

Before we prove this equation, we must define a simplification of the symbol for multiplication: The quantity ab can also be written as $a \cdot b$.

Thus the distributive law becomes

$$a(b + c) = ab + ac$$

Returning to the proof of the distributive property, we exhibit the following:

$$n(A)[n(B) + n(C)] = n(A)[n(B \cup C)]$$

$$\text{where } B \cap C = \varnothing \qquad \text{Def. of } +$$

$$= n[A \times (B \cup C)]$$

$$\text{where } B \cap C = \varnothing \qquad \text{Def. of } \cdot$$

$$= n[(A \times B) \cup (A \times C)] \qquad \text{Dist. Property of}$$
$$\cdot \text{ over } \cup$$

$$(A \times B) \cap (A \times C) = \varnothing$$

$$= n(A \times B) + n(A \times C)$$

$$\text{if } (A \times B) \cap (A \times C) = \varnothing \qquad \text{Def. of } +$$

$$= n(A)n(B) + n(A)n(C), \qquad \text{Def. of } \cdot$$

$$(A \times B) \cap (A \times C) = \varnothing$$

Hence, since we can justify every step (and its restrictions), the distributive property for multiplication over addition holds for elements of set N. Consider the following example:

$$5(6 + 7) = 5 \cdot 6 + 5 \cdot 7$$

The distributive property actually says that each side of the equality names the same number, i.e., the left side, $5(6 + 7)$, equals $5 \cdot 13$, or 65. The right side, $5 \cdot 6 + 5 \cdot 7$, equals $30 + 35$, or 65.

It is interesting to note that the right side is actually the easier to work. Suppose we were asked to multiply 8 by 17. In our ordinary manner of working the problem, we would arrive at 136 for an answer. But if we write $8 \cdot 17$ and use the distributive law, we can write $8 \cdot 17 = 8(10 + 7) = 80 + 56, = 136$. This method is shorter and makes greater use of the "multiplication facts." Thinking back over our ordinary multiplication process, we see that the same numbers are computed, but in a different arrangement.

The distributive property that we demonstrated earlier in this section properly should be called the left-hand distributive property for multiplication over addition. The right-hand distribution, $(b + c)a =$

$ba + ca$, can be proven in much the same way as the left-hand:

$$(b + c)a = a(b + c) \qquad \text{Why?}$$
$$= ab + ac \qquad \text{Why?}$$
$$= ba + ca \qquad \text{Why?}$$

The right-hand distributive property follows directly from the left-hand with use of the commutative property for multiplication.

4.11   The Distributive Property for Addition over Multiplication

Our next problem is to determine if the distributive property for addition over multiplication also holds for elements of set W and the operations of addition and multiplication. In other words, is the following equation true:

$$a + bc = (a + b)(a + c) \quad \text{where } a, b, c \in W$$

If we can show that, in general, the two quantities $a + bc$ and $(a + b)(a + c)$ do not name the same element of W, then the distributive property for addition over multiplication does not hold. If the two quantities always name the same element of W, then we must produce some proof which would justify this for every possible case of a, b and c.

Consider then what $a + bc$ is equal to and what $(a + b)(a + c)$ is equal to. If $a = n(A)$, $b = n(B)$ and $c = n(C)$, then

$$(a + b)(a + c) = [n(A) + n(B)][n(A) + n(C)]$$
$$= [n(A \cup B)] \cdot [n(A \cup C)]$$
$$= n[(A \cup B) \times (A \cup C)]$$

Also

$$a + bc = n(A) + n(B)n(C)$$
$$= n(A) + n(B \times C)$$
$$= n[A \cup (B \times C)]$$

If $n[A \cup (B \times C)]$ and $n[(A \cup B) \times (A \cup C)]$ were equal, then we could complete the proof. But we do not know if they are equal. However, we do know that $A \cup (B \times C)$ will consist of elements of A and elements which are pairs (with one element from B and one element from C). On the other hand, $(A \cup B) \times (A \cup C)$ will consist entirely of pairs of elements. Since the two quantities do not name the same set (why?), then they cannot be equal. Even though the two sets are not equal, they could contain the same number of elements; however, with information we have about the three sets A, B and C, we do not know if they do. This line of thought has not produced a proof, nor has it actually shown that the distributive law does not hold.

A simple way to show that a given property is false is to construct an example where it does not hold. For example, let $a = 2$, $b = 5$ and $c = 7$. Then

$$a + bc = 2 + 5 \cdot 7 = 2 + 35 = 37$$

Also,

$$(a + b)(a + c) = (2 + 5)(2 + 7) = 7 \cdot 9 = 63$$

Obviously, $a + bc$ is not equal to $(a + b)(a + c)$ for the example in question, and the distributive property for addition over multiplication is not valid for *all* $a, b, c \in W$.

In this last instance we have shown that a mathematical property is not valid by finding an example which does not satisfy the supposed property. This is not the only example we might find which does not satisfy this supposed property, but one example is enough to prove it false. Try constructing an example of your own for which this property does not hold.

This should not be construed to mean that the property might not be a valid one in some instances. But, in mathematics, we are not normally interested in properties which are valid only in certain circumstances, especially when we do not know what the circumstances are. An example which does make this distributive property valid exists when $a = 0$, and b and c are any elements of W. Then, $a + bc = bc$ and $(a + b)(a + c) = (0 + b)(0 + c) = bc$. Another example occurs when $a = 1$, $b = 0$ and $c = 0$. Then, $a + bc = 1$, and $(a + b)(a + c) = 1$. However, these are the exceptions rather than the rule. One example is not enough to prove a rule, but it is always enough to prove that the rule is not always true. When we construct or find an example to show that a statement is not true, such an example is called a *counter example*. Mathematicians use counter examples to prove that a statement is not true.

Exercises

1.   In the proof of Equation (9), show that the restrictions, as listed, are valid restrictions and that each follows from the preceding one.

2.   Find the following products by using the distributive property for multiplication over addition:
(a) $8 \cdot 21$ (b) $17 \cdot 9$
(c) $35 \cdot 64$ (d) $101 \cdot 305$

3.   Verify the following:
(a) $2 \cdot 14 = 2 \cdot 6 + 2 \cdot 8$ (b) $4 \cdot 16 = 4 \cdot 10 + 4 \cdot 6$
(c) $6 \cdot 7 = 4 \cdot 7 + 2 \cdot 7$ (d) $5 \cdot 5 = 5 \cdot 1 + 5 \cdot 4$

4.   Prove the following:
(a) $a(b + c + d) = ab + ac + ad$
(b) $a(b + c) = ca + ba$
(c) $(a + b)(c + d) = ac + ad + bc + bd$
(d) $(a + b)(a + b) = a^2 + 2ab + b^2$

5.   Can you describe the conditions (in terms of restrictions on a, b and c) when the distributive property for addition over multiplication will hold? If it is easier to describe when it will not hold for elements of set W, do so.

4.12   The Size of W

Thus far we have developed the commutative and associative properties for addition and multiplication and the distributive property for multiplication over addition. We have not examined any characteristics of the set of elements itself, nor have we discussed any characteristics of the elements other than the concepts implied by $n(A)$.

One of the first thoughts regarding set W is whether it is a finite or an infinite set. Does it have a "last" element in terms of counting the number of its elements? Suppose that it does have a last element in terms of counting. Call its number p, and let A represent a set which contains this number of elements. Then p is the number of elements in A, and $n(A) = p$. But we can construct a set B such that A is contained in B or is a proper subset of B by merely putting one more element in set A. Thus, B is also a set which has an $n(B)$, and hence, $n(B)$ belongs to W. But $n(B) = n(A) + 1$, or $n(B) = p + 1$. Thus, the additional element is now the last element in terms of counting, and the element p is not the last. This contradicts our assumption that p is the last element, and therefore our assumption must be false. Hence, set W has no last element or, in other words, W contains an infinite number of elements; there is no largest natural number.

4.13   Some Types of Elements of W—The Primes

The numbers of set W are the natural numbers, i.e., 1, 2, 3, . . ., and zero (or counting numbers as they are sometimes called). But are these numbers all odd numbers, or all even numbers? Are there "perfect" numbers among the elements of W? Are there primes in W? In order to specifically answer such questions, we need to know a description of each of these types of numbers and then find one or more which fit this description.

Consider first the prime numbers. A prime number is a natural number which is divisible by only two numbers, 1 and itself. (By *divisible*, we mean that the number can be divided evenly with zero remainder.) With this yardstick we can begin to examine the natural numbers in W. *One* is divisible only by 1 and itself; hence, 1 is not a prime. *Two* is divisible by 1 and 2, and no others; hence, 2 is a prime number. *Three* is divisible only by 1 and 3; hence, 3 is a prime number. *Four* is divisible by 1, 2 and 4 and, therefore, does not fit the description of a prime number.* We could continue indefinitely and still never determine if every element of W is a prime. What we need is a way of determining for any given $x \in W$ whether x is a prime or not.

In table 4.1 are given numbers which are products of two numbers, each of which is greater than 1. If we examine the products of the table carefully, we will observe that certain numbers are missing. Among the missing numbers are 1, 2, 3, 5, 7, 11, 13, 17 and 19. Since one is not a prime number it must be removed from this list and the following partial list of missing numbers remains:

$$2, \quad 3, \quad 5, \quad 7, \quad 11, \quad 13, \quad 17 \quad \text{and} \quad 19$$

all of which are prime numbers. All missing numbers in the product part of the table are also primes. Every product of the table is the product of two numbers neither of which is 1 or the number itself. Hence the product is divisible by 1, by the number itself and by the two numbers which are multiplied to give the product. The number may also be divisible by other numbers but this is immaterial. That a given product is divisible by four numbers is enough to prevent the number from being a prime. For example, to determine whether 27 is prime, we look at table 4.1 and note that 27 is a product and that $3 \cdot 9 = 27$. Hence, 27 is divisible by 3 and 9 and by 1 and 27; thus it is not a prime. To determine if 23 is a prime, look for it in the product part of the table. Since every row or column has a last entry larger than 23, and since 23 is not in the table, it must be a prime. For numbers larger than 23, the table might be extended and the same determination made.

---

* Any natural number greater than 1 which is not a prime is called a *composite* number.

TABLE 4.1

·	2	3	4	5	6	7	8	9	10	11	12
2	4	6	8	10	12	14	16	18	20	22	24
3	6	9	12	15	18	21	24	27	30	33	36
4	8	12	16	20	24	28	32	36	40	44	48
5	10	15	20	25	30	35	40	45	50	55	60
6	12	18	24	30	36	42	48	54	60	66	72
7	14	21	28	35	42	49	56	63	70	77	84
8	16	24	32	40	48	56	64	72	80	88	96
9	18	27	36	45	54	63	72	81	90	99	108
10	20	30	40	50	60	70	80	90	100	110	120
11	22	33	44	55	66	77	88	99	110	121	132
12	24	36	48	60	72	84	96	108	120	132	144

Exercises

1. Determine which of the following are primes and which are composite:

(a) 3   (b) 6
(c) 16   (d) 21
(e) 51   (f) 97

2. Is it possible to express every natural number as the product of primes? For example, $21 = 7 \cdot 3$. If so, how does one go about finding all the primes involved in the product of primes?

4.14   Fundamental Theorem of Arithmetic

Every nonprime natural number can be expressed as the product of primes. The fundamental theorem of arithmetic states that any nonprime natural number is expressible uniquely as the product of primes.

For example,

$$21 = 7 \cdot 3$$
$$38 = 2 \cdot 19$$
$$100 = 2 \cdot 2 \cdot 5 \cdot 5$$

If a number is a prime, it is not expressible as the product of primes. The proof of this theorem is beyond the scope of this book. However, we shall use the theorem in chapter 7 when we discuss rational numbers.

4.15   More Types of Numbers in W—Odd and Even

The set of *even* natural numbers consists of natural numbers which are divisible by 2, including 2 itself. A number which is not an even natural number is called an *odd* number. (Remember, we are concerned at this point only with numbers in set W.) Some even numbers are

$$2, 4, 6, 8, 10, 12, \ldots$$

and some odd numbers are

$$1, 3, 5, 7, 9, 11, 13, \ldots$$

Even numbers may be written in the form $2k$, where k is a natural number. Odd numbers can be written in the form $2k + 1$, where k is zero or a natural number.

The even natural numbers form a set of numbers which we shall denote by E, and the odd natural numbers form a set which we shall denote by θ. For sets E and θ, $E \cap \theta = \varnothing$, because the definition given in the preceding paragraph defines the two sets to be mutually exclusive, i.e., $E \cap \theta = \varnothing$.

Given $x \in E$ and $y \in E$, it is true that $(x + y) \in E$? Let $x = 2k$ and $y = 2p$, where k and p are natural numbers. Then

$$2k + 2p = 2(k + p) \qquad \text{Why?}$$

We know that $k + p$ is a natural number, because set W is closed for the operation of addition and neither k nor p is zero. Then

$$2(k + p) = 2q \quad \text{where } q = k + p$$

But $2q$ is divisible by 2, and is therefore an even number. Hence $(x + y) \in E$.

Given $x \in E$ and $y \in \theta$, to which set does $x + y$ belong? Again, let $x = 2k$ and let $y = 2p + 1$, where k and p are natural numbers. Then

$$x + y = 2k + (2p + 1)$$
$$= (2k + 2p) + 1$$
$$= 2(k + p) + 1$$
$$= 2r + 1 \quad \text{where } r = k + p$$

Therefore, $2r + 1$ is in the same form as an odd natural number, and if $x \in E$ and $y \in \theta$, then $(x + y) \in \theta$.

Given $x \in \theta$ and $y \in \theta$, is it true that $(x + y) \in \theta$? Let $x = 2k + 1$ and $y = 2p + 1$. Then

$$x + y = (2k + 1) + (2p + 1)$$
$$= 2k + [1 + (2p + 1)]$$
$$= 2k + [(1 + 2p) + 1]$$
$$= 2k + [(2p + 1) + 1]$$
$$= [2k + (2p + 1)] + 1$$
$$= [(2k + 2p) + 1] + 1$$
$$= (2k + 2p) + (1 + 1)$$
$$= 2(k + p) + 2$$
$$= 2(k + p) + 2 \cdot 1$$
$$= [(k + p) + 1]$$
$$= 2q \quad \text{where } q = (k + p) + 1$$

Hence, $x + y$ is an even number, not an odd. Therefore, if $x \in \theta$ and $y \in \theta$, then $(x + y) \in E$. The student is urged to verify that each step of the above argument is valid and that he can supply the reason for each line in the argument.

From the three preceding examples, it is possible to construct an addition table for odd and even numbers which contains all this information. Table 4.2 tells us what the sum of any two elements, either even or odd, is and, as such, contains all the information of the three preceding examples: The sum of an even and an even is an even, and the sum of an even and an odd is an odd.

TABLE 4.2

+	E	θ
E	E	θ
θ	θ	E

It is also possible to arrive at the same type of table illustrating the products of odds and evens. To determine if xy is odd or even when x is even and y is odd, let $x = 2k$ and $y = 2p + 1$. Then

$$xy = (2k)(2p + 1)$$

$$= 2[k(2p + 1)] \quad \text{Why?}$$

$$= 2q \quad \text{where } q = k(2p + 1)$$

Since xy is in the form of $2q$, it is an even number. Therefore, if x is even and y is odd, xy is even.

If x is an odd number and y is an odd number, is xy odd or even? Let $x = 2k + 1$ and $y = 2p + 1$. Then

$$xy = (2k + 1)(2p + 1)$$

$$= (2k + 1)(2p) + (2k + 1)1 \qquad \text{Why?}$$

$$= [(2k)(2p) + 1(2p)] + [(2k)1 + 1 \cdot 1] \quad \text{Why?}$$

$$= [(2k)(2p) + 1 \cdot (2p) + (2k) \cdot 1] + 1 \cdot 1 \quad \text{Why?}$$

$$= [2(k \cdot (2p)) + 2p + 2k] + 1 \qquad \text{Why? (several reasons)}$$

$$= 2[(k \cdot (2p)) + p + k] + 1$$

This number is of the form $2 \cdot r + 1$, where $r = k \cdot (2p) + p + k$, and r is a natural number. Therefore, $2r + 1$ is odd. Hence, xy must be odd.

4.16   Still More Types of Numbers in W

In addition to the prime, even and odd numbers which belong to set W, there are other numbers perhaps not as well known. For instance, there are the *triangular* numbers consisting of 1, 3, 6, 10, 15, ..., so-called because if dots are used to represent the number of elements in the set which each number represents, the dots may be arranged in triangular form. Figure 4.1 shows such an arrangement.

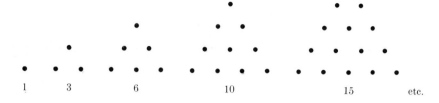

FIGURE 4.1

There are also the *square* numbers, 1, 4, 9, 16, 25, etc, shown in figure 4.2, and *rectangular* numbers, such as 2, 6, 12, 20, etc.

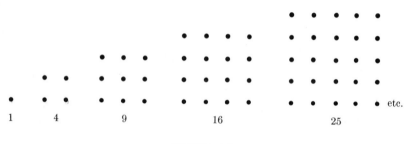

FIGURE 4.2

A *perfect* number is equal to the sum of its divisors which are less than the number itself. The number 1 is not a perfect number. The first perfect number, in terms of size, is 6, for $6 = 1 + 2 + 3$. The next perfect number is 28. Can you find another one?

Other numbers are called *deficient* and *surplus* numbers, so named because the sums of their proper divisors* are either less than or greater than the number itself. Thus 4 is a deficient number and 12 is a surplus number.

We could list numerous other types of numbers which belong to set W, but it is not our intent to treat properties of the numbers themselves. It is interesting to observe that we could study the numbers themselves in almost any of the systems of numeration we have mentioned (and some we have not mentioned) and the results would always be the same. Some of the processes might be involved and complicated, but the results are the same. For example, the number 6 is a perfect number if we write it as 6, VI, ||| or 110_2.

---

* Proper divisors of a number p are divisors of p which are less than p.

Exercises

1. Prove that the associative property for addition holds if the elements are odd or even. In other words, prove that $(a + b) + c = a + (b + c)$, where a, b and c, are either even or odd.

2. Prove that the associative property for multiplication holds if the elements are odd or even numbers.

3. Prove that the product of two even numbers is an even number.

4. If 1, 3, 6, 10 and 15 represent the first five triangular numbers, what are the next five triangular numbers in the sequence?

5. If 1, 4, 9, 16 and 25 represent the first five square numbers, what are the next five square numbers?

6. If 2, 6, 12 and 20 represent the first four rectangular numbers, what are the next four rectangular numbers in this sequence?

7. Is it possible to construct another sequence of rectangular numbers, other than the one in Exercise 6? If so, construct the first eight numbers of the sequence.

8. List five deficient numbers.

9. List five surplus numbers.

4.17   Is Less than and Is Greater than

We are all aware that things around us vary in size. We often compare objects by using expressions such as *smaller* and *larger*. A similar concept exists in mathematics, but it is defined with much greater precision. Mathematical comparisons are made in terms of *less than*, denoted by the symbol $<$, and *greater than*, denoted by the symbol $>$. "Is less than" can be defined using set notation or mathematical properties of set W. For the set definition we have the following: Let $a = n(A)$ and $b = n(B)$, and let A be a proper subset of B. Then we say "a is less than b," denoted by $a < b$. Thus to say that 2 is less than 5 we must know that 2 is the cardinality of some set A, 5 is the cardinality of some set B and A is a proper subset of B. One obvious difficulty occurs with this definition. Suppose $2 = n\{3, 4\}$ and $5 = n\{1, 2, 6, 7, 8\}$. Since $\{3, 4\}$ is not a proper subset of $\{1, 2, 6, 7, 8\}$, we are not able to say $2 < 5$ even if we know it to be true. The solution to the difficulty lies in a wise choice of the set which has cardinality 2. Since we know $n\{3, 4\} = n\{6, 7\}$, we can select $\{6, 7\}$ as the set which has cardinality 2. Then $\{6, 7\}$ is a proper subset of $\{1, 2, 6, 7, 8\}$ and we can say that 2 is less than 5.

The second definition of "is less than" is equivalent to the first but is expressed without referring to sets. This second definition is used in the remaining discussions, and use of the notation $a < b$ is continued.

DEFINITION 4.4 a is less than $b (a < b)$ if and only if there exists a natural number c such that $a + c = b$.

First, in Definition 4.4, note that c is nonzero. If $c = 0$, then $a + 0 = b$ and $a = b$, which contradicts the statement that $a < b$. Second, the definition makes use of the operation of addition and thus relates to a previously established concept in set W. Moreover, in its definition the addition operation requires that sets A and C [where $a = n(A)$ and $c = n(C)$] be disjoint. Hence, since $C = \varnothing$, B contains at least one element not in A, so A (if properly chosen) is a proper subset of B.

To determine if "is less than" is an equivalence relation, we need to determine first if it is reflexive, symmetric and transitive. For "is less than" to be reflexive, a must be less than a. By definition, $a < a$ is true if and only if there exists a $c \neq 0$ such that $a + c = a$. But the only c for which $a + c = a$ is true is $c = 0$. Hence, there is no $c \neq 0: a + c = a$ and a is not less than a. Thus, "is less than" is neither a reflexive nor an equivalence relation.

For $<$ to be symmetric the following must be true: If $a < b$, then $b < a$. To show that $>$ is not symmetric we must prove that the following is false: If $a < b$, then $b < a$. If $a < b$, then there exists a $c \neq 0$ such that $a + c = b$. If $b < a$, there exists some $d \neq 0$ such that $b + d = a$. Using the transitive property of equality, we can write

$$(b + d) + c = b$$

$$b + (d + c) = b$$

Since d and c are both nonzero, the sum $d + c$ is nonzero. Hence, there exists a number $\neq 0$ such that b plus that number is b. Hence, by the definition of $<$, we have $b < b$. Since this is false, our supposition cannot be true (i.e., $b < a$ is true). Hence, "is less than" is not a symmetric relation.

This last proof relies upon the technique of proof by contradiction. A proof by contradiction usually involves choosing two statements and showing that they conflict by producing some false statement. Since one of the two statements is the hypothesis of the theorem, it is always assumed to be true. Thus we find the contrary of the conclusion and show that they conflict. In the last proof, we showed that "is less than" is not symmetric, i.e., "if $a < b$, then $b < a$" is false. We assumed that $a < b$ is true (always true, since it is the hypothesis of the theorem) and $b < a$ is true (the contrary of the conclusion). This eventually produced the statement that $b < b$. Since $b < b$ is a false statement, it must be the consequence of a false statement, for true statements can have only true statements as consequences. Since $a < b$ is always true, then "$b < b$ must be the consequence of $b < a$" is true. Hence, "$b < a$ is true" is a false statement, so "$b < a$ is false" is a true statement.

In order to prove that "is less than" is transitive, we show the following.

THEOREM 4.2   If $a < b$ and $b < c$, then $a < c$.

Proof   If $a < b$, then there exists a $d \neq 0: a + d = b$. If $b < c$, then there exists an $e \neq 0: b + e = c$. By substitution we obtain

$$(a + d) + e = c$$

Thus

$$a + (d + e) = c$$

Since $d + e \neq 0$, $a < c$. Thus "is less than" is transitive, but not reflexive or symmetric.

The "is less than" relation enables us to order the elements of set W. For example, given 2, 3 and 4, we can establish the following true statements:

$$2 < 3, \quad 2 < 4 \quad \text{and} \quad 3 < 4$$

Thus 2, 3 and 4 can be put in the following order: $2 < 3 < 4$. In fact, the set of whole numbers can be written in the following order using $<$:

$$0 < 1 < 2 < 3 < 4 < 5 < \cdots$$

We shall use this property when we talk about number lines in the next chapter.

Since "is less than" has been defined, it is also possible to define "is greater than."

DEFINITION 4.5 b is greater than a if and only if $a < b$.

We denote "b is greater than a" by $b > a$. It follows from our previous discussion that "is greater than" is a transitive relation, but not symmetric or reflexive.

An important consequence of defining "is less than" and "is greater than" is that it is possible that the trichotomy property holds for numbers in set W. The trichotomy property for elements of set W is stated in the following manner.

THEOREM 4.3   If a, $b \in W$, then one and only one of the following statements is true:

$$1.\ a = b$$

$$2.\ a < b$$

$$3.\ a > b$$

Of course, which one of the statements is true depends upon a and b. Clearly one of three (hence, the name *trichotomy*) must be true. To prove this requires the consideration of several cases; we will prove one case and leave the others as exercises. The cases involve showing that if one statement is true, the other two are false. For example, if $a = b$, then $a < b$ is false, as is $b < a$. In addition, if $a < b$ is true, then $a > b$ and $a = b$ are false. We will prove that if $a = b$ then $a < b$ is false. This proof will serve as a pattern for other cases.

Proof   If $a = b$ and $a < b$, then there exists a $c \neq 0$ such that $a + c = b$. But $a = b$, so by the transitive property we have $a + c = a$. By the definition of "is less than," $a < a$. However, this is false; hence, by our technique of proof by contradiction, $a < b$ is not true.

Other cases of the trichotomy property are given as exercises.

Exercises

1.   Prove the following:
(a) If $a = b$, then $b > a$ is false.
(b) If $a < b$, then $a = b$ and $b > a$ are false.
(c) If $a > b$, then $a = b$ and $a < b$ are false.

2.   If $2 < 5$, is $2 + 7 < 5 + 7$? Is $2 + 12 < 5 + 12$? Is $2 + 0 < 5 + 0$? Given $a < b$, write a general statement which is true and includes these three examples.

3. If $3 < 7$, is $3 \cdot 4 < 7 \cdot 4$? Is $3 \cdot 5 < 7 \cdot 5$? Is $3 \cdot 0 < 7 \cdot 7$? Is $3 \cdot 1 < 7 \cdot 1$? Given $a < b$, write a general statement which includes the given examples which had *yes* answers. Is the example $3 \cdot 0 < 7 \cdot 0$ the only possible one which has a *no* answer?

4. If $5 < 6$, is $5 < 6 + 7$? Is $5 < 6 + 9$? Is $5 < 6 + 1{,}000$? Given $a < b$, write a general statement including these examples. Is it true for all possible examples?

4.18   Subtraction

Subtraction can be defined in terms of sets, but we define it using the concept of addition. (The exercises at the end of this section contain the basic set approach.)

DEFINITION 4.6   If a, b and c are whole numbers, then $a - b = c$ if and only if $a = b + c$.

For example,

$$5 - 2 = c \quad \text{if and only if } 5 = 2 + c$$

where c is a whole number. If there is a whole number c such that $5 = 2 + c$, then $c = 5 - 2$. Since $2 + 3 = 5$, $c = 3$, and $5 - 2 = 3$. Consider the following:

$$2 - 5 = d \quad \text{if and only if } 2 = 5 + d$$

where d is a whole number. There is no whole number d such that $5 + d = 2$. Hence, $2 - 5$ has no whole number answer.

The operation of subtraction is not closed. In fact, no subtraction problem $a - b$ has an answer if $a < b$; that is, if $a - b = c$ and $a < b$, then $a = b + c$ by definition. But if $a < b$, then $a < b + c$. Hence, there is no c, $c \in W$, such that $a = b + c$. Hence, there is no whole number answer for $a - b$.

The definition of subtraction applies if and only if c is a whole number such that $a = b + c$. Thus subtraction is defined only for the case when $a = b$ or $a > b$.

Subtraction is neither commutative nor associative, as can be proven with counter examples. For the commutative property, while $5 - 2$ is defined, $2 - 5$ is not defined. Hence, $5 - 2 \neq 2 - 5$. In fact,

$a - b \neq b - a$ for any pairs a and b. For the associative property,

$$(17 - 5) - 4 = 12 - 4 = 8$$

But $17 - (5 - 4) = 17 - 1 = 16$, and $16 \neq 8$. Hence, subtraction is not associative.

There is one property which does hold true for subtraction, the distributive property for multiplication over subtraction:

$$a(b - c) = ab - ac$$

where a, b, $c \in W$ and the subtraction operation is defined on both sides of the equality. In other words, subtraction is defined when $b > c$ or $b = c$.

Since $b - c$ is defined, then there exists a $d : b = c + d$, where $b - c = d$. If $b = c + d$, then

$$ab = a(c + d) \quad \text{and} \quad ab = ac + ad$$

Applying the definition of subtraction, we can write this last statement in the form

$$ab - ac = ad$$

But $d = b - c$, so

$$ab - ac = a(b - c)$$

This is a statement of the distributive property for multiplication over subtraction.

Exercises

1. Find the following by applying the definition of subtraction:
(a) $14 - 6$ (b) $27 - 19$
(c) $2 - 0$ (d) $8 - 3$

2. Given that set A is a subset of set B, we define the complement of set A to be the set of all x such that $x \in B$ and $x \in A$. Using this definition, find the complement of A (denote this by $\bar{A}$) in the following:
(a) $A = \{1, 2, 4\}$, $B = \{1, 2, 4, 9, 16\}$
(b) $A = \{2\}$, $B = \{1, 2, 4, 9\}$
(c) $A = \{\}$, $B = \{1, 2\}$
(d) $A = \{1, 2, 3\}$, $B = \{1, 2, 3\}$

3. In Exercise 2, find $n(A)$, $n(B)$ and $n(\bar{A})$ for a, b, c, d. In each case write a statement that relates the three numbers found. Generalize by

writing a definition of the operation of subtraction using sets and the concept of a complement of a set.

4.   Compute by using the distributive property for multiplication over subtraction:

(a) $7 \cdot 19$ (Hint: Let $19 = 20 - 1$.)

(b) $13 \cdot 8$

(c) $9 \cdot 14$

(d) $101 \cdot 99$

5.   In Exercise 4(d) we wrote 99 as $100 - 1$. Suppose we also write 101 as $100 + 1$. Work this problem using the distributive property for multiplication over subtraction. Make no calculations until the problem is completely written out. From looking at the problem, can you write out the answer for another problem such as $52 \cdot 48$? (Hint: Write 52 as $50 + 2$ and 48 as $50 - 2$.)

4.19   Division

The last operation to be defined on the set of whole numbers is the operation of division. As in the case of subtraction, we could define division in terms of sets, but we choose to use an alternate definition. The definition follows.

DEFINITION 4.7 $a \div b = c$ if and only if $a = b \cdot c$ where $a, b, c \in W$ and $b \neq 0$.

Definition 4.7 does not define all possible division problems. For example,

$$7 \div 5 = c \quad \text{if and only if } 7 = 5 \cdot c$$

where $c \in W$. However, there is no c in W which satisfies this criterion. Hence, $7 \div 5$ is undefined (at this point). However, $16 \div 2$ is defined because there exists a $c \in W$ such that $16 = 2 \cdot c$, namely, $c = 8$.

The definition also requires that b be nonzero; thus division by zero is undefined. Consider the problem $7 \div 0$. If the definition is applicable in this case, then there must exist a c where $7 \div 0 = c$ such that $7 = 0 \cdot c$. However, there is no c that when multiplied by 0 would give 7. Zero times c is always 0, no matter the value of c. Hence, there is no possible answer when dividing by zero, so we exclude it from the definition.

Division is neither commutative nor associative. We just noted that $16 \div 2 = 8$. The problem $2 \div 16$ does not produce a whole number; hence $2 \div 16$ cannot be the same as $16 \div 2$. Therefore, by counter example we have shown that $\div$ is not commutative. For the associative property, consider the following:

$$(32 \div 8) \div 4 = 32 \div (8 \div 4)$$

$$(32 \div 8) \div 4 = 4 \div 4 = 1$$

$$32 \div (8 \div 4) = 32 \div 2 = 16$$

But $1 \neq 16$, so division is not associative.

It is not as easy to write out conditions which tell us when $a \div b$ is defined or has meaning. To specify simply that $a > b$ is not sufficient, as in the case of subtraction (for example, $7 \div 2$). However, if a is some multiple of b, then $a \div b$ is defined. Since the multiplication table contains all defined division problems, by examining all multiplication problems we could identify all division problems. Refer to table 4.1 and find the division problems which are defined from the products in the table.

Exercises

1.   Work the following by definition:
(a) $16 \div 4$ (b) $32 \div 8$
(c) $4 \div 4$ (d) $0 \div 6$
(e) $1 \div 1$

2.   See if you can devise a way to define division by using sets. No new operation on sets is needed.

3.   Suppose division by zero were possible through our definition. What is the answer to the problem $0 \div 0$? Is there more than one answer?

4.20   Cancellation Properties

In addition to the previously mentioned properties of the operations, there are several properties which relate the operations and relations (*relations* being "is equal to" and "is less than") in the same statements. For example:

$$\text{If } a + b = a + c, \text{ then } a = b. \tag{1}$$

$$\text{If } a \cdot c = b \cdot c \text{ and } c \neq 0, \text{ then } a = b. \tag{2}$$

The first is a cancellation property of addition applied to an equality. We could also write the following:

$$\text{If } a + c < b + c, \text{ then } a < b. \tag{3}$$

This equation is the same cancellation property applied to an inequality. In addition, we have the following:

$$\text{If } a \cdot c < b \cdot c \text{ and } c > 0, \text{ then } a < b. \tag{4}$$

In each of these statements, a number is removed or canceled out. Thus these statements are called *cancellation* properties. We shall prove (3) and leave (1), (2) and (4) as exercises.

For the proof of (3) we begin with the hypothesis that $a + c < b + c$. By the definition of "is less than," there exists a $d > 0$ such that

$$(a + c) + d = b + c$$

Rewriting this, we can obtain

$$(a + d) + c = b + c$$

By Equation (1), if $(a + d) + c = b + c$, then $a + d = b$. But $a + d = b$ is, by definition, the condition to be satisfied when $a < b$. Hence

$$a < b$$

Thus, we have the proof of the statement, if $a + c < b + c$, then $a < b$. Each of the four statements given in this section also has a converse:

$$\text{If } a = b, \text{ then } a + c = b + c. \tag{5}$$

$$\text{If } a + b, \text{ then } a \cdot c = b \cdot c. \tag{6}$$

$$\text{If } a < b, \text{ then } a + c < b + c. \tag{7}$$

$$\text{If } a < b, \text{ then } a \cdot c < b \cdot c, \text{ if } c \neq 0. \tag{8}$$

The proofs are omitted but the student should write examples of each to feel reasonably sure that each is valid.

4.21   Summary

In this chapter, we have been concerned with the set of natural numbers and zero. This set, called W, and the operations of addition and multiplication have been related in such a way that a mathematical system has been formed. This system consists of set W, addition and multiplication and has the following properties:

1. Set W is closed for the operation of addition.
2. Set W is closed for the operation of multiplication.
3. $a + b = b + a$, for $a, b \in W$.
4. $ab = ba$, for $a, b, \in W$.
5. $(a + b) + c = a + (b + c)$, for $a, b, c \in W$.
6. $(ab)c = a(bc)$, for $a, b, c \in W$.
7. $a(b + c) = ab + ac$, for $a, b, c \in W$.
8. $a = a + 0$, for every $a \in W$.
9. $0b = 0$, for every $b \in W$.
10. $1 \cdot a = a$, for every $a \in W$.

From these properties we were able to deduce others. For example,

$$(b + c)a = ba + ca$$
$$a + 0 = a$$
$$b0 = 0$$

In addition, we had the following two statements: (1) There is a unique b, such that $a + b = a$ ($b = 0$); and (2) There is a unique b, such that $ab = a$ ($b = 1$). We also noted that W contains no last number in the sequence of natural numbers; hence, it contains an infinite number of elements.

Set W also contains various types of numbers and we discussed the primes, odds and evens in some detail. We also noted that a mathematical system can be constructed with elements E and θ (E for even and θ for odd) with operations of addition and multiplication; this system possesses the same characteristics as set W with its operations of addition and multiplication. (If two mathematical systems possess the same characteristics, then we can say they are *isomorphic* to each other.) We also found that set W contains an identity element for addition and an identity element for multiplication, and we discussed the cancellation properties:

1. If $a + b = b + c$, then $a = b$.
2. If $a \cdot c = b \cdot c$ and $c \neq 0$, then $a = b$.
3. If $a + c < b + c$, then $a < b$.
4. If $a \cdot c < b \cdot c$ and $c \neq 0$, then $a < b$.
5. If $a = b$, then $a + c = b + c$.
6. If $a = b$, then $a \cdot c = b \cdot c$.
7. If $a < b$, then $a + c < b + c$.
8. If $a < b$, then $a \cdot c < b \cdot c$, if $c \neq 0$.

5

ALGORITHMS FOR OPERATIONS WITH WHOLE NUMBERS

5.1   Introduction

One rather striking observation can be made about the ideas in chapter 4. We defined operations on the set of whole numbers and, in most cases, derived some properties of these operations. However, upon examination of these statements in chapter 4, it becomes obvious that we have defined such concepts as addition on the set of whole numbers but have not shown how to actually add these numbers; that is, using solely these concepts, we would not be able to add a column of numbers. Moreover, multiplication of whole numbers was defined, but the definition did not tell us how to multiply one whole number by another. It told us that there is one whole number, and if we apply the definition, we can find which one it is. Therefore, in this chapter we extend the ideas of chapter 4 to produce the normal working processes we use in arithmetic.

5.2   Addition Processes with Whole Numbers

When developing the actual computational processes, keep in mind that the addition operation defined in chapter 4 can be applied only to the whole numbers and that the computational processes are normally developed in stages or steps which are sequential and which depend upon previously developed stages. The beginning point for this sequential development is the definition of addition. By applying the definition we are able to show that $2 + 3$ is 5. In elementary school such a sum is usually proven by concrete examples in which the union of two sets (for example, two apples and three apples) is formed and in which a whole number is determined for $A \cup B$ by counting or some other comparable process. The same process can be applied to $1,234,567 + 987,654$, but it is obvious that this technique would be very time-consuming. Thus we will develop some shortcuts.

Suppose a youngster has learned the various combinations of addition up through $5 + 5$ only from the definition of addition, but he wants to find $5 + 6$. He may write $5 + 6$ as $5 + (5 + 1)$, and, by applying the associative property, he can write

$$5 + (5 + 1) = (5 + 5) + 1$$

Since he knows that $(5 + 5)$ is 10, he can write

$$5 + 6 = 10 + 1$$

He can determine $10 + 1$ by noting that $10 + 1$ is the next number in the sequence of ordered whole numbers, i.e., 11. An alternate way of determining that $10 + 1$ is 11 is to use the place value system notation: $10 + 1$ becomes $1 \cdot 10 + 1 \cdot 1$, written as 11. In a similar manner other combinations can be found which yield 11 as an answer. The process can now be extended to problems such as $5 + 7$, for example,

$$5 + 7 = 5 + (6 + 1)$$
$$= (5 + 6) + 1$$
$$= 11 + 1$$
$$= 12$$

If a student already knows $5 + 6$, the associative property and the next number after 11 in the ordered sequence of whole numbers, he can find $5 + 7$ with little difficulty. Another way of looking at the same problem follows:

$$(5 + 7) = 5 + (5 + 2)$$
$$= (5 + 5) + 2$$
$$= 10 + 2$$

At this point the student is asked to find the second number after 10, 12; hence $10 + 2 = 12$. Again he can treat $10 + 2$ as $1 \cdot 10 + 2 \cdot 1$ and use the place value notation approach to obtain 12. In fact, this approach has the advantage of being related to our "column addition" process and thereby should be used in teaching elementary arithmetic. With sufficient work of this nature the student soon recognizes that $10 + 5$ is 15, $10 + 7$ is 17, etc., and that there is a sequence of problems in addition, the solutions of which do not depend directly upon the definition of addition. One develops the combinations of $10 + a$, $a < 10$, and if the development is carefully done, the generalization we desire begins to take place. Now try $10 + 10$:

$$10 + 10 = 10 + (9 + 1)$$
$$= (10 + 9) + 1$$
$$= 19 + 1$$

and the successor for 19 (i.e., $19 + 1$) is 20. This idea of using the successor of 19 means that the student must previously know the sequence of symbols to represent the whole numbers. We may also use the place value notation to arrive at the same answer. For example,

$$10 + 10 = 1 \cdot 10 + 1 \cdot 10$$
$$= (1 + 1) \cdot 10$$
$$= 2 \cdot 10$$
$$= 20$$

Here we have used several of the properties of addition and multiplication. Notice that the previous example used properties of addition plus the concept of successor. In either case the basic properties of operations are essential to developing the algorithms.

The idea is extended further in the following manner:

$$10 + 11 = 10 + (10 + 1)$$
$$= (10 + 10) + 1$$
$$= 20 + 1 \text{ or } 21$$

This leads to problems such as

$$10 + 14 = 10 + (10 + 4)$$
$$= (10 + 10) + 4$$
$$= 20 + 4 \text{ or } 24$$

and still further to problems such as

$$12 + 14 = (10 + 2) + (10 + 4)$$
$$= [(10 + 2) + 10] + 4$$
$$= [10 + (10 + 2)] + 4$$
$$= [(10 + 10) + 2] + 4$$
$$= (10 + 10) + (2 + 4)$$
$$= 20 + 6$$
$$= 26$$

Again note that we are using properties previously developed to find a sum. The place value system is an integral part and could be clearly indicated if we were to rewrite the last example in the following form:

$$12 + 14 = (1 \cdot 10 + 2 \cdot 1) + (1 \cdot 10 + 4 \cdot 1)$$
$$= [(1 \cdot 10 + 2 \cdot 1) + 1 \cdot 10] + 4 \cdot 1$$
$$= [1 \cdot 10 + (1 \cdot 10 + 2 \cdot 1)] + 4 \cdot 1$$
$$= [(1 \cdot 10 + 1 \cdot 10) + 2 \cdot 1] + 4 \cdot 1$$
$$= (1 \cdot 10 + 1 \cdot 10) + (2 \cdot 1 + 4 \cdot 1)$$
$$= (1 + 1) \cdot 10 + (2 + 4) \cdot 1$$
$$= 2 \cdot 10 + 6 \cdot 1$$
$$= 26$$

This last form has some distinct advantages for teaching. It depends heavily upon the place value notation, which is the key to the development of the addition algorithm. While we have not been writing reasons for all the steps we have taken, the student should be able to give them.

The student should also write all examples out in the place value form, as that is how he will probably encounter it in the elementary arithmetic texts.

One may continue this method of attack on addition combinations and be fairly successful in developing several notions needed in computing sums. One can even handle problems requiring the process we refer to as *carrying*. For example,

$$16 + 17 = (10 + 6) + (10 + 7)$$
$$= [(10 + 6) + 10] + 7$$
$$= [10 + (10 + 6)] + 7$$
$$= [(10 + 10) + 6] + 7$$
$$= (10 + 10) + (6 + 7)$$
$$= 20 + 13$$
$$= 20 + (10 + 3)$$
$$= (20 + 10) + 3$$
$$= 33$$

But these examples seem to require more and more steps, all of which are necessary unless we shortcut somewhere; the computational process does shortcut much of this through use of a process called an *algorithm*.

If we write $16 + 17$ as

$$\begin{array}{r} 16 \\ 17 \\ \hline \end{array}$$

we can find in the problem the two sums $6 + 7$ and $10 + 10$. Moreover, such pairs of sums occur in all previous examples. Thus the addition problem could look like this:

$$\begin{array}{r} 16 \\ 17 \\ \hline 13 \\ 20 \\ \hline 33 \end{array}$$

If we try another example, we note the same pattern. Thus

$$34 + 28 = (30 + 4) + (20 + 8)$$
$$= (30 + 4 + 20) + 8$$
$$= (30 + 20 + 4) + 8$$
$$= (30 + 20) + (4 + 8)$$
$$= 50 + 12$$
$$= 50 + (10 + 2)$$
$$= (50 + 10) + 2$$
$$= 60 + 2$$
$$= 62$$

or in the suggested form, $34 + 28$ becomes

$$\begin{array}{r} 34 \\ 28 \\ \hline \end{array}$$

and we have

$$\begin{array}{r} 34 \\ 28 \\ \hline 12 \\ 50 \\ \hline 62 \end{array}$$

The partial sums, 12 and 50, can be determined by two very elementary additions without going through all the steps of the last example. It is possible to prove that this process works for all such addition problems. We have deduced an alternative procedure for finding sums of this type of problem. We no longer need to rely upon the definition and subsequent manipulations using the various properties of addition. We *know* that $34 + 28 = 50 + 12$ and finally that $50 + 12 = 62$.

There are additional patterns which emerge in our work with mathematics. For example, in the $50 + 12$ pattern, the 2 in the 12 ends up as the 2 in 62. Since the partial sum like 12 has two digits, we can write down the last digit (2) and add the first digit (1) to the first digit of the 50 and thus get 6, which is then put in the tens digit place in the answer. In other words, further shortcuts can be devised until we finally arrive at the usual process used in addition. This technique, called *carrying*, can greatly streamline the addition algorithm and can be extended to all other types of addition problems involving whole numbers.

Discovering patterns and shortcuts can be very rewarding for every student, regardless of his ability. Let the student be creative and generate his own shortcuts in the beginning. It matters not that a fact has been previously established in mathematics for millions of others, but it matters a great deal to each student who discovers the process of shortcutting. When a student is aware that he *can* establish a shortcut procedure, then he is ready to do so and thereby skip all the involved steps which appear in the last example. Such shortcuts come only after the comprehension and understanding of the mathematical principles involved. Whatever a teacher does to help students learn computational procedures must never be done at the expense of understanding why something works.

A thinking student can produce some interesting variations for some problems. For example, $30 + 19$ might be determined in the following manner:

$$30 + 19 = 30 + (20 - 1)$$
$$= (30 + 20) - 1$$
$$= 50 - 1$$
$$= 49$$

This certainly is a different twist and not beyond the grasp of many youngsters. But what a creative thought in mathematics for the youngster who did this!

The developmental pattern outlined above for the sum of two two-digit numbers can be repeated for problems which require more than the one carrying process. For example,

$$57 + 64 = (50 + 7) + (60 + 4)$$
$$= (50 + 60) + (7 + 4)$$
$$= [50 + (50 + 10)] + (10 + 1)$$
$$= 100 + 10 + 10 + 1$$
$$= 121$$

This process can be repeated for problems involving three, four or more digits in each addend; the shortcut process discovered (or created) for problems like $34 + 28$ can be applied to any addition problem. Hence, we now have a speedy efficient way of finding the sum of two numbers without depending only on the definition of addition. It is also obvious that the notion described here can be extended to the sum of several numbers and need not be revised in any way.

All of these concepts are not developed in a short period of time but are extended over several grades in the elementary school program in mathematics.

Exercises

1.　In the example illustrating that $12 + 14 = 26$, supply the reasons necessary for the various steps used to obtain 26.

2.　Illustrate how to find $26 + 37$ and $49 + 65$ without using the carrying process.

3.　Suppose the only addition facts we know are those up to $5 + 5$. Show how we might derive $10 + 9$ without using the addition algorithm.

4.　Must addition by an algorithm always be done from right to left? Try to find $34 + 48$ by starting on the left in a column addition sense.

5.　Describe a relationship between the definition of addition and the addition algorithm.

6.　What is the definition of the word *algorithm*?

7.　Examine a given textbook series in elementary school mathematics to determine the amount of time it takes to actually develop the addition algorithm.

8.　Construct a table showing all the sums of numbers between 0 and 10 inclusive. Is it necessary to have the addition algorithm for finding these sums?

5.3　Additional Comments on Addition Processes

The checking of answers that is commonly found in elementary school mathematics programs is not related to addition. To check the sum in an addition problem, we must do the addition a second time. We frequently suggest that if we add *down* a column of figures to get the first answer, we should add *up* the column to check this answer. In reality, we work the problem *again* and compare the answers. If the answers are the same, then we conclude that the answer is correct, a false conclusion. A valid conclusion is that the answer is probably, or very nearly certainly, the correct one. There is, of course, the possibility of making a mistake each time of such a nature to produce the same answers, but such errors are rare. Thus we have developed a degree of confidence in this procedure and frequently depend upon it to insure that our answers are correct.

A second idea related to addition is the emphasis upon certain addition facts such as $6 + 4$, $7 + 3$, $8 + 2$, $5 + 5$, etc. These combinations all yield 10 as the sum, and we frequently stress the notion that we should look for these in column addition problems. Presumably these combinations are easier to remember and thereby make column addition easier, or, if not easier, faster. It is unreasonable to suggest that $7 + 3$ is an easier combination to remember than $4 + 5$. In fact, if one devotes equal time to all combinations or addition facts, each should be equally easy to recall and apply. What is usually overlooked in this procedure is that we are making liberal use of the commutative and associative properties for addition on cardinal numbers and we could "jump around" selecting combinations at will unless these properties held for the operation of addition. These *properties* make time-saving possible in such instances; the *combinations* chosen do not necessarily make the process of addition more efficient. Whatever efficiency there is in looking for the combinations such as $6 + 4$ and $7 + 3$ could not be utilized without the commutative and associative properties.

In connection with the subject of efficiency in addition problems, one frequently questions the need for rapid calculation. Why is it necessary to develop such skills? Adding machines can do it faster than most humans and are usually more dependable. Moreover, if calculations are really important, we usually take the time to be sure that they are correct. What we must remember is that speed is not important in and of itself; what is important is reasonable speed with a high degree of accuracy. Together these enable a person to make the maximum use of time for other things; this should be the prime motivating factor for speed or time drills in addition. In fact, it is precisely this efficient use of time that motivates us to develop the shortcut procedures outlined in Section 5.2. Some educators have estimated that we spend up to 50 percent of our time in arithmetic instruction developing shortcuts and achieving speed.

5.4   Zero and Addition

In developing the properties of addition on the set of whole numbers, we noted that zero possessed a very unique property with respect to addition. Zero is called the additive identity element, indicated by the statement

$$a + 0 = a$$

We can make efficient use of the additive identity element in column addition. For example,

$$
\begin{array}{r}
32 \\
60 \\
45 \\
\hline
\end{array}
$$

In the units column we say $5 + 2$ is 7 and write the 7 as part of the answer. Note that we did not even include the zero in our thinking. Actually we observe that the identity property for addition of the number zero would occur as $7 + 0 = 7$, and then we write down 7. This last step can be eliminated *because* of the identity property and, even though we do not say so or think so in so many words, we have actually recognized that this property is there. If we did not know this, we would have to include the step $7 + 0$, thereby lengthening our computational time.

5.5 The Number Line and Addition

Many textbooks in elementary school mathematics either suggest or use the number line as a device whereby youngsters may understand simple addition combinations. It is quite true that the number line has many uses or values, but it also has some disadvantages both in learning mathematics and in the mathematics itself.

First, we examine the notion of a number line itself, as used in elementary school mathematics. Take a given straight line on which we place marks or identify certain points as follows:

We select one of these points and label it 0 and label the other points in order by the numerals 1, 2, 3, etc:

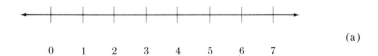

(a)

Or should we have one of the following?

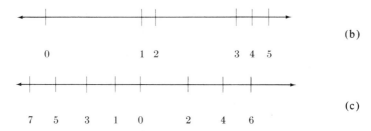

(b)

(c)

Perhaps none of these suffices as a number line. What characteristics must a number line have to be useful for demonstration work in elementary school mathematics? In particular, what characteristics are necessary for us to adapt it to the addition process?

Let's take the problem 2 + 3 and try to fit it onto the three number lines suggested above. First, we must interpret this addition problem to make it fit onto any number line. Suppose we say that since the first number is 2, we intend to start at the position labeled 2. Then what? What does it mean then to *add* 3? If we remember the set notation and concepts, we know that 3 refers to the cardinality of a given equivalent class of sets. We also know that 2 apples + 3 apples type of interpretation means that we put three apples with the two we already have. But what does it mean to *add* 3 on the number line? Here we must make some sort of interpretation. Quite obviously whatever the interpretation is, we must end up at 5 or we are in trouble. Suppose we think of adding 3 as moving three points from 2. If we move to the right from 2, the third point on number line (a) is 5. If we move to the left from 2, we never find a point beyond the second one which is labeled with a numeral for a whole number. On number line (b) the same thing happens. Obviously going to the left is not a good interpretation for these number lines.

Now try number line (c) and the same set of interpretations. If we move to the right 3 points we arrive at 8; if we move the left 3 points we arrive at 3. Neither of these seems to be related to the statement 2 + 3 = 5. So we recognize that this set of interpretations does not apply to number line (c). We have a choice—either get a new set of interpretations or use a different kind of number line. It appears that our interpretation of 2 + 3 works fairly well on number lines (a) and (b), so these are the types of number lines we want. [We could interpret 2 + 3 differently and make it work with number line (c). Can you find such an interpretation? Will it work on either of the other two number lines?] Moreover, our example suggests that if adding 3 is to be interpreted as moving 3 points, such a movement must be to the right and not to the left.

The numerals are arranged along the line from left to right in precisely the same manner that the whole numbers are ordered by the "is less than" relation. Thus the arrangement of number lines (a) and (b) could be a geometric interpretation of this relationship. Number line (c) does not exhibit this relationship. Using a diagram, we see that $2 + 3$ would look like this:

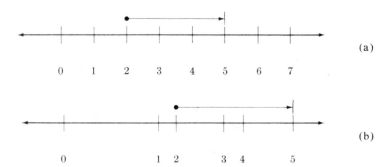

The same interpretation on $3 + 2$ produces the following:

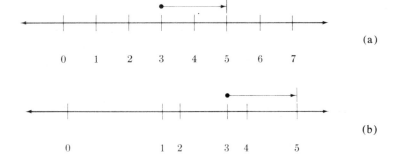

We have a wide choice of number lines which we could use; if we wish no further characteristics for a number line, we could use either (a) or (b).

In our contacts with the physical world we use various devices which are very similar to number lines, for example, a ruler. On a ruler the numerals are assigned to points along the edge (which serves as a line) in a uniformly distributed fashion. Number line (a) exhibits the same characteristic, while number line (b) does not. The reason for uniform distribution on a ruler is based upon a concept from measurement, i.e., consistency. We expect an inch to be an inch, not so long here and a different length somewhere else. Moreover, we expect two objects 1 inch in length when placed end to end to *measure* 2 inches long. If the ruler were not uniformly divided this would not happen.

What obviously follows from this last observation is that the choice of number lines should be reserved for those like number line (a). It serves our purpose of illustration of our interpretation of addition problems, *plus* it could be used later to develop the notions of measurement. Hence, all number lines ought to look like (a), and a number line must possess the following characteristics:

1. The points which are assigned names along the line must be uniformly distributed.

2. The names (numerals) assigned must be in an order left to right (or right to left) which preserves the "is less than" relation for the numbers represented.

With these characteristics and our interpretation of $2 + 3$, we can use the number line to illustrate that $2 + 3 = 5$. Moreover, all basic addition facts can be illustrated in the same manner. Hence, we have a second way in which addition facts can be determined. (The first was through the application of the union of disjoint sets, as was done in chapter 4.)

Other interpretations can be applied to $2 + 3$ if we keep number line (a). For example, suppose we always start at 0. Then the 2 means to move 2 points to the right, and adding 3 means to move 3 more points to the right. Thus we have

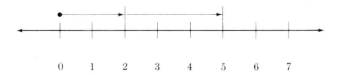

This interpretation is slightly better, for it is more closely related to measurement concepts; that is, an object 2 units long placed end to end with an object 3 units long is the same as one object 5 units long.

There is some criticism of the use of number lines to teach addition facts. The principal objection is based upon the fact that to adequately develop the concept of a number line requires much mathematical knowledge which most primary students do not possess. Furthermore, the students must apply an interpretation to the $a + b$ statement—likewise not an obvious idea. Users of the number line also tend to ignore the definition of addition of whole numbers, and this, mathematically, is unfortunate. Some educators claim that the number line becomes a crutch for students (and teachers?) and that it persists in use after it has served its purpose. On the other hand, it is a useful mathematical idea with many applications. It should be used wisely.

Exercises

1.   Illustrate the following addition problems on a number line:
(a) 3 + 1   (b) 4 + 2
(c) 2 + 4   (d) (3 + 1) + 5
(e) 3 + (1 + 5)   (f) 6 + 0
(g) 0 + 0

2.   In Exercise 1, do (b) and (c) end up at the same point? What does this mean as far as addition is concerned?

3.   In Exercise 1, do (d) and (e) end up at the same point? What does this mean?

4.   On the number line, what is to the left of zero? Is there a number between 1 and 2 on *this* number line?

5.   Suppose the number line were as follows:

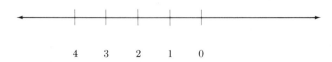

Would this make a difference in our interpretation of addition? If so, in what way?

6.   Would it be possible to have a vertical number line? If so, construct one and describe the interpretation of addition necessary for this number line.

5.6   The Multiplication Algorithm for Whole Numbers

The operation of multiplication is also defined only for whole numbers; moreover, the definition of multiplication in chapter 4 does not tell us how to compute products. Either we must rely upon the definition as the means of determining the product of two whole numbers, or we must develop some rule or algorithm. The development of this algorithm is the purpose of this section.

We first determine certain products by using the definition of multiplication as related to whole numbers. We determine, for example, that $2 \cdot 3 = 6$ by applying the definition or by using concrete examples which illustrate the definition. Suppose that a student already knows that $2 \cdot 3 = 6$ and that he now wishes to determine $2 \cdot 4$. Since $2 \cdot 4 =$

$2 \cdot (3 + 1)$, and by the distributive property of multiplication over addition, we know that

$$2 \cdot (3 + 1) = 2 \cdot 3 + 2 \cdot 1$$

Each of the products $2 \cdot 3$ and $2 \cdot 1$ is already known, so we have

$$2 \cdot 3 + 2 = 1 = 6 + 2$$
$$= 8$$

We know now that $2 \cdot 4 = 8$ and we have a new fact at our disposal. By applying the commutative property for multiplication, we know that $2 \cdot 4 = 4 \cdot 2 = 8$. What is $4 \cdot 3$?

$$4 \cdot 3 = 4(2 + 1)$$
$$= 4 \cdot 2 + 4 \cdot 1$$
$$= 8 + 4$$
$$= 12$$

Repeating this process, we can complete the multiplication facts through $9 \cdot 9$. Knowing all these facts enables us to further extend our information about multiplication. For example,

$$8 \cdot 10 = 8 \cdot (9 + 1)$$
$$= 8 \cdot 9 + 8 \cdot 1$$
$$= 72 + 8$$
$$= 80$$

Here we are able to find $8 \cdot 10$ when we know multiplication facts only through $9 \cdot 9$; the distributive property for multiplication over addition makes this computation possible. Another example will illustrate further:

$$6 \cdot 10 = 6 \cdot (7 + 3)$$
$$= 6 \cdot 7 + 6 \cdot 3$$
$$= 42 + 18$$
$$= 60$$

Again the distributive property allowed us to break an unknown problem into two problems for which we knew the solutions. This is the last technique we will use repeatedly to develop the multiplication algorithm.

If we apply the above pattern to $7 \cdot 10$, we will get 70. Hence, to multiply a number represented by a single-digit numeral by 10, we simply write the single digit with a zero after it, creating a new two-digit numeral. This is, in essence, the familiar shortcut to multiplying by 10.

We can also rely upon the place value notation to find the product $8 \cdot 10$. For example,

$$
\begin{aligned}
8 \cdot 10 &= 8 \cdot 10 + 0 && \text{Additive identity} \\
&= 8 \cdot 10 + 0 \cdot 1 && \text{Multiplicative identity} \\
&= 80 && \text{Place value notation}
\end{aligned}
$$

Each of these approaches has merit and could serve in an elementary instructional program in multiplying by 10. Whichever we use, we can arrive at the algorithmic process for multiplying by 10. Moreover, it is not difficult to extend the notion to include multiplying by any multiple of 10. For example,

$$
\begin{aligned}
8 \cdot 20 &= 8 \cdot (2 \cdot 10) \\
&= (8 \cdot 2) \cdot 10 \\
&= 16 \cdot 10 \\
&= (10 + 6) \cdot 10 \\
&= 10 \cdot 10 + 6 \cdot 10 \\
&= 100 + 60 \\
&= 160
\end{aligned}
$$

Notice that we used the associative property to convert the multiplication by 20 to multiplying by 10. The place value notation is also applicable, and we observe within the problem that our shortcut also applies to multiplying two-digit numerals by 10 $(16 \cdot 10 = 160)$.

Consider this example from the place value notation point of view:

$$
\begin{aligned}
8 \cdot 100 &= 8 \cdot 100 + 0 \cdot 10 + 0 \cdot 1 \\
&= 800
\end{aligned}
$$

Here we see the shortcut extended to apply to multiplying by 100. In a similar pattern we could extend it to multiplying by multiples of 100. The pattern is repeatable for 1,000 and multiples of 1,000, etc. Knowing how to multiply by 10 enables us to obtain other facts.

In this developmental stage, one might expect students to be somewhat creative and not necessarily write down a sequence of steps which the teacher had in mind. The following example indicates alternative ways of determining certain products:

$$5 \cdot 9 = 5 \cdot (10 - 1)$$
$$= 5 \cdot 10 - 5 \cdot 1$$
$$= 50 - 5$$
$$= 45$$

This approach makes use of the distributive property for multiplication over subtraction as it could be defined on the set of whole numbers. This type of creative effort certainly needs to be encouraged in every student of mathematics.

After we have developed the products of two one-digit numbers and developed the shortcut in multiplying by multiples of 10, we are ready to extend this to additional types of problems. For example,

$$12 \cdot 3 = (10 + 2) \cdot 3$$
$$= 10 \cdot 3 + 2 \cdot 3$$
$$= 30 + 6$$
$$= 36$$

Here we choose to write 12 as $10 + 2$ to take advantage of the results in the form of $30 + 6$, which uses the place value notations. Moreover, we wish to work toward the idea of multiplying using the algorithm, and this form is a good example of the first stage of the development of the algorithm. Another example illustrates the point:

$$17 \cdot 8 = (10 + 7) \cdot 8$$
$$= 10 \cdot 8 + 7 \cdot 8$$
$$= 80 + 56$$
$$= 136$$

We should note that we must already know how to add certain combinations, as we must use them consistently in multiplication. Hence, certain addition combinations must be taught before certain multiplication combinations can be presented. Care must be taken in seeing that this is done properly and in a good sequence for arithmetic to be meaningful.

The last example shows again how it is possible to convert $17 \cdot 8$ to multiplication problems we already know how to do, i.e., $10 \cdot 8$ and $7 \cdot 8$. Moreover, by careful observation we see that a pattern begins to emerge. Another example reveals the same pattern:

$$18 \cdot 6 = (10 + 8) \cdot 6$$
$$= 10 \cdot 6 + 8 \cdot 6$$
$$= 60 + 48$$

We stop here to examine the last line. Each of the two preceding examples has a corresponding line similar to this: $30 + 6$ in the first, and $80 + 56$ in the second. Before pursuing this idea further, we look at a couple of examples of the products of two two-digit numbers. To do this, we must first know how to multiply a two-digit number by a one-digit number, for example, $12 \cdot 15$:

$$12 \cdot 15 = 12 \cdot (10 + 5)$$
$$= 12 \cdot 10 + 12 \cdot 5$$

If we know how to do $12 \cdot 10$ and $12 \cdot 5$, we have

$$12 \cdot 10 + 12 \cdot 5 = 120 + 60$$
$$= 180$$

Also,

$$23 \cdot 45 = 23(40 + 5)$$
$$= 23 \cdot 40 + 23 \cdot 5$$

If we know how to do $23 \cdot 40$ and $23 \cdot 5$, we have

$$23 \cdot 40 + 23 \cdot 5 = 920 + 115$$
$$= 1,035$$

Such examples show how it is possible to apply the distributive property for multiplication over addition, and other known properties for addition and multiplication, and find products of two two-digit numbers. The last example also suggests that there must be a shortcut, for it is time-consuming and requires many steps to complete. A shortcut to all this is obtainable only if we recognize that certain patterns are present each and every time in every similar problem. In the last two examples, two basic types of problems occur, and all remaining steps are involved in solving them:

$$12 \cdot 10, \quad 23 \cdot 40, \quad 10 \cdot 8, \quad 10 \cdot 6 \qquad \text{Type (a)}$$
$$12 \cdot 5, \quad 23 \cdot 5, \quad 23 \cdot 5, \quad 23 \cdot 4 \qquad \text{Type (b)}$$

plus the various products up through $9 \cdot 9$. Since we have already suggested that Type (a) problems can be shortened, we shall look first at Type (b) problems:

$12 \cdot 5$ turns out to be $50 + 10$.

$23 \cdot 5$ turns out to be $100 + 15$.

$23 \cdot 4$ turns out to be $80 + 12$.

As we look at the steps in $12 \cdot 5$, we observe that the 12 is divided into 10's and 1's and that each is multiplied by 5. We might write this in the following manner:

$$\begin{array}{r} 12 \\ 5 \\ \hline ? \end{array}$$

First, multiply $2 \cdot 5$:

$$\begin{array}{r} 12 \\ 5 \\ \hline 10 \end{array}$$

Secondly, multiply the 1 in 12 (which really stands for one 10) by 5 to obtain 50. Write it as follows:

$$\begin{array}{r} 12 \\ 5 \\ \hline 10 \\ 50 \end{array}$$

Then add the two partial products thus obtained. Thus the whole process looks like this:

$$\begin{array}{r} 12 \\ 5 \\ \hline 10 \\ +50 \\ \hline 60 \end{array}$$

This certainly is shorter to write down than what we wrote in the example in the first place. With a little more refinement on this process we finally may arrive at the following: In words, $2 \cdot 5$ is 10; write down the 0 and remember the 1. Then $5 \cdot 10$ is 50, plus the 1 which really represents one 10, and we have 60. However, this product always ends in zero and we need only the tens portion of it, or 6. Put the 6 in the tens position of the answer. We can be somewhat systematic about this if we pattern our process in the following manner:

$$12 \longleftarrow \text{Tens digit of the product } 2 \cdot 5$$
$$\cdot 5$$
$$\overline{}$$
$$6\ 0 \longleftarrow \text{Units digit of the product } 2 \cdot 5$$
$$\underline{} \longleftarrow \text{Tens digit of } 10 \cdot 5 \text{ plus the tens digit of } 2 \cdot 5$$

For $23 \cdot 4$ the process becomes

$$1 \longleftarrow \text{Tens digit of } 3 \cdot 4$$
$$23$$
$$\cdot 4$$
$$\overline{}$$
$$9\ 2 \longleftarrow \text{Units digit of } 3 \cdot 4$$
$$\underline{} \longleftarrow \text{Tens digit of } 20 \cdot 4 \text{ plus the tens digit of } 3 \cdot 4$$

This process certainly saves writing and makes it possible to quickly compute certain products. However, this process is a gimmick, a device or a trick to permit us to save time. We should not be in too big a rush to teach this pattern, for the elementary student needs to know and understand what is going on in a multiplication problem *before* he looks for or develops shortcuts.

Type (a) problems have already been discussed and are either like $12 \cdot 10$ (which we already know how to handle via a shortcut) or like $23 \cdot 40$. The $23 \cdot 40$ can be quickly computed by considering $(23 \cdot 4) \cdot 10$, which involves a Type (a) and a Type (b) problem. These we now know how to treat, so our examples now may be shortened to the following:

$$12 \cdot 15 = 12(10 + 5)$$
$$= 12 \cdot 10 + 12 \cdot 5$$
$$= 120 + 60$$
$$= 180$$

and

$$23 \cdot 45 = 23(40 + 5)$$
$$= 23 \cdot 40 + 23 \cdot 5$$
$$= 920 + 115$$
$$= 1{,}035$$

These are considerably shorter and much easier to complete. However, this procedure is still not the multiplication process that we normally use and can be shortened further. In fact, if we apply the pattern to additional steps, we might reduce the number of steps still further. The last example can be made to appear as follows:

$$23 \cdot 45 = 920 + 115 = 1{,}035$$

This is left to the student to justify.

In this chapter we have suggested how to start with the definitions and properties of chapter 4 and evolve an algorithm on the product of two whole numbers. While we have not given all the steps necessary in the complete evolution of the multiplication algorithm, we have indicated, in a general way, a sequence of steps which would be followed. What is important to remember is that the algorithm is an outgrowth of the various properties; the distributive property for multiplication over addition is most important. Great care must be taken to develop a clear understanding of this distributive property; otherwise the multiplication algorithm is not clearly motivated or properly placed in the sequence of mathematical ideas taught in elementary school.

Exercises

1. Explain why we handle the zero in 306 in the product $245 \cdot 306$ as we do.

2. In working the problem $8 \cdot 20 = 160$, give reasons for all steps involved.

3. In the "creative" example of $5 \cdot 9$, why is $5(10 - 1)$ equal to $5 \cdot 10 - 5 \cdot 1$? What property does this exemplify? Does this property hold on the set of cardinal numbers?

4. In the example of $23 \cdot 45$, enumerate all facts and properties we need to know before we can show that $23 \cdot 45$ is 1,035.

5. In applying the multiplication algorithm to the product of 204

and 306, how do we handle the zero in the multiplier? What do we do to shortcut this step even further?

6.   Would it be possible to develop a multiplication algorithm where we multiply from left to right rather than right to left? Try it on $46 \cdot 35$.

7.   Can you multiply 12 by 4 without using the algorithm or the distributive property for multiplication over addition?

5.7   Zero and Multiplication

In examining the various properties of multiplication in chapter 4, we noted that a very special property was exhibited by the number zero:

$$a \cdot 0 = 0 \quad \text{for all } a \in \{\text{whole numbers}\}$$

This useful property is recognized and accounted for in the multiplication algorithm as applied to products such as $254 \cdot 306$. It enables us to shorten further certain problems.

An equally interesting question relating to multiplication and zero is posed in the following: If $a \cdot b = 0$, where a and b are whole numbers, must a or b be zero? If either a or b is zero, then it is a valid statement and precisely the same type of statement as indicated in the preceding paragraph. If both a and b are zero, then $0 \cdot 0 = 0$ and $a \cdot 0 = 0$ for all whole numbers a (and that includes $a = 0$). But the question asks, Must a or b be 0 if $a \cdot b = 0$; that is, if the product of two whole numbers is zero, must *one* of the numbers be zero? Suppose $a \cdot b = 0$. If $a = n(A)$ and $b = n(B)$, then $n(A) \cdot n(B) = 0$. By definition, $n(A) \cdot n(B) = n(A \times B) = 0$. This last equality must mean that $A \times B = \varnothing$, which is true if and only if $A = \varnothing$ or $B = \varnothing$. If $A = \varnothing$, then $a = 0$. If $B = \varnothing$, then $b = 0$. Hence we have the following important property.

THEOREM 5.1   If $a \cdot b = 0$, a and b being whole numbers, then $a = 0$ or $b = 0$, or both a and b = zero.

Theorem 5.1 has many applications in our mathematics. For example, given $(x - 5)(y - 6) = 0$, find an x and a y which make this statement true. Since the product of $(x - 5)$ and $(y - 6)$ is zero, then $x - 5 = 0$ or $y - 6 = 0$ or both. If $x - 5 = 0$, then $x = 5$. If $y - 6 = 0$, then $y = 6$. Thus $x = 5$ or $y = 6$, or both of these facts make the given statement true.

Exercises

1.   Without using the property that $a \cdot 0 = 0$, show that $6 \cdot 0$ is equal to zero.

2.   If $a \cdot b = 0$, then either $a = 0$ or $b = 0$. Use this to solve for x and y:

(a) $(x - 5)(y - 7) = 0$ (b) $(x - z)(y - 1) = 0$

(c) $x(y - 3) = 0$ (d) $(x - 1)(y - 1) = 0$

(e) $(x - z)(y - 3)(z - 4) = 0$

5.8   Interpretations of Multiplication with Whole Numbers

Elementary mathematics textbooks commonly consider multiplication as repeated addition. For example,

$$3 \cdot 4 = 4 + 4 + 4$$

$$5 \cdot 6 = 6 + 6 + 6 + 6 + 6$$

Here we say $3 \cdot 4$ means three 4's, $4 + 4 + 4$; $4 + 4 + 4$ and $3 \cdot 4$ name the same number. Moreover, this interpretation of multiplication as repeated addition fits many problems in our surrounding physical world. For example, $3 \cdot 4$ could be a statement which represents the total number of apples in three pans if each pan contains four apples. We can consider the problem as $4 + 4 + 4$ or as $3 \cdot 4$; in either case the answer is 12. Such an interpretation is almost essential if one tries to relate $3 \cdot 4$ to the number line. One must think of $3 \cdot 4$ as 3 sets of 4 each; on the number line the problem appears as follows:

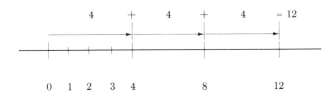

This interpretation actually says that a multiplication problem is an addition problem. Since we already know how to add on the number line we can multiply on the number line.

Can multiplication *always* be interpreted as repeated addition? Consider the following products:

4·3 can be interpreted 4 + 4 + 4.

3·4 can be interpreted as 3 + 3 + 3 + 3.

10·2 can be interpreted as 10 + 10.

1·2 can be interpreted as 1 + 1.

1·1 can be interpreted as _____.

1·0 can be interpreted as _____.

0·0 can be interpreted as _____.

The problem 1·1 cannot be interpreted as a repeated addition problem. In fact, to have addition at all, at least two numbers are necessary, for addition is a binary operation. Therefore, the interpretation is not a valid one for 1·1. Also, it is not a valid interpretation for 1·0 or 0·0. Hence, it seems to be questionable as to whether such an interpretation should be allowed at all unless it works every time. Also, this interpretation of multiplication as repeated addition does not apply to other types of products. For example, it does not apply to $1/2 \cdot 2/3$, $\pi\sqrt{2}$, $(-2)(-3)$ and many other types of products.

We have a choice at this point. Do we keep this interpretation for the product of two whole numbers *even if* it does not describe all such products? Do we find another interpretation and hope that it describes all products? Repeated addition works fairly well and is adaptable to the number line. Moreover, such an interpretation of the product may be closely related to other properties which we know. If this were true, then we would have more and better reasons to use it.

Consider again 3·4. If we rename 4, we have 3·4 = 3(1 + 1 + 1 + 1). Applying the distributive property for multiplication over addition, we have

$$3 \cdot 4 = 3(1 + 1 + 1 + 1) = 3 \cdot 1 + 3 \cdot 1 + 3 \cdot 1 + 3 \cdot 1$$

Since 3·1 = 3, then 3·4 = 3 + 3 + 3 + 3. Our interpretation is no longer an interpretation, but a proven mathematical fact! A small catch is the 3·1 = 3, but this need not hold us back because 1 is the multiplicative identity element and we know (from chapter 4) that $a \cdot 1 = a$ for all a. Is it possible to repeat the method with the products 1·1, 1·0 and 0·0? Try 1·1. From the statement $a + 0 = a$ for all a, let $a = 1$. Then 1 + 0 = 1. Therefore,

$$1 \cdot 1 = 1 \cdot (1 + 0) = 1 \cdot 1 + 1 \cdot 0$$

But this brings us back to $1 \cdot 1$ and we have accomplished nothing. Try $1 \cdot 0$, or $0 \cdot 0$:

$$1 \cdot 0 = 1 \cdot (0 + 0) = 1 \cdot 0 = 1 \cdot 0$$
$$0 \cdot 0 = 0(0 + 0) = 0 \cdot 0 + 0 \cdot 0$$

Each attempt to relate these three products to an addition problem produces the same products. However, these three products are all very special and need not be explained or illustrated. They are very special cases of $a \cdot 1 = a$ and $a \cdot 0 = 0$.

Although it seems that we might have failed in our attempt to express all products of whole numbers as addition problems, our attempt did do us a great service. It showed us that we need not interpret a product as an addition problem but can show or prove that almost all products of whole numbers can be changed to addition problems by using the distributive property for multiplication over addition. With this added bit of information, it seems desirable to keep the "interpretation" of a product of two whole numbers. However, we no longer need to call it an interpretation, because it is not. It is a derivable fact for nearly all such products. Hence, we may use this as it was suggested in connection with the number line.

Exercises

1.   Show that $4 \cdot 5 = 4 + 4 + 4 + 4 + 4$.

2.   Show that $5 \cdot 4 = 4 + 4 + 4 + 4 + 4$.

3.   Is it possible to show that a product such as $4 \cdot 5$ is a *certain* addition problem such as $4 + 4 + 4 + 4 + 4$ without using the distributive property? If so, show how.

4.   Show how to illustrate $3 \cdot 2$ on a number line. Show how to illustrate $2 \cdot 3$ on a number line. Do you obtain the same answer for each?

5.   Give an illustration of $1 \cdot 4$ on the number line. Give one for $4 \cdot 1$.

6.   Is it possible to give an illustration for $0 \cdot 0$ on a number line?

5.9   Other Techniques for Multiplication

Shortly after the Hindu-Arabic system of notation was introduced into Western culture, it was necessary to devise ways to multiply. In the 1500s several methods appeared in textbooks and at least one such book gave at least eight ways to perform the multiplication of whole numbers.

This is interesting for several reasons. It reflects mankind's attempt to arrive at the shortcut procedure we now use and it illustrates some alternatives to what we do use. Moreover, it indicates that arithmetic was (and is) a developing and growing subject.

An historically significant technique of multiplication, called the lattice method, is not much different from our own. The framework of the problem resembles a lattice work. We illustrate with an example.

Example 5.1   Find 325·641. First, construct a 3 by 3 square and then subdivide it into nine squares. We obtain figure 5.1. Divide each square with a diagonal from upper right to lower left (fig. 5.2). Place 325 on top of the square as indicated and 641 on the right as indicated. Next write the various products in the nine squares in such a manner that the tens digit, if any, is above the diagonal and the units digit is below. For the 6 row we have figure 5.3. Upon completion of the other two rows, we have figure 5.4. Now add down each diagonal starting with the lower right-hand one by the 1 in 641 and write the sum below the large square. We obtain for the first two such operations 5 and 2, re-

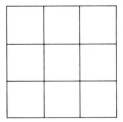

FIGURE 5.1

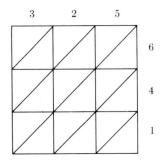

FIGURE 5.2

spectively. In the third diagonal column, we obtain 13. Put down the 3 and carry 1 to the next diagonal column. Here we have the completed problem in figure 5.5. Thus $325 \cdot 641 = 208,325$.

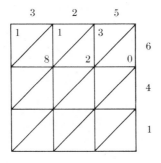

FIGURE 5.3

The procedure seems quite different from ours, yet if we examine it in detail we observe precisely the same substeps found in ours. The substeps appear in different sequences, and the lattice method ignores which side we start with. Moreover, the lattice technique requires only the knowledge of multiplication facts up through $9 \cdot 9$ and knowledge of addition.

Does the lattice method seem easier to do? Is it easier to justify in terms of what we know about the properties of multiplication? These answers depend entirely upon the person who is answering. One obvious product of looking at the lattice method is that we could use this for enrichment material for youngsters after they already know the usual process. Experience has shown that youngsters really like it and learn from studying it.

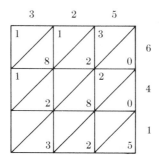

FIGURE 5.4

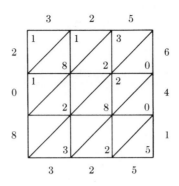

FIGURE 5.5

Exercises

1. Find the following products by using the lattice method:
(a) $293 \cdot 414$ (b) $209 \cdot 68$
(c) $14 \cdot 10$ (d) $9 \cdot 8$
(e) $13 \cdot 0$

2. Look up the various methods of multiplication described by D. E. Smith in his book, *History of Mathematics*. Compare them with the method we normally use.

3. Find $3,456 \cdot 11$ by some shortcut method other than those referred to or given in this text. Is this method shorter than the one we normally use? Should it be used in elementary school? Why?

5.10   Algorithm for Subtraction on Whole Numbers

In chapter 4, we defined subtraction on the set of whole numbers by the following definition:

$a - b = c$ such that $a = b + c$, where a, b and c are whole numbers

As the result of this definition we found that the set of whole numbers is not closed for the operation of subtraction. This discovery resulted from those problems in which $b > a$, in which case there is no whole number c such that $a = b + c$. In effect, this means that a must be greater than or equal to b before we can consider subtraction as an operation on the set of whole numbers. In other words, we can only subtract the smaller number from the larger.

We also noted in chapter 4 that subtraction was not a commutative or an associative operation. However, we did observe that the distributive property for multiplication over subtraction holds for whole numbers, provided that the subtraction operation is defined for whole numbers involved.

Since subtraction is, by definition, related to addition and since we already know the basic addition facts, we can readily determine the basic subtraction facts. For example, if $2 + 3 = 5$, then $5 - 3 = 2$ and $5 - 2 = 3$. It is probably wise to teach such relations at the same time; the following patterns can be used to firmly establish these relations:

$$2 + 3 = 5 \quad 2 + \square = 5 \quad 3 + \triangle = 5 \quad 5 - 3 = \square \quad 5 - 2 = \triangle$$

Since we know the addition combinations through $9 + 9$, we know as many subtraction facts, including some which appear to require some techniques not yet developed. For example, since $9 + 9 = 18$, we know that $18 - 9$ is 9 although we do not know how to subtract where borrowing is concerned.

Consider then some problems which are beyond the basic addition facts, for example, (a) $57 - 34$, and (b) $64 - 36$. In Example (a) it is possible to subtract without "borrowing," and this class of subtraction problem is handled readily. One needs only to refer to the "such that" part of the definition and determine that $34 + \square = 57$. Since column addition has already been developed, we use its techniques to find $57 - 34$. We know that $3 + 4$ is 7 and $2 + 3$ is 5. Therefore, our answer to $57 - 34$ must be 23. Moreover, the subtraction process may be done from right to left *or* left to right.

	Right to Left				Left to Right		
	57		57		57		57
First	34	Then	34	First	34	Then	34
	3		23		2		23

It is fairly obvious that either of the teaching approaches to subtraction applies equally well to this class of problems.

Consider Example (b), $64 - 36$. Column subtraction is complicated here because $4 - 6$ in the units column does not fit our definition of subtraction, so we must try something else. We offer the following techniques which are quite similar to the addition techniques used to develop the carrying concept:

$$64 - 36 = (8 + 56) - 36$$
$$= 8 + (56 - 36) \qquad \text{Why? Subtraction is not an associative}$$
$$= 8 + (20) \qquad\qquad \text{operation.}$$
$$= 28$$

or

$$64 - 36 = (28 + 36) - 36$$
$$= 28$$

or

$$64 - 36 = (50 + 14) - (30 + 6)$$
$$= (50 - 30) + (14 - 6) \qquad \text{Why?}$$
$$= 20 + 8$$
$$= 28$$

or

$$64 - 36 = (64 + 4) - (36 + 4) \qquad \text{Why?}$$
$$= 68 - 40$$
$$= 28$$

All of the techniques used here to obtain the answer 28 are valid but not all have been previously considered. In fact, we have used some properties we have not yet developed! What is more important is that we do not recognize a pattern in these that suggests an algorithm for subtraction, so we try some other technique. Since 64 means $6 \cdot 10 + 4 \cdot 1$ and 36 means $3 \cdot 10 + 6 \cdot 1$, column subtraction would be possible if we could rewrite the $6 \cdot 10 + 4 \cdot 1$ expression to get more 1's. We could do so by taking one of the 10's and making it ten 1's. Thus we have

$$\begin{array}{r} 64 \\ -36 \\ \hline \end{array} \text{ is the same as } \begin{array}{r} 6 \cdot 10 + 4 \cdot 1 \\ -(3 \cdot 10 + 6 \cdot 1) \\ \hline \end{array}$$

$$\text{and is the same as } \begin{array}{r} 5 \cdot 10 + 14 \cdot 1 \\ -(3 \cdot 10 + 6 \cdot 1) \\ \hline \end{array}$$

Now we can subtract six 1's from fourteen 1's and get eight 1's, and three 10's subtracted from five 10's gives two 10's. This gives us two

10's and eight 1's, or 28. The possibility of establishing an algorithm could be assured if we could devise a shortcut way of handling the shifting of one 10 to ten 1's. This can be easily done by the process we call *borrowing*, sometimes called *regrouping* or *renaming*. Whatever it is called, it is still the same process; it is a valid procedure (other problems are worked the same way as the above example) and can be learned as the algorithm for subtraction. We work another example to illustrate the borrowing concept.

Example 5.2   Find $82 - 49$.

$$\begin{array}{r} 82 \\ -49 \\ \hline \end{array} \text{ is the same as } \begin{array}{r} 8 \cdot 10 + 2 \cdot 1 \\ -(4 \cdot 10 + 9 \cdot 1) \\ \hline \end{array} \text{ is the same as } \begin{array}{r} 7 \cdot 10 + 12 \cdot 1 \\ -(4 \cdot 10 + \;\; 9 \cdot 1) \\ \hline \end{array}$$

Now $9 \cdot 1$ from $12 \cdot 1$ gives $3 \cdot 1$, and $4 \cdot 10$ from $7 \cdot 10$ gives $3 \cdot 10$. Hence, $82 - 49 = 33$.

The previous type of problem which does not involve borrowing also fits into this pattern. For instance, $57 - 34$ means

$$\begin{array}{r} 5 \cdot 10 + 7 \cdot 1 \\ -(3 \cdot 10 + 4 \cdot 1) \\ \hline \end{array}$$

and we obtain $2 \cdot 10 + 3 \cdot 1$ or 23. Note that the subtraction algorithm depends heavily upon the place value system of writing numerals. (To really see this, try $LVII - XXXIV$ in Roman numerals. The algorithm becomes something else for Roman numerals because it depends upon the way the numerals are written.)

One should observe that the process of borrowing is, in a sense, the reverse of the carrying process of the addition algorithm, because of the nature of the definition of subtraction. Subtraction is defined in terms of addition because the "such that" part of the definition is an addition problem.

Exercises

1.   Subtract without borrowing:
(a) $57 - 34$ (b) $69 - 18$
(c) $43 - 36$ (d) $121 - 98$

2.   Develop an algorithm for subtracting from left to right. Is it easier to handle than the one we normally use?

3.   What are the two principal teaching approaches to subtraction? How are they related to our development of a subtraction definition and subtraction algorithm?

4.　In one of the four illustrations of $64 - 36$, we find the following statement:

$$(50 + 14) - (30 + 6) = (50 - 30) + (14 - 6)$$

Why is this true? Is $(a + b) - c = a + (b - c)$?

5.　Is $64 - 36 = (64 + 4) - (36 + 4)$? Why? If $a - b = c$, does $(a + d) - (b + d) = c$? Can you prove it?

5.11　Subtraction and the Number Line

Because subtraction is defined in terms of an addition situation, we would expect to have a comparable interpretation for use on a number line. For example, $2 + 3 = 5$ is expressible as $5 - 2 = 3$. Now $5 - 2$ is 3, and if we start the subtraction on the number line in the same way as the addition interpretation, we have

Since $5 - 2 = 3$, we want to end up at 3. To do so, we must go from 5 to the *left* to get 3. Therefore, if we wish to subtract 2 we must go to the left 2 units. Therefore, our number line looks like this:

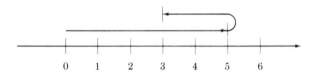

To find $4 - 3$, start at 0, then go 4 to the right. Then turn and go 3 to the left. We end up at 1. Therefore $4 - 3 = 1$.

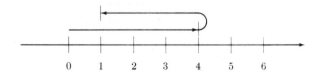

One might note that $4 - 5$ does not have a meaning on the number

line, for example,

There is no whole number located to the left of 0. Therefore, there is no whole number which is equal to $4 - 5$.

Exercises

1. Illustrate the following on the number line:
(a) $10 - 4$ (b) $6 - 2$ (c) $5 - 5$

2. Use the number line to show that the associative property for subtraction does not hold.

3. We sometimes have people read the subtraction problem $12 - 8$ as "12 take away 8." What do we mean by "take away"? Can this be expressed in set language to be more precise?

5.12   Algorithm for Division on Whole Numbers

In chapter 4, we defined division on the set of whole numbers as follows:

$a \div b = c$ such that $a = b \cdot c$,   where a, b, and c are whole numbers

The set of whole numbers is not closed for this operation because for some a and b, c is not a whole number. The operation is neither commutative nor associative. Moreover, division by zero must be excluded because there would be no whole number c which would satisfy the above definition for division.

Because the definition is expressed in terms of multiplication, we know many division facts. For example, $6 \div 3$ is 2 because $6 = 3 \cdot 2$, only one example from the multiplication table of facts which can also be written as a division problem. This suggests an excellent way to teach basic division facts. Frequently the combinations expressed in the multiplication table which are written as division problems or facts are referred to as exact division problems, that is, $a \div b$ is exactly the whole number c because $a = b \cdot c$. Such division problems have a zero remainder. Not all division problems involving whole numbers have a zero remainder. For example, $17 \div 5$ is not a whole number because it has a remainder of 2. Because such a division problem is not an exact division, we wish to express the relationship in some convenient form involving only whole numbers. We know that $5 \cdot 3$ is less than 17 and that $5 \cdot 4$ is greater than 17. We also know that 17 can be written as $5 \cdot 3 + 2$. This suggests that every whole number can be written in the form $aq + r$, where a, q and r are whole numbers. In general, if p is a whole number, then

$$p = aq + r \quad \text{where } r \text{ is less than } a$$

This is frequently referred to as the *remainder theorem* because of its relation to the division process. Another example might help clarify the statement of the remainder theorem:

$$23 = 3 \cdot 4 + 11$$

is a statement of 23 in the form of the theorem. It says that $23 \div 3$ will give us 4 with a remainder of 11. We also know that we can express this with numbers other than 4 and 11. For example, $23 \div 3$ will give us 5 with a remainder of 8. Also $23 \div 3$ will give us 7 with a remainder of 2. Thus 23 may be written as

$$23 = 3 \cdot 4 + 11$$

or

$$23 = 3 \cdot 5 + 8$$

or

$$23 = 3 \cdot 7 + 2$$

There is an expression for any whole number in the form $aq + r$, where $r < a$. Only in the last instance where $23 = 3 \cdot 7 + 2$ was the restriction on r ($r < a$) satisfied. This is the form which the remainder theorem requires. Moreover, the theorem says that there exists a q such that r is less than a. Such a q is called the *quotient* and the resulting r is called the *remainder*.

If $r = 0$, then $p = aq$ which may also be written as $p \div a = q$. (This is the case of exact division mentioned a moment earlier.) If $r \neq$ zero, then the division form of $p = aq + r$ is $p \div a = q$ plus a remainder of r.

Consider the example $76 \div 6$: $76 = 6q + r$ and we wish to find a q and an r such that $r < 6$. Suppose we think q should be 10. Then we would have $76 = 6 \cdot 10 + r$; r must be 16 for this to be a true statement. However, 16 is not less than 6, so q must not be large enough. We recall that $6 \cdot 2$ is 12 and $16 - 12 = 4$, which is less than 6. Therefore,

$$76 = 6 \cdot 10 + 16$$
$$= 6 \cdot 10 + (6 \cdot 2 + 4)$$
$$= (6 \cdot 10 + 6 \cdot 2) + 4$$
$$= 6(10 + 2) + 4$$
$$= 6 \cdot 12 + 4$$

This states that there are twelve 6's and four 1's in 76, or in other words, $76 \div 6$ is 12 with a remainder of 4.

In reality then, the remainder theorem gives us a way of dividing one whole number by another. Our only task is to find a q such that $0 \leq r < a$. If we find an x such that $b = 0$, then we have exact division. The division algorithm must, therefore, be a way of finding this q. In the last example, we obtained the desired q by trial and error. After 10 proved unsuccessful, we did not start all over but took the r term, 16, and removed any multiples of 6 from it. By applying certain properties we rearranged terms until we obtained the desired $aq + r$ form. Will this method always be applicable? Try this example: $651 \div 24 = ?$ Writing $651 = 24 \cdot q + r$, we try to guess q, for example $q = 20$. Then $651 = 24 \cdot 20 + r$ and $r = 651 - 24 \cdot 20$, or $r = 651 - 480 = 171$. But 171 is not less than 24. Therefore, q is not large enough. We proceed as follows: $651 = 24 \cdot 20 + (24 \cdot y + c)$, where $24y + c = 171$. (Here y and c play the role of q and r, respectively.) It looks like y might be 5. If $y = 5$, then

$$651 = 24 \cdot 20 + (24 \cdot 5 + c)$$

and we determine that c must be $171 - 24 \cdot 5$, or $171 - 120 = 51$. Therefore,

$$651 = (24 \cdot 20 + 24 \cdot 5) + 71$$

But again 51 is too large, so there must be more 24's in the remainder term, 51. Quite obviously there must be two more 24's, and we obtain

$$651 = (24 \cdot 20 + 24 \cdot 5) + 24 \cdot 2 + 3$$
$$= 24(20 + 5 + 2) + 3$$
$$= 24 \cdot 27 + 3$$

All of this suggests that there must be a more convenient form in which this can be done, for example,

$$
\begin{array}{r|r}
24 & 651 \\
 & -480 \\
\hline
 & 171 \\
 & -120 \\
\hline
 & 51 \\
 & -48 \\
\hline
 & 3
\end{array}
$$

Try 20; then $20 \cdot 24 = 480$. Subtract from 651. Now try 5 more. Then $5 \cdot 24 = 120$; subtract from 171. Try 2 more; then $2 \cdot 24 = 48$. Subtract from 51. Now we have left 3, which is less than 24, so r must be 3. Therefore, $20 + 5 + 2$ must be q and $651 = 24 \cdot 27 + 3$.

The suggested form is convenient and eliminates a lot of writing. However, our guess for q did not turn out to be too close the first time, but with a little practice we could get closer to the final value for q. However, it appears that our first choice for q might always be a multiple of 10 and we would have an easy computational step. Let's try another example.

Example 5.3 $876 \div 62 = ?$ Using our convenient form, we have

$$
\begin{array}{r|l}
62 & 876 \\
 & -620 \qquad \text{Try } 10 \\
\hline
 & 256 \\
 & -248 \qquad \text{Try } 4 \\
\hline
 & 8
\end{array}
$$

Therefore, $876 = 62 \cdot 14 + 8$ and $876 \div 62 = 14$ with a remainder of 8.

The suggested form works fairly effectively and is reasonably efficient as far as time is concerned. However, it has not yet reached the form we usually use in division. It is reasonably close and with a few minor modifications we should be able to change it to what we usually use.

The 14 in Example 5.3 is scattered down the right side. There is no particular reason for this, but note that 620 is $62 \cdot 10$ and $248 =$

62·4; the 10 and the 14 could be written above the dividend:

$$
\begin{array}{r}
4 \\
10 \\
62 \enclose{longdiv}{876}
\end{array}
$$

The zero in 10 can be omitted in writing if the 1 is properly placed, and the 0 in 620 can be omitted at the same time, provided we bring down the 6 in 876 after the first subtraction is completed. In reality these are simple changes in format and do not constitute major changes in form. We simply replace some writing with some memory operations with the same result. This last phase should not be attempted until the student is well aware of what has gone on before. Understanding should not be sacrificed for speed. In the final form, the division process may evolve to the following steps:

$$
\textbf{(1)} \quad
\begin{array}{r}
1 \\
62 \enclose{longdiv}{876} \\
62 \\
\hline
25
\end{array}
\qquad
\textbf{(2)} \quad
\begin{array}{r}
1 \\
62 \enclose{longdiv}{876} \\
62 \\
\hline
256
\end{array}
\qquad
\textbf{(3)} \quad
\begin{array}{r}
14 \\
62 \enclose{longdiv}{876} \\
62 \\
\hline
256 \\
248 \\
\hline
8
\end{array}
$$

The problem of determining the various digits in 14 is strictly a process of trial and error. If either is too small, then after we subtract, the remainder term will be larger than the divisor, in which case, we know we could have selected a larger q in the $aq + r$ form. We could repeat the process, adjusting to a larger q, or we could erase and start over. With experience, we can usually make the proper selection in the beginning for any portion of the problem and thus shorten the time involved.

5.13   Division on the Number Line

Division is difficult to interpret on the number line; only exact division is attempted and only in terms of multiplication. For example, $12 \div 3 = ?$ On the number line we locate 12, as indicated:

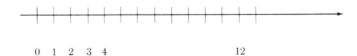

How many moves of 3 units each are necessary to reach 12? We start at 0 and move by successive steps of 3:

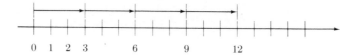

We find there are 4 moves necessary. Therefore $12 \div 3 = 4$.

For $11 \div 4$, the same procedure can be used except that if we move by 4 unit steps we never arrive at 11. We have either

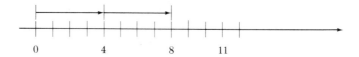

or

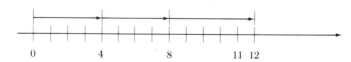

Therefore there are two 4-unit moves plus 3 more units, but these 3 units are not enough to make a 4-unit move. Thus we have

$$11 = 4 \cdot 2 + 3$$

and the 3 is the remainder portion. Therefore $11 \div 4 = 2$ with a remainder of 3.

The number line is limited in its use because it is quite impractical to try $876 \div 62$ on a number line. The time required would be prohibitive in such a problem. The number line is useful to illustrate or interpret the meaning of division on whole numbers, but its usefulness is limited to division problems involving small whole numbers only.

5.14 The Role of Algorithms

Throughout our discussion of algorithms we have consistently mentioned time, efficiency and other related concepts. It is important to recognize that we were looking for a process which provides an answer to a given problem (be it addition, subtraction, multiplication or division) in as short a time as possible and which is related to or deduced from the various definitions. Such a search for an algorithm should not be attempted until the definitions are clearly understood, and even then it must be an extension of the appropriate definition. A person who does not know the appropriate algorithm for a given operation can produce an answer on the basis of the definition only. That person is mathematically competent to a higher degree than a person who can produce an answer by using an algorithm which he has memorized but does not understand.

Exercises

1. Apply the division algorithm to the following problems and note any differences in the various problems:

(a) $689 \div 23$ (b) $802 \div 15$
(c) $482 \div 15$ (d) $593 \div 30$
(f) $25 \div 32$ (No decimals please!)

2. Illustrate $16 \div 5$ on the number line.

3. If we used the remainder theorem $p = aq + r$ and $p = 17$ and $a = 4$, and we guessed that q might be 5, what would r be? What does this tell us about our choice for q?

4. What is the relation of division form $6 \lfloor 126$ to the division form $6 \lceil 126$?

5. If $7 \lceil 29$ is 4 with a remainder of 1, write it in the remainder theorem form. What relationship does either of these have with the statement $29 \div 7 = 4 + 1/7$?

6. Illustrate on a number line how $1/7$ can be explained as the result of division being interpreted on a number line.

7. Express the following in form of the remainder theorem with $0 \le r < a$:

(a) $18 \div 4$ (b) $37 \div 12$
(c) $129 \div 3$ (d) $4 \div 4$
(e) $0 \div 5$

8. Is it true that $a \div a$ (where $a \ne 0$) is always 1? Can you prove it?

9. Answer the following questions:
(a) Is $(45 - 9) \div 3$ the same as $(45 \div 3) - (9 \div 3)$?
(b) Is $(96 - 16) \div 8$ the same as $(96 \div 8) - (16 \div 8)$?
(c) Express a general statement for all a, b and c. (Assume, of course, that the subtraction must be defined.)

References

Periodicals

Amstutz, Mildred G. "Lets 'Place' the Decimal Point, Not 'Move' It." *Arithmetic Teacher*, 10 April 1963. pp. 205–7.

Bechtel, Robert D., and Dixon, Lyle J. "Multiplication: Repeated Addition?" *Arithmetic Teacher*, May 1967.

Coon, Lewis H. "Work Backwards! Why Not?" *Arithmetic Teacher*, 12 April 1965, pp. 285–87.

Cunningham, George S. "Three Views of the Multiplier." *Arithmetic Teacher*, 12 April 1965, pp. 275–76.

Dye, David. "A Different Way of Subtracting." *Arithmetic Teacher*, 12 January 1965, pp. 56–66.

Gibney, Thomas. "Uses and Abuses of the Number Line." *Arithmetic Teacher*, 11 November 1964, pp. 478–82.

Neureiter, Paul R. "The Ultimate Form of Subtraction Algorithm." *Arithmetic Teacher*, 12 April 1965, pp. 277–81.

Rivera, Emilo. "Adding by Endings: Some Important Considerations." *Arithmetic Teacher*, 12 March 1965, pp. 204–6.

Robinson, Donald K. "Addition, Regrouping Addends." *Arithmetic Teacher*, 11 October 1964, pp. 423–25.

Books

Keedy, Mervin L. *Number Systems: A Modern Introduction*. Reading: Addison-Wesley, 1965.

National Council of Teachers of Mathematics. Booklet from *Topics in Mathematics for Elementary School Teachers*. Washington, D.C., 1964.

Peterson, John A., and Hashisaki, Joseph. *Theory of Arithmetic*. New York: John Wiley and Sons, 1963.

School Mathematics Study Group. *Studies in Mathematics*. Vol. 9. Rev. ed. Leland Stanford University, 1963.

6

ADDITIONAL POSITIONAL SYSTEMS OF NUMERATION

6.1   Introduction

In chapter 1 we examined some systems of numeration and their characteristics and discussed how numbers are represented by various symbols. In chapter 2 we continued by examining our own Hindu-Arabic,
positional system of numeration, and by discussing exponents and developing the expanded form of numerals in a positional system. In
this chapter we will continue the examination of positional systems of
numeration by studying positional systems with different bases. Systems with different bases have many characteristics similar to those of
our own system.

6.2   Numerals in Base Five System

Suppose we were created with only one hand, that everyone for generations past had only one hand and that we began to develop a system of numeration based upon five as the basic group. (Such a supposition parallels in many respects what we believe actually happened in the development of the base ten system.) Suppose still further that we recognize that a positional system of notation is the better choice of several other types of systems. Now with these restrictions or guidelines, let us construct a system of numeration based on five symbols.

First, we must select five distinct symbols, to be used in various combinations to create other symbols as additional numerals. The five symbols could be any five we might want to use, but to simplify the amount of memory work we choose 0, 1, 2, 3 and 4. Moreover, we order these in the same order as in our base ten system. Thus 0 is zero, 1 is one, 2 is two, 3 is three and 4 is four. There are other reasons for this choice which will become obvious as we progress with the development of the system.

Now that we have selected the first five symbols and their order, we begin to list succeeding symbols and what they represent. To represent five in this positional system we must compose symbols by forming a combination of two or more of the first five distinct symbols, for example, 10 represents five. Be careful here not to read 10 as "ten" because it is not ten. In order to be specific in our language and not confuse these symbols with our base ten system, we should read 10 as "one-zero" and write it as 10_5, where the subscript 5 denotes the system that we are developing.

Then let 11_5 represent six, 12_5 represent seven, and so on. By comparison with our present system, the symbols might look like the following:

Number Represented	zero	one	two	three	four	five	six	seven	eight	nine	ten
Hindu-Arabic Base Ten	0	1	2	3	4	5	6	7	8	9	10
Base Five	0	1	2	3	4	10	11	12	13	14	20

The sequence or pattern is continued in the manner indicated by the following tables:

Number Represented	eleven	twelve	thirteen	fourteen	fifteen	sixteen	seventeen
Hindu-Arabic Base Ten	11	12	13	14	15	16	17
Base Five	21	22	23	24	30	31	32

Number Represented	eighteen	nineteen	twenty	twenty-one	twenty-two	twenty-three
Hindu-Arabic Base Ten	18	19	20	21	22	23
Base Five	33	34	40	41	42	43

Number Represented	twenty-four	twenty-five	twenty-six	twenty-seven
Hindu-Arabic Base Ten	24	25	26	27
Base Five	44	100	101	102

There are many interesting relationships emerging from the tables, for example, $10_5 = 5$, $20_5 = 10$, $30_5 = 15$, $40_5 = 20$, $100_5 = 25$ and other similar expressions. The odd part about such expressions is the result of our choice of the five distinct symbols. If we had chosen $*$, #, !, ? and $ as the symbols (in order), then we would have expressions such as $\#* = 5$, $!* = 10$, $?* = 15$, $\$* = 20$ and $\#** = 25$. Perhaps these are just as odd but not quite as confusing. The student is reminded that 14 in the base five can and does represent a different number from 14 in our base ten system of notation.

We digress for a moment to remind the student of the number of different ways we have seen to represent or write nine, for example,

$$\text{nine,} \quad 9, \quad \begin{matrix} ||| \\ ||| \\ ||| \end{matrix}, \quad \text{VIIII,} \quad \text{IX,} \quad 14_5$$

All the symbols listed are "names" for the same number. Are there others?

Exercises

1.   Find the corresponding Hindu-Arabic numeral in base ten for the following base five numerals:
(a) 13
(b) 24
(c) 32
(d) 111
(e) 201
(f) 1,000
(g) 25 (Is something wrong here?)

2.   Find the corresponding base five numeral for the following base ten numerals:

(a) 8   (b) 11
(c) 19   (d) 39
(e) 100   (f) 0
(g) 3

6.3   Conversion from Base Five to Base Ten

Suppose we are given a numeral in the base five and are asked to find the corresponding numeral in the base ten. Such a question was posed in Problem 1 in the above set of exercises. Is there a systematic way of doing this? Did you find such a way in working Exercise 1? First, we could extend the table of Section 6.2 which compares the Hindu-Arabic notation in base ten with the base five notation. If the table were extended far enough, we could find the corresponding base ten symbol for any given base five symbol. However, this would not be practical, especially if the base five numeral represented a large number. The table would become too bulky to be practical, and would have to be available for all such conversion problems. There is another, more systematic way to convert from base five to base ten which depends upon a characteristic of any positional system.

We noted in chapters 1 and 2 how a Hindu-Arabic numeral is written in expanded notation. For example, 8,654 can be written as

$$8 \cdot 10^3 + 6 \cdot 10^2 + 5 \cdot 10^1 + 4 \cdot 10^0$$

Since the system is based upon 10, each digit represents an independent numeral times a power of 10. Thus, in the above example, the 8 digit represents 8 one thousands, and one thousand can be expressed 10^3. Since the base five is a positional system based upon fives, we may also apply the same interpretation. We look at several examples to clarify this point.

Example 6.1 The first two-digit number in base five is 10, which represents five in the base ten. Thus 10_5 means one five and zero ones.

Example 6.2 23_5 represents 13 in the base ten. Thus 23_5 means two fives and three ones, or 13.

Example 6.3 From the table in Section 6.2 we know that 35_5 represents 19. Again the 3 in 34 represents three fives and the 4 represents four ones. Thus, 34_5 represents three fives and four ones, or $15 + 4 = 19$.

Example 6.4 From the table we know that 104_5 represents 29. Thus the 1 in 104 represents one twenty-five, the 0 represents zero fives and the 4 represents four ones.

From the examples we can see that the various digits in a base five numeral represent powers of 5. This corresponds to the expanded form of the earlier chapters. The four examples can be written in expanded form as follows:

Example 6.1 $10_5 = 1 \cdot 5^1 + 0 \cdot 5^0$.

Example 6.2 $23_5 = 2 \cdot 5^1 + 3 \cdot 5^0$.

Example 6.3 $34_5 = 3 \cdot 5^1 + 4 \cdot 5^0$.

Example 6.4 $104_5 = 1 \cdot 5^2 + 0 \cdot 5^1 + 4 \cdot 5^0$.

Other examples further illustrate the expanded form for the base five positional system of numeration.

Example 6.5 $231_5 = 2 \cdot 5^1 + 3 \cdot 5^1 + 1 \cdot 5^0.$

Example 6.6 $4103_5 = 4 \cdot 5^3 + 1 \cdot 5^2 + 0 \cdot 5^1 + 3 \cdot 5^0.$

Example 6.7 $213421_5 = 2 \cdot 5^5 + 1 \cdot 5^4 + 3 \cdot 5^3 + 4 \cdot 5^2 + 2 \cdot 5^1 + 1 \cdot 5^0.$

Since the right-hand sides of the expressions of these seven examples involve fives and there is no symbol 5 in base five, then the various expression must be written in base ten symbols. Thus, in Example 6.5, we may write the following:

$$2 \cdot 5^2 + 3 \cdot 5^1 + 1 \cdot 5^0 = 2 \cdot 25 + 3 \cdot 5 + 1 \cdot 1$$
$$= 50 + 15 + 1$$
$$= 66_{10}$$

Thus 231_5 represents the same number as 66_{10}. Similarly

$$4103_5 = 4 \cdot 5^3 + 1 \cdot 5^2 + 0 \cdot 5^1 + 3 \cdot 5^0 = 4 \cdot 125 + 1 \cdot 25 + 0 \cdot 5 + 3 \cdot 1$$
$$= 500 + 25 + 3$$
$$= 528_{10}$$

and 4103_5 represents the same number as 528_{10}.

Exercises

1.   Convert the following base five numerals into numerals in the base ten:

(a) 13   (b) 24
(c) 43   (d) 101
(e) 214   (f) 414
(g) 300   (h) 2040

2.   Apply the expanded form technique to Exercise 1 following Section 6.2.

3.   In the base ten system of numeration, an even number can be identified by checking the units digit of its numeral to determine if the digit is 0, 2, 4, 6 or 8. How do we identify an even number if its numeral is written in the base five?

4.   In base ten, the multiples of 10 end in zero. In base five, how do the multiples of 5 end?

5.   In base ten, the multiples of 5 end in 5 or 0. In base five, how do the multiples of 5 end?

6.   In base ten, the perfect squares are numbers m such that $n \cdot n = m$, for example, 0, 1, 4, 9, 16, 25, 36, 49, 64 and 81. Write each of these numbers in base five notation and describe any characteristics of the numerals obtained. Will a perfect square written in base five notation ever end in a 2? A 3?

6.4   Conversion from Base Ten to Base Five

If we are given a numeral in the base ten and asked what the corresponding numeral is in the base five, we have a problem which is the reverse of that described in Section 6.3. The first thought is, Can we reverse the procedure of that section and thereby arrive at a technique to convert from a base ten numeral to a base five numeral? The answer is yes, but we may have to do a little extra work to accomplish the task.

Take Example 6.6, where we converted 4103_5 to 528_{10}, and write the detailed steps in reverse order:

$$528 = 500 + 25 + 3 \qquad\qquad \text{Step (1)}$$
$$= 4 \cdot 125 + 1 \cdot 25 + 0 \cdot 5 + 3 \cdot 1 \qquad \text{Step (2)}$$
$$= 4 \cdot 5^3 + 1 \cdot 5^2 + 0 \cdot 5^1 + 3 \cdot 5^0 \qquad \text{Step (3)}$$
$$= 4103_5 \qquad\qquad\qquad \text{Step (4)}$$

How do we know to write 528 as we did in Step (1) and later as we did in Step (2)? The answer, of course, is that we wish to express 538 as sums of various powers of 5 (the expanded numeral form for base five). Moreover, there cannot be more than four of any of these powers of 5. (Why?)

The real question involved here is the number of digits in the base five numeral, which we can determine by a little checking at the beginning. Once the number is established, the remaining steps are quite simple. We determine the number of digits by comparing 528 to the various powers of 5. For example, 528 is greater than 5^0, 5^1, 5^2 and 5^3, but not greater than 5^4 or any larger power of 5. Therefore, there are no (5^4)'s, or larger powers of 5, in 528. Hence the numeral 528, when expressed as sums of powers of 5, can be represented only by powers of

5^3, 5^2, 5^1 and 5^0. If this is true, then the numeral in base five contains only four digits (the number of powers of 5 less than 528). Immediately we know

$$528 = \underline{\quad} \cdot 5^3 + \underline{\quad} \cdot 5^2 + \underline{\quad} \cdot 5^1 + \underline{\quad} \cdot 5^0$$

and we need only determine what goes in the blanks to arrive at the expanded numeral form of our base five numeral. To determine what goes in the blanks, ask how many (5^3)'s are in 528. Since 5^3 is 125, we can determine that there are four 125's with 28 leftover. Hence, we put 4 in the blank before 5^3. Thus we have

$$528 = 4 \cdot 5^3 + \underline{\quad} \cdot 5^2 + \underline{\quad} \cdot 5^1 + \underline{\quad} \cdot 5^0$$

The remaining powers of 5 must be used to represent the remaining part of 528 or 28. We repeat the process. How many (5^2)'s are in 28? Since 5^2 is 25, the answer is 1, with 3 leftover. Putting the 1 in the blank in front of 5^2, we have

$$528 = 4 \cdot 5^3 + 1 \cdot 5^2 + \underline{\quad} \cdot 5^1 + \underline{\quad} \cdot 5^0$$

Since we still have 3 left it must be represented by the remaining powers of 5. Since 5^1 is larger than 3, there are zero 5's, and consequently there must be three (5^0)'s. Thus, we have

$$528 = 4 \cdot 5^3 + 1 \cdot 5^2 + 0 \cdot 5^1 + 3 \cdot 5^0$$

and the right-hand part of this equality is exactly the expanded numeral form (in base five) of 4103_5. Hence, $528 = 4103_5$!

This procedure involves the same steps as converting 4103_5 to 528 except for some minor differences in calculations. Hence, converting from base ten to base five is the reverse of the process of converting from base five to base ten, except we must first determine how many digits will be in the base five numeral we are looking for. This is easily done as illustrated in the above example.

Exercises

1.   Convert the following base ten numerals to base five numerals:
(a) 14   (b) 7
(c) 23   (d) 100
(e) 131   (f) 456
(g) 1,019   (h) 6,971

2.   Verify your answers to Exercise 1 at the end of Section 6.3 by converting them back to base five numerals.

3.   How many digits will a base ten numeral between 25 and 125 have in base five notation? A base ten numeral between 125 and 625?

6.5   Addition in Base Five

To add numbers in the base five system of numeration, we need to know two things. First, we need to know some of the basic combinations of addition. This corresponds to our knowledge of a hundred or so combinations in the base ten which we frequently use. Second, we need to know how to accomplish other additions which are beyond the scope of the basic combinations; thus we need to know how to perform column addition and how to "carry."

Since our base five system is positional, it behaves as the base ten system. Hence, we can conclude that the procedures of adding are alike; that is, if we know how to add in base ten, we know how to add in base five. The only change or difference is in how we write the numerals. This is clearly seen if we construct an addition table showing certain basic addition facts as they are written in base five notation. (See table 6.1.)

TABLE 6.1

Addition in Base Five

+	0	1	2	3	4
0	0	1	2	3	4
1	1	2	3	4	10
2	2	3	4	10	11
3	3	4	10	11	12
4	4	10	11	12	13

Some statements in table 6.1 are quite different from those we normally see in base ten, for example, $4 + 3 = 12$. Since this problem is in base five, the 12 is not "twelve" of base ten, but "one-two" in base five language, and one-two in base five is 7 in base ten. Hence, $4 + 3 = 12$ is a valid statement in a base five which says exactly the same thing as $4 + 3 = 7$ does in base ten.

If we were to use the base five system a great deal, then we should probably memorize the addition facts presented in the above table. This would be the most efficient way to have the information available. However, for our purposes, memorization is not advisable. In fact, these facts might hinder our use of those which we normally use. The student is expected to refer to this table and others which will follow whenever he needs to. (A convenient way to do this is to put the tables on file cards for handy reference.)

Consider the following examples in base five notation.

Example 6.8 $(1 + 2) + 1 = ?$ Since $(1 + 2) = 3$, then $(1 + 2) + 1 = 3 + 1$ and $3 + 1 = 4$. Therefore, $(1 + 2) + 1 = 4$.

Example 6.9 $(3 + 2) + 4 = ?$ Since $(3 + 2) = 10$, then $(3 + 2) + 4 = 10 + 4$. But $10 + 4$ is not in the table. However, we know from our experience with a positional system that to add 10 and 4, we can add 0 and 4 to get 4 and the answer should be 14 (in base five, of course!). Therefore, $(3 + 2) + 4 = 10 + 4 = 14$.

Example 6.10 $4 + (3 + 4) = ?$ $4 + (3 + 4) = 4 + (12) = 21$. Why?

Example 6.11 $11 + 23 = ?$ $11 + 23 = (10 + 1) + (20 + 3) = (10 + 20) + (1 + 3) = 30 + 4 = 34$.

Example 6.12 $34 + 242 = 331$ (in base five).

Example 6.11 could also be done by means of column addition, as Example 6.12 was done. In Example 6.12 we also were required to use the carrying process. The procedure was as follows:

$$
\begin{array}{r}
34 \\
+242 \\
\hline
\end{array}
$$

Add 4 and 2; obtain 11. Put down 1, carry 1. Thus,

$$
\begin{array}{r}
{}^{1} \\
34 \\
242 \\
\hline
1
\end{array}
$$

Then $1 + 3$ is 4 and $4 + 4$ is 13. Put down 3 and carry 1. We have

$$
\begin{array}{r}
{\scriptstyle 1} \\
{\scriptstyle 1}34 \\
242 \\
\hline
31
\end{array}
$$

Finally $1 + 2 = 3$ and $34 + 242 = 331$.

Exercises

1. Find the following sums in base five:
(a) $4 + 10$ (b) $4 + 3$
(c) $11 + 34$ (d) $34 + 11$
(e) $(3 + 4) + 1$ (f) $3 + (4 + 1)$
(g) $24 + 33$ (h) $314 + 432$

2. Are the answers for 1(c) and 1(d) the same? Why? Are the answers for 1(e) and 1(f) the same? Why?

3. Although subtraction in base five was not discussed in Section 6.5, perform the following:
(a) $13 - 4$ (b) $11 - 2$
(c) $14 - 10$ (d) $24 - 13$
(e) $32 - 24$ (f) $100 - 21$

4. What does the following addition problem mean? Find its answer: $212_5 + 36_{10}$.

6.6   Multiplication in Base Five

The comments about addition in base five also apply to multiplication. We must start with a basic set of facts, i.e., a multiplication table, and we must have a multiplication algorithm. (See table 6.2.) Any multiplications are performed in the same manner as they are in base ten. Again it is recommended that the student use this table rather than try to memorize the products. Since we shall be looking at some additional bases, the memory may become a little crowded.

Since the multiplication covers all problems which involve the products of two one-digit numerals, we need only look at other products. In finding these products we need to remember that we are dealing with a positional number system and that what we know about these problems in base ten applies to the same type of problem in base five. Consider the following examples.

TABLE 6.2

Multiplication in Base Five

·	0	1	2	3	4
0	0	0	0	0	0
1	0	1	2	3	4
2	0	2	4	11	13
3	0	3	11	14	22
4	0	4	13	22	31

Example 6.13 $(14)(3) = ?$

$$
\begin{array}{r}
14 \\
3 \\
\hline
102
\end{array}
$$

Example 6.14 $(14)(10) = 140.$

Example 6.15 $(23)(11) = ?$

$$
\begin{array}{r}
23 \\
11 \\
\hline
23 \\
23 \\
\hline
303
\end{array}
$$

Example 6.16 $(341)(123) = ?$

$$
\begin{array}{r}
341 \\
123 \\
\hline
2123 \\
1232 \\
341 \\
\hline
104043
\end{array}
$$

Exercises

1.   Find the following products in base five:
(a) $(11)(10)$ (b) $(21)(4)$

(c) $(34)(11)$

(d) $(11)(34)$

(e) $(4) \cdot (3) \cdot 4$

(f) $4 \cdot (3 \cdot 4)$

(g) $(23)(22)$

(h) $(123)(32)$

(i) $(100)(201)$

2.   Give an algorithm for multiplying by 100 in base five.

3.   Is it possible to determine whether the statement $(10)(10) = 100$ is in base ten or in base five?

6.7   Base Two Numerals and Conversion Techniques

If a positional number system were to be constructed with a base of two rather than five or ten, the procedure would be quite similar to the process outlined in the preceding sections for base five. The one significant distinction would be the number of independent symbols involved. For the base two, we would have only two such symbols. For convenience, we choose 0 and 1. The sequence of numerals would follow the pattern suggested in the table below:

Number Represented	zero	one	two	three	four	five	six	seven	eight	nine
Base Ten	0	1	2	3	4	5	6	7	8	9
Base Two	0	1	10	11	100	101	110	111	1000	1001

Thus 111_2 is 7_{10}. The table is extendable to include other comparisons, and the student should develop it further to fully recognize the base two pattern of writing numerals.

One obvious conclusion can be drawn from examining the base two numerals: To represent a small number requires many digits. For example, it takes a four-digit numeral in the base two to represent the base ten number nine. This is the result of a limited number of independent symbols available in base two.

The base two has practical applications, for example, electrical circuits frequently make use of the absence or presence of electrical current, represented by 0 and 1, respectively. The base two is frequently used in designing and building electronic computers. The programmer must convert from base ten to base two; the machine works the problem gives an answer in base two. The operator must then convert the answer back into base ten to determine the solution. "Converter" units may also be built to handle this job. In more recent years the language of the computer includes the base of the system used (for example, base two is called a *binary system*), thus eliminating this conversion task.

To convert a base two numeral to base ten, follow the pattern established in Section 6.3 on base five, but note that a 2 appears wherever a 5 appeared before. For example,

$$11101_2 = 1 \cdot 2^4 + 1 \cdot 2^3 + 1 \cdot 2^2 + 0 \cdot 2^1 + 1 \cdot 2^0$$
$$= 16 + 8 + 4 + 1$$
$$= 29_{10}$$

Note that 2 appears as the base symbol in the expanded numeral form. Another example follows.

$$1011010_2 = 1 \cdot 2^6 + 0 \cdot 2^5 + 1 \cdot 2^4 + 1 \cdot 2^3 + 0 \cdot 2^2 + 1 \cdot 2^1 + 1 \cdot 2^0$$
$$= 64 + 0 + 16 + 8 + 0 + 2 + 0$$
$$= 90_{10}$$

The problem of converting from base ten to base two is handled as indicated in Section 6.3. First, determine the number of digits by comparing the base ten numeral with various powers of 2. For example, 79_{10} is larger than 2^6 (64) but smaller than 2^7 (128). Hence, there must be seven digits in the base two numeral. We proceed as follows:

$$79_{10} = \underline{\qquad} \cdot 2^6 + \underline{\qquad} \cdot 2^5 + \underline{\qquad} \cdot 2^4$$
$$+ \underline{\qquad} \cdot 2^3 + \underline{\qquad} \cdot 2^2 + \underline{\qquad} \cdot 2^1 + \underline{\qquad} \cdot 2^0$$

Since $2^6 = 64$, there must be one term involving 2^6 in 79, and the remainder of 15 must be represented by the remaining digits. Thus we have

$$79_{10} = 1 \cdot 2^6 + \underline{\qquad} \cdot 2^5 + \underline{\qquad} \cdot 2^4$$
$$+ \underline{\qquad} \cdot 2^3 + \underline{\qquad} \cdot 2^2 + \underline{\qquad} \cdot 2^1 + \underline{\qquad} \cdot 2^0$$

Since 2^5 and 2^4 are both larger than 15, there must be none of these terms and consequently one term of 2^3 in 15. We have then

$$79_{10} = 1 \cdot 2^6 + 0 \cdot 2^5 + 0 \cdot 2^4 + 1 \cdot 2^3 + \underline{\qquad} \cdot 2^2 + \underline{\qquad} \cdot 2^1 + \underline{\qquad} \cdot 2^0$$

and $15 - 2^3 = 7$; that is, the remaining digits must represent 7. From the table in the early part of this section, we know that $7_{10} = 111_2$.

Therefore,

$$79_{10} = 1\cdot2^6 + 0\cdot2^5 + 0\cdot2^4 + 1\cdot2^3 + 1\cdot2^2 + 1\cdot2^1 + 1\cdot2^0$$

or

$$79_{10} = 1001111_2$$

All problems of converting from base ten to base two can be solved in this same manner.

Exercises

1. Convert the following base two numerals to base ten numerals:
(a) 101   (b) 11
(c) 111   (d) 1011
(e) 10110   (f) 11111
(g) 10000   (h) 11011001

2. Convert the following base ten numerals to base two numerals:
(a) 13   (b) 19
(c) 7   (d) 42
(e) 71   (f) 119
(g) 162   (h) 1,000

3. Take 28 and divide by 2, and write any remainder to one side. Take the quotient and divide by 2 again. Again write the remainder to one side. Repeat this process until you obtain a zero as a quotient, and write down any remainder. The procedure outlined might appear as follows:

$$
\begin{array}{r}
2 \,\underline{|\,28\phantom{\text{ R 0}}} \\
2 \,\underline{|\,14 \text{ R } 0} \\
2 \,\underline{|\,7 \text{ R } 0} \\
2 \,\underline{|\,3 \text{ R } 0} \\
2 \,\underline{|\,1 \text{ R } 1} \\
0 \text{ R } 1
\end{array}
$$

Examine this result carefully and see if you can determine the base two numeral which represents the numeral 28. Repeat the process using 79 in place of 28. Did you find the corresponding numeral for 79 in base two? Will this procedure work on converting any base ten numeral to base two?

4. Try the procedure of Exercise 3 on 79, but divide by 5 rather than 2. Do you obtain the base five numeral for 79?

6.8   Addition and Multiplication in Base Two

As in the case of base five, we need to establish the basic addition and multiplication facts in base two:

+	0	1
0	0	1
1	1	10

·	0	1
0	0	0
1	0	1

Since base two is a positional system, the algorithms of addition and multiplication apply, and we should be able to find sums and products without much difficulty.

Example 6.17 $111 + 1011 = 10010$.

Example 6.18 $(101)(111) = 100011$ because

$$
\begin{array}{r}
101 \\
111 \\
\hline
101 \\
101 \\
101 \\
\hline
100011
\end{array}
$$

The student should check these answers by working the corresponding problems in base ten.

Multiplication in the base two is quite easy, and although it seems to involve more addition than multiplication, it does not actually. Because the multiplication facts are quite simple, the addition aspect of the algorithm takes on greater significance.

Exercises

1.   Add in base two:
(a) $1011 + 1101$
(b) $111 + 111$
(c) $110 + 100$
(d) $10110 + 11001$
(e) $11010100 + 101100011$

2.   Multiply in base two:
(a) $(11)(10)$
(b) $(101)(101)$
(c) $(1101)(11)$
(d) $(1011)(1000)$
(e) $(1111)(111)$

3.   In the base ten, an even number ends in 0, 2, 4, 6 or 8. What does an even number end with in the base two? An odd number?

6.9   Base Twelve

The base twelve system of numeration (sometimes called the duo-decimal system) is quite similar to base two and base five, with the exception that there are twelve independent symbols involved. We use all of the base ten symbols, 0, 2, 3, 4, 5, 6, 7, 8 and 9, but we need two more. For convenience, let the next two symbols be respectively T and E. We may have numerals such as 2T3, T0E, ET213T and others in which T and E appear as digits.

Since base twelve is also a positional system, each numeral may be expressed in expanded numeral form. For example,

$$2T49 = 2 \cdot 12^3 + T \cdot 12^2 + 4 \cdot 12^1 + 9 \cdot 12^0 \qquad (1)$$

and remembering that T represents ten, we may also write

$$2T49 = 2 \cdot 12^3 + 10 \cdot 12^2 + 4 \cdot 12^1 + 9 \cdot 12^0 \qquad (2)$$

From this form we can calculate the corresponding base ten numeral by computing the various terms on the right of Equation (2). Thus we see that $2T49_{12} = 6953_{10}$.

The conversion of a base ten numeral into a base twelve numeral is accomplished in the manner previously described. Exercise 3 of Section 6.7 provides an alternate technique which also applies to base ten–base twelve conversion problems.

Exercises

1.   Convert from base twelve numerals to base ten numerals:
(a) 32   (b) 64
(c) T4   (d) E9
(e) 213   (f) 4T2
(g) T00T   (h) TEE
(i) 12TE

2.   Convert the following base ten numerals to base twelve numerals:
(a) 63   (b) 156
(c) 916   (d) 2,461
(e) 10,000   (f) 6,241

3.   In what digits in base twelve do even numbers end? Odd numbers?

6.10   Addition and Multiplication in Base Twelve

Tables 6.3 and 6.4 contain addition and multiplication facts in base twelve. The procedures of addition and multiplication are the same as in base five, base two or base ten. Examples 6.19 and 6.20 illustrate both procedures.

Example 6.19   Find $2TE4 + 3162$. Since $4 + 2 = 6$, $E + 6 = 15$, $T + 1 = E$, $2 + 3 = 5$, then $2TE4_{12} + 3162_{12} = 6056_{12}$.

Example 6.20   Find $(3T6)(E14)$. Since

$$
\begin{array}{ccc}
\overset{32}{(3T6)} & 3T6 & \overset{95}{3T6} \\
4 & 10 \quad \text{and} & E00 \\
\hline
1360 & 3T60 & 367600
\end{array}
$$

TABLE 6.3

Addition in Base Twelve

+	0	1	2	3	4	5	6	7	8	9	T	E
0	0	1	2	3	4	5	6	7	8	9	T	E
1	1	2	3	4	5	6	7	8	9	T	E	10
2	2	3	4	5	6	7	8	9	T	E	10	11
3	3	4	5	6	7	8	9	T	E	10	11	12
4	4	5	6	7	8	9	T	E	10	11	12	13
5	5	6	7	8	9	T	E	10	11	12	13	14
6	6	7	8	9	T	E	10	11	12	13	14	15
7	7	8	9	T	E	10	11	12	13	14	15	16
8	8	9	T	E	10	11	12	13	14	15	16	17
9	9	T	E	10	11	12	13	14	15	16	17	18
T	T	E	10	11	12	13	14	15	16	17	18	19
E	E	10	11	12	13	14	15	16	17	18	19	1T

we have

$$
\begin{array}{r}
3T6 \\
E14 \\
\hline
1360 \\
3T60 \\
367600 \\
\hline
370{,}800
\end{array}
$$

The procedures are not difficult to follow, but the basic or elementary facts appear to be very different to us. They are different because we have not "learned" these in the same manner as we have the corresponding facts for base ten. As we work the exercises that follow, we will have to continually refer to the tables given at the beginning of this section.

It is interesting to note that the duo-decimal system of numeration has been advocated as a replacement for our base ten system; in fact,

TABLE 6.4

Multiplication in Base Twelve

·	0	1	2	3	4	5	6	7	8	9	T	E
0	0	0	0	0	0	0	0	0	0	0	0	0
1	0	1	2	3	4	5	6	7	8	9	T	E
2	0	2	4	6	8	T	10	12	14	16	18	1T
3	0	3	6	9	10	13	16	19	20	23	26	29
4	0	4	8	10	14	18	20	24	28	30	34	38
5	0	5	T	13	18	21	26	2E	34	39	42	47
6	0	6	10	16	20	26	30	36	40	46	50	56
7	0	7	12	19	24	2E	36	41	48	53	5T	65
8	0	8	14	20	28	34	40	48	54	60	68	74
9	0	9	16	23	30	39	46	53	60	69	76	83
T	0	T	18	26	34	42	50	5T	68	76	84	92
E	0	E	1T	29	38	47	56	65	74	83	92	T1

a society in the United States has this as its objective. There are good reasons for this suggested change, particularly if we are to continue using the English system of weights and measures.

Exercises

1. Find the following in base twelve:
(a) 23 + 14
(b) 312 + 616
(c) 2T + E3
(d) 2E1 + T06
(e) T0E + T0E
(f) 24TE + TE19
(g) 2000 + T000

2. Find the following products in base twelve:
(a) (23)(32)
(b) (64)(T)
(c) (3E)(9)
(d) (2T)(E3)
(e) (2T3)(46E)
(f) (T00)(6E4)
(g) (100)(ET9)
(h) (T00T)(T0E)

6.11   Questions for Discussion

The following set of questions examines several aspects of the positional number system which are readily observable in all except the binary system. The aspects are also present in the binary system, but they are not so obvious.

1. Take a good look at the base twelve multiplication table. Are there any observable patterns present in this table? Examine the numerals in a given row and see if you can detect some pattern in the numerals that appear. For example, in the 6 row, all numerals end in 0 or 6. Is there a similar situation anywhere in the base ten multiplication table? Where? Is there a pattern present in the E row? Is such a pattern present in the base ten table? Base five? Base two? Construct a base seven multiplication table. Is the same pattern found there?
2. Is there an observable pattern in all addition tables, regardless of the base of the system?
3. Is it possible to describe one rule which identifies even numbers in any base system? Why?
4. Describe some advantages and disadvantages of the binary system, and the base five, ten and twelve systems. What system of numeration will probably be used in A.D. 2000?

5. If we were to decide to change the system of numeration which we are using to, say, the binary system, what would be some of the problems we might encounter in making this change?

6.12   Comment

The author has chosen to treat base five, base two and base twelve representations and problems in separate sections to prevent the confusion of representations which sometimes occurs when the different systems are presented at the same time. There is, however, a fundamental principle common to all base representations and their uses in arithmetic. All such bases are place value systems of numeration, and as such, the algorithmic processes which were used to compute problems in the different bases were the same processes we use in base ten. If the student has not reached this conclusion from the preceding sections, he should take a second look. The addition process in base five and the addition process in base two were exactly the same process. The basic facts were written differently for each base, but the carrying process was the algorithmic way in which we obtained sums. The same is true for base twelve. Check the multiplication problems; the same is true there. Thus, working with base systems other than base ten is, in effect, working with place value systems. Herein lies the objective of teaching bases other than ten, not only to prospective elementary teachers, but also to their future students.

7

THE SET OF FRACTIONS

7.1   Definition of Fraction

We are familiar with fractions from our elementary school experiences when we used symbols such as

$$\frac{1}{2}, \frac{2}{3}, \frac{5}{6}, \frac{6}{5}, \frac{1}{4}, \text{ etc.}$$

These symbols are constructed by using two natural numbers, called a *numerator* and a *denominator*. A fraction is, in reality, an ordered pair of whole numbers, represented by a numerator and a denominator in that order. Thus 2/3 is readily distinguished from 3/2, as the order of 2 and 3 is different. Since fractions are simply ordered pairs of whole numbers, there are an infinite number of different possible fractional symbols, for example,

$$\frac{9}{4}, \frac{1}{2}, \frac{2}{3}, \frac{4}{9}, \frac{19}{29}, \frac{0}{7}, \frac{5}{5}, \frac{9}{0}, \text{ etc.}$$

Each of the numbers above the fraction bar is a numerator and each below is a denominator. The bar identifies the order.

In the next section we formalize a technique to determine if two or more fraction symbols represent the same number.

7.2 Equality of Fractions

We know from previous experience with fractions that 1/2 and 2/4 are equal. They are equal in the sense that they are two different symbols which represent the same number. We wish to formalize a definition which makes it possible to determine when any two fractions represent the same number. We will approach this definition from a mathematical point of view, although we would not necessarily use such a method in first teaching the idea to elementary school students. There we depend upon concrete examples, such as 1/2 pie and 2/4 pie, to show that these symbols represent the same thing. Moreover, we usually develop some algorithmic way of converting one fractional symbol into another fractional symbol (as we shall also do later in the chapter) and this allows us to generate other representations for a given fraction.

We now return to our definition.

DEFINITION 7.1 $a/b = c/d$ if and only if $a \cdot d = b \cdot c$. Thus $1/2 = 2/4$ because $1 \cdot 4 = 2 \cdot 2$, and $7/10 = 35/50$ because $7 \cdot 50 = 35 \cdot 10$.

The definition of two equal fractions permits us to write several different representations of the same number. In fact, there are an infinite number of representations for the same fractional number. For example,

$$\frac{1}{2} = \frac{2}{4} = \frac{3}{6} = \frac{4}{8} = \frac{5}{10} = \frac{6}{12} = \cdots$$

This is new to our development of arithmetic at this point and can be formalized by saying that *a fractional number can be represented by a member of an equivalence class of ordered pairs (that is, fractions), and the symbols in each class can be used interchangeably with others in the same class.* Moreover, the equivalence class which can be used to represent one fraction is disjoint from every other equivalence class. For example, if

$$\frac{1}{2} = \frac{2}{4} = \frac{3}{6} = \frac{4}{8} = \frac{5}{10} = \cdots$$

and

$$\frac{1}{3} = \frac{2}{6} = \frac{3}{9} = \frac{4}{12} = \frac{5}{15} = \cdots$$

then, by our definition, no symbol for 1/2 can be found which represents 1/3. In fact, $1/2 \neq 1/3$ for $1 \cdot 3 \neq 1 \cdot 2$.

There is one problem which does occur in the application of the definition. Consider, for example, the fractions 1/2, 1/3 and 0/0. The fraction 0/0 has been previously excluded from the arithmetic of our elementary schooling, but we include it here. By the definition of equality we see that

$$\frac{1}{2} = \frac{0}{0} \quad \text{because } 1 \cdot 0 = 2 \cdot 0$$

and

$$\frac{1}{3} = \frac{0}{0} \quad \text{because } 1 \cdot 0 = 3 \cdot 0$$

Hence, 0/0 belongs to both equivalence classes for 1/2 and 1/3—just the opposite of what we have been saying. Moreover, if $1/2 = 0/0$ and $1/3 = 0/0$, is it possible that $1/2 = 1/3$ as a result of these equalities? This is possible only if equality is transitive (see chapter 3). But if the equality of fractions is transitive, then (from this example) $1/2 = 1/3$. The difficulty occurs because of two occurrences. First, we want equality to be defined such that it is an equivalence relation (i.e., equality is reflexive, symmetric and transitive) and we want 0/0 to be included in our set of fractions. But this is not really possible, so we choose the transitive property; then the fractional symbol 0/0 will have to be excluded from our collection of symbols and we will, therefore, have no fractional number with this symbolic representation.

In addition, it is easy to see that any fraction with zero in the denominator also would have to be excluded. For example, let $a/0$, where $a \neq 0$, and 0/0 be two fractions. Then $a/0 = 0/0$ because $a \cdot 0 =$

$0 \cdot 0$. Hence $a/0$ belongs to the same equivalence class as $0/0$ and, therefore, must also be excluded. (This is, of course, based upon the assumption that these ordered pairs obey the same definition of equality as other ordered pairs.) Therefore, we alter our original definition of the set of fractions to exclude those fractional symbols with zero in the denominator; thus the definition of equality in this section applies *only* to fractions with nonzero denominators.

THEOREM 7.1 The equality for fractions is an equivalence relation.

It is easy to show that equality for fractions is reflexive. For equality to be reflexive, we need to show that $a/b = a/b$ for all fractions a/b. But $a/b = a/b$ if and only if $a \cdot b = b \cdot a$; since a and b are whole numbers, we know $a \cdot b = b \cdot a$ and, therefore, $a/b = a/b$. Hence, equality is reflexive.

To prove symmetry we need to show that if $a/b = c/d$, then $c/d = a/b$. If $a/b = c/d$ is true, then $a \cdot d = b \cdot c$, which can be rewritten as $c \cdot b = d \cdot a$ by using the symmetric property of equality on the whole numbers (note that this is known already) and the commutative property for multiplication. If $c \cdot b = d \cdot a$, then, by the definition of equality, we know $c/d = a/b$, and equality is symmetric.

It remains to be shown that equality satisfies the transitive property and, if it does, then equality of fractions can be said to be an equivalence relation. We leave this last part as an exercise for the student. If equality for fractions is an equivalence relation, then it has the same properties as equality on whole numbers or equality on sets. Thus we can use the symbol $=$ for fractions, just as we do for whole numbers.

Exercises

1. Show that equality on fractions is a transitive relation. (Hint: Show that if $a/b = c/d$ and $c/d = e/f$, then $a/b = e/f$.)

2. Suppose the definition of equality also covers the fractions with zero denominators and nonzero numerators. Which of the following are true?

(a) $1/2 = 4/8$
(c) $10/5 = 2/1$
(e) $0/3 = 0/7$
(g) $0/3 = 7/0$

(b) $2/3 = 7/10$
(d) $4/0 = 9/0$
(f) $1/1 = 7/7$

7.3　Addition

The defining of an operation on the set of fractions gives us an opportunity to distinguish between two aspects of mathematics which are often ignored by those concerned with elementary school mathematics. We refer to a definition of a mathematical operation in the mathematical sense as opposed to the definition of a mathematical operation from the pedagogical sense. While we do not wish to involve ourselves in a lengthy discussion of pedagogy, it is still important to recognize that the choice of definition (or idea) determines in large part how we can teach the concept to young students. It certainly is true that the psychology of learning plays a large role in how successful we are in teaching mathematics, and the alternatives available in mathematical definitions at this point affect our teaching success with fractions. In this section we develop two different mathematical approaches to the addition of fractions; one parallels the elementary school development, and the other is a more abstract approach. We treat the elementary school approach first.

We begin by defining the sum of two fractions when these fractions have the same denominator.

DEFINITION 7.2　　$a/b + c/b = (a + c)/b.$

This is the usual definition illustrated by example in the primary grades. For example,

$$\frac{1}{3} + \frac{1}{3} = \frac{1 + 1}{3} = \frac{2}{3}$$

We can illustrate the example by considering the following diagrams. Take a rectangle (or a pie) and divide it into thirds, as in figure 7.1. Then put 1/3 of the rectangle with another 1/3, which represents 2/3 of the rectangle. (See figure 7.2.) By using such illustrations (via teaching aids) we can see a plausible justification of the above definition.

FIGURE 7.1

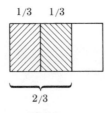

1/3   1/3

2/3

FIGURE 7.2

There are at least two observations which can be made about this definition of addition of fractions. First, it is limited to those addition problems in which the two fractions have the same denominators. It does not apply directly to such problems as

$$\frac{1}{2} + \frac{1}{3} \quad \text{or} \quad \frac{3}{4} + \frac{5}{9}$$

and if we are to be able to add such problems, we will have to develop some other technique. Second, whenever we add two fractions, we obtain another fraction, indicating that the operation (when defined) is a closed operation. Note that thus far we have not indicated any connection between fractions such as 4/2 and any other numbers. This will be presented later, and the student is urged, for the present, to refrain from using other forms of writing certain fractions. The object is to identify what actually happens in adding fractions first and later refine any answer obtained. For example,

$$\frac{3}{4} + \frac{3}{4} = \frac{6}{4}$$

For the present, we stop with that answer.

We return now to the problem of adding fractions which do not have the same denominators, for example, 1/2 + 1/3. (Remember, at this point we know only about equality of fractions and the above definition of addition of fractions.) First, consider the equivalence classes represented by 1/2 and 1/3.

$$\frac{1}{2} = \frac{2}{4} = \frac{3}{6} = \frac{4}{8} = \frac{5}{10} = \frac{6}{12} = \cdots$$

and

$$\frac{1}{3} = \frac{2}{6} = \frac{3}{9} = \frac{4}{12} = \frac{5}{15} = \frac{6}{18} = \cdots$$

Certain members of the first equivalence class have the same denominators as certain members of the second, for example, 3/6 and 2/6, or

6/12 and 4/12. If the lists were continued further, we would find 9/18 and 6/18 and many other such pairs. Since

$$\frac{1}{2} = \frac{3}{6} \quad \text{and} \quad \frac{1}{3} = \frac{2}{6}$$

we could write

$$\frac{1}{2} + \frac{1}{3} = \frac{3}{6} + \frac{2}{6}$$

and then be able to apply the definition of addition and obtain

$$\frac{1}{2} + \frac{1}{3} = \frac{3}{6} + \frac{2}{6} = \frac{5}{6}$$

or

$$\frac{1}{2} + \frac{1}{3} = \frac{6}{12} + \frac{4}{12} = \frac{10}{12}$$

or

$$\frac{1}{2} + \frac{1}{3} = \frac{9}{18} + \frac{6}{18} = \frac{15}{18}$$

In fact, we could write an infinite number of such expressions for $1/2 + 1/3$. The answers obtained for the three additions in this example are the same number because

$$\frac{5}{6} = \frac{10}{12} = \frac{15}{18} = \cdots$$

All the answers belong to the same equivalence class. This example suggests that when we have a problem such as $1/2 + 1/3$, we can find the sum by looking at the equivalence classes of both fractions and *finding* a pair (one in each class) with the same denominators, replacing each of the given fractions by these two and then adding. Thus, if we apply this procedure, we can *always* find the sum of any two fractions, even if their denominators are different.

Most people have been taught that an answer such as 10/12 or 15/18 should be "reduced" to 5/6. They have been taught this probably for pedagogical rather than mathematical reasons. The definition of addition says nothing about reducing; moreover, 5/6, 10/12 and 15/18 all belong to the same equivalence class and *all are acceptable mathematical answers*. Why, then, were we taught to reduce fractions? To *reduce* a fraction means to find another fraction such that the numerator and denominator have no common divisor other than 1. That is, 1 is the largest number which divides both numerator and denominator; thus 5/6 is the reduced form of 10/12 and 15/18. Moreover, there is one and only one reduced form in any given equivalence class of fractions. Hence, we could always reduce whatever answer we get to one fraction in a given class. Here we see a logical pedagogical reason for asking the students to add fractions and then reduce their answers. All students would come up with precisely same fraction (like 5/6 in our example), which would certainly make it easier to grade papers! In fact, this seems to be the only justification for asking students to reduce fractions wherever possible. It contributes little to the knowledge of arithmetic; and the expression *reduce* is not the best choice of words to use to describe the process.

Since the fractional form of an answer is immaterial, we might assume that there is one and only one answer to the sum of two fractions. Indeed this is true but for other reasons. The proof that there is exactly one sum for a pair of fractions (one sum, but many possible forms, in that equivalence class) follows. Let

$$\frac{a}{b} + \frac{c}{b} = \frac{e}{b}$$

and let

$$\frac{a}{b} + \frac{c}{b} = \frac{f}{b} \quad \text{where } \frac{e}{b} \neq \frac{f}{b}$$

Thus we have two different numbers, e/b and f/b, as sums for $a/b + c/b$. But, by the transitive property of equality, if

$$\frac{e}{b} = \frac{a}{b} + \frac{c}{b} \quad \text{and} \quad \frac{a}{b} + \frac{c}{b} = \frac{f}{b}$$

then

$$\frac{e}{b} = \frac{f}{b}$$

But this contradicts our assumption that there are two different numbers for the sum of a/b and c/b. Hence, our assumption must be wrong and the sum of a/b and c/b is unique.

Exercises

1. Using the definition of addition, find the following:
(a) $2/1 + 1/2$
(b) $0/3 + 2/5$
(c) $1/2 + 1/2$ (Be careful how you write the answer.)
(d) $(1/4 + 1/4) + 1/4$
(e) $1/4 + (1/4 + 1/4)$

2. Find the equivalence classes for each of the following pairs of fractions; then find the sum of the pair:
(a) 1/2, 2/3   (b) 3/4, 5/6
(c) 5/3, 3/4   (d) 3/1, 0/4

3. Which of the following fractions are "reducible"?
(a) 1/2   (b) 3/4
(c) 7/9   (d) 10/15
(e) 24/32   (f) 100/20,000

4. Which of the following statements are true?
(a) $2/3 = 15/18$ (b) $5/6 = 10/12$
(c) $21/39 = 537/984$ (d) $2/2 = 5/5$
(e) $7/3 = 35/15$ (f) $17/9 = 102/54$

7.4   Properties of Addition for Fractions

In chapter 4, we found that the operations on the whole numbers possess the associative and commutative properties, and we defined the identity element. In this section we will see that these same properties are also true for the operation of addition on fractions. Before we develop these properties, one important observation needs to be made. We have used the word *addition* to describe two operations, one on the set of fractions and one on the set of whole numbers. This can be misleading because we might think of addition as being the same algorithm wherever used. If it were, we would not need to consider the properties of addition on fractions, since we already know them. However, we have *two* definitions for addition, one for each set of numbers. In fact, we could have written the definition for addition of fractions as

$$\frac{a}{c} \oplus \frac{b}{c} = \frac{a+b}{c}$$

where $\oplus$ means addition on fractions and $+$ means addition on whole numbers. To add fractions ($\oplus$), we perform a certain problem in addition ($+$); the new operation of addition ($\oplus$) is being defined in terms of the previous operation. Using this concept, we shall generate other ideas for operations on different sets of numbers. We shall not continue the use of $\oplus$ as a symbol for addition of fractions but will use the symbol $+$ and from the context of the statement determine the correct meaning. For example, $2 + 3$ means addition on the set of whole numbers, and $1/2 + 1/4$ means addition on the set of fractions. We shall have more to say on this point in a later section of this chapter on similar uses of addition in other situations.

We turn now to proving some properties of addition on the set of fractions. We consider first the commutative property. If addition is commutative, then

$$\frac{a}{c} + \frac{b}{c} = \frac{b}{c} + \frac{a}{c}$$

We prove this in the following manner:

$$\frac{a}{c} + \frac{b}{c} = \frac{a+b}{c} \qquad \text{Definition of } +$$

Since $a + b = b + a$ (the commutative property for addition of whole numbers),

$$\frac{a+b}{c} = \frac{b+a}{c}$$

But $(b + a)/c$ is, by definition of addition, $b/c + a/c$. Hence

$$\frac{a}{c} + \frac{b}{c} = \frac{b}{c} + \frac{a}{c}$$

and addition on fractions is a commutative operation. Note that the proof depends upon our knowing about commutativity for addition on whole numbers ($a + b = b + a$); clearly there is a connection between the two operations, but they are *not* the *same* operation.

If addition on fractions is associative,

$$\left(\frac{a}{c} + \frac{b}{c}\right) + \frac{d}{c} = \frac{a}{c} + \left(\frac{b}{c} + \frac{d}{c}\right)$$

First, recall that every operation we have defined on a set of numbers is a binary operation and that the parentheses here indicate which addition is to be done first. The proof is as follows:

$$\left(\frac{a}{c} + \frac{b}{c}\right) + \frac{d}{c} = \frac{a+b}{c} + \frac{d}{c} \qquad \text{Definition of } +$$

$$= \frac{(a+b)+d}{c} \qquad \text{Definition of } +$$

$$= \frac{a+(b+d)}{c} \qquad \text{Why?}$$

$$= \frac{a}{c} + \frac{b+d}{c} \qquad \text{Definition of } +$$

$$= \frac{a}{c} + \left(\frac{b}{c} + \frac{d}{c}\right) \qquad \text{Definition of } +$$

Hence, addition on fractions is associative.

We next wish to determine if there is an additive identity element for the set of fractions. If there is an additive identity element for fractions, there must be a fraction x/c such that

$$\frac{a}{c} + \frac{x}{c} = \frac{a}{c} \quad \text{for all fractions } \frac{a}{c}$$

We will determine what the fraction x/c must be for this to be true. Consider the following:

$$\frac{a}{c} + \frac{x}{c} = \frac{a+x}{c} \qquad \text{Definition of } +$$

For the fraction $(a + x)/c$ to be equal to a/c, we must have $c(a + x) = c \cdot a$ (definition of equality). If $c(a + x) = c \cdot a$, then $a + x = a$ (by a cancellation property on whole numbers). Since a is any whole number, x must be zero. Hence, $x/c = 0/c$, and there is an additive identity element.

It is also possible to prove that $0/c$ is the only fraction which satisfies this condition. Let $0/c$ be an additive identity element and let y/c be another additive identity element such that

$$\frac{0}{c} \neq \frac{y}{c}$$

Then

$$\frac{a}{c} + \frac{0}{c} = \frac{a}{c} \qquad \text{Definition of Additive Identity}$$

and

$$\frac{a}{c} + \frac{y}{c} = \frac{a}{c} \qquad \text{Definition of Additive Identity}$$

Hence, by the transitive property of equality,

$$\frac{a}{c} + \frac{0}{c} = \frac{a}{c} + \frac{y}{c}$$

$$= \frac{a+0}{c} = \frac{a}{c}$$

and

$$\frac{a}{c} + \frac{y}{c} = \frac{a+y}{c}$$

Then

$$\frac{a}{c} = \frac{a+y}{c}$$

and, by definition of equality,

$$ac = c(a+y)$$

Then $a = a + y$; therefore, y must be 0. But this contradicts our assumption that $y/c \neq 0/c$, so there is one and only one additive identity element.

Exercises

1.   Work the following by the definition of addition. Do not reduce.
(a) 8/3 + 2/3   (b) 0/5 + 2/5
(c) 1/5 + 4/5   (d) 2/1 + 3/1
(e) 1/1 + 1/1   (f) 4/3 + 8/3

2.   Find the following *and reduce* the answer. Show how to reduce by using only the definition of equal fractions. Answers must be fractions.
(a) 5/3 + 3/3   (b) 3/7 + 4/7
(c) 4/2 + 8/2   (d) 13/8 + 15/8

3. Find the following sums. Show how to add these using equal fractions. Do not reduce.

(a) $2/3 + 3/4$

(b) $2/1 + 4/3$

(c) $6/9 + 2/3$

(d) $0/5 + 2/7$

(e) $(2/3 + 1/2) + 1/4$

7.5 Alternate Definition of Addition

Our first definition of addition for fractions was based upon the elementary school approach where the denominators of the two fractions were the same. If they were not, then we devised a way to rewrite them with the same denominators. Now we give a more abstract definition of addition which covers all cases.

Definition 7.3 $a/b + c/d = (ad + bc)/bd.$

Definition 7.3 is applicable to all problems, including those with fractions which have the same denominators. For example, let $b = d$. Then

$$\frac{a}{b} + \frac{c}{b} = \frac{ab + bc}{b \cdot b}$$

$$= \frac{(a + c) \cdot b}{b \cdot b}$$

$$= \frac{a + c}{b} \qquad \text{Why?}$$

Thus the alternate definition covers the cases of the first definition *plus* all other addition problems. Mathematically, it is a superior definition, as it works regardless of circumstance. However, this definition has no clear relation to part of a pie or a rectangle and no intuitive basis for a primary school youngster; hence, it rarely appears in elementary school texts. However, in the beginning study of algebra, it is frequently given as the definition of addition of algebraic fractions.

It is possible to show that the two definitions are equivalent; that is, given one definition we can derive the other one. We completed half of the proof above when we considered the case $b = d$. It remains to be shown that if $a/c + b/c = (a + b)/c$, then the other definition also works. Consider $a/b + c/d$. By the first definition the denominators must be the same. Using the idea of equal fractions, we obtain

$$\frac{a}{b} = \frac{ad}{bd} \quad \text{and} \quad \frac{c}{d} = \frac{bc}{bd}$$

Hence,

$$\frac{a}{b} + \frac{c}{d} = \frac{ad}{bd} + \frac{bc}{bd}$$

$$= \frac{ad + bc}{bd}$$

and the first definition produces the second definition. Hence, the definitions are equivalent.

The student should go back to the exercises in Section 7.7, rework the problems using the alternate definition, then compare his answers (which should be the same).

7.6   Multiplication of Fractions

We are now ready to define a second operation on the set of fractions. We shall give an intuitive illustration to make our subsequent definition meaningful. Consider the following example.

Example 7.1   Find $1/2 \cdot 3/4$. We illustrate $3/4$ by the shaded region in the rectangle in figure 7.3. Thus $3/4$ means three of the four equal parts of the region in the rectangle. To multiply $1/2$ and $3/4$ means to take $1/2$ of the region denoted by $3/4$; to do so, we divide the rectangle into two equal parts the other way (fig. 7.4). Thus $1/2$ of this region denoted by $3/4$ is denoted by the shaded region in figure 7.5. There are eight small rectangles, three of which are shaded. Hence $1/2 \cdot 3/4$ must be $3/8$, if our interpretations are to be consistent.

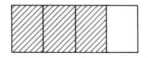

FIGURE 7.3

3/4

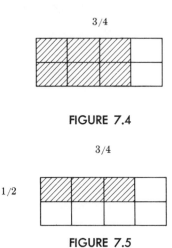

FIGURE 7.4

3/4

1/2

FIGURE 7.5

Example 7.1 motivates the definition of the multiplication operation for the set of fractions.

DEFINITION 7.4 $a/b \odot c/d = (a \cdot c)/(b \cdot d)$.

The multiplication sign on the left $\odot$ is for fractions, and those on the right are for whole numbers. Our previous comments on $\oplus$ and $+$ could apply equally well here for $\odot$ and $\cdot$.

The product of two fractions is also a fraction, so the operation is closed on the set of fractions. Moreover, since $a \cdot c$ and $b \cdot d$ are unique whole numbers, the answer obtained is also unique. We can write this answer in many ways (as found in an equivalence class of fractional representations for a fraction). We do not have the difficulty as with addition where the denominators had to be the same. In fact, there is no distinction between the definitions for elementary school and for algebra; they are the same. Earlier comments about reducing also apply here for multiplication.

7.7   Properties of Multiplication

We first show that the operation of multiplication for fractions is commutative. Consider the following:

$$\frac{a}{b} \cdot \frac{c}{d} = \frac{a \cdot c}{b \cdot d} \quad \text{Definition of Multiplication}$$

$$= \frac{c \cdot a}{d \cdot b} \quad \begin{array}{l}\text{Commutative Property of}\\ \text{Multiplication on Whole Numbers}\end{array}$$

$$= \frac{c}{d} \cdot \frac{a}{b} \quad \text{Definition of Multiplication}$$

Hence,

$$\frac{a}{b} \cdot \frac{c}{d} = \frac{c}{d} \cdot \frac{a}{b}$$

which is a statement of the commutative property for multiplication on fractions.

We prove now that multiplication of fractions is associative. The proof is similar to that for the associative property for addition of fractions:

$$\left(\frac{a}{b} \cdot \frac{c}{d}\right) \cdot \frac{e}{f} = \left(\frac{a \cdot c}{b \cdot d}\right) \cdot \frac{e}{f} \qquad \text{Why?}$$

$$= \frac{(a \cdot c) \cdot e}{(b \cdot d) \cdot f} \qquad \text{Why?}$$

$$= \frac{a \cdot (c \cdot e)}{b \cdot (d \cdot f)} \qquad \text{Why?}$$

$$= \frac{a}{b} \cdot \frac{c \cdot e}{d \cdot f} \qquad \text{Why?}$$

$$= \frac{a}{b} \cdot \left(\frac{c}{d} \cdot \frac{e}{f}\right) \qquad \text{Why?}$$

Hence,

$$\left(\frac{a}{b} \cdot \frac{c}{d}\right) \cdot \frac{e}{f} = \frac{a}{b} \cdot \left(\frac{c}{d} \cdot \frac{e}{f}\right)$$

and multiplication is associative.

Next, we show the existence of a multiplication identity element in the set of fractions. If there is an identity element, say, x/y, then the following must be true:

$$\frac{a}{b} \cdot \frac{x}{y} = \frac{a}{b} \qquad a \neq 0, b \neq 0$$

Since

$$\frac{a}{b} \cdot \frac{x}{y} = \frac{ax}{by}$$

we have $ax/by = a/b$. By definition of equality of fractions,

$$(ax)b = a(by) \quad \text{or} \quad (ab) \cdot x = (ab) \cdot y$$

By the cancellation property, $x = y$. Thus, the multiplicative identity element must be the fraction x/x, or a member of that equivalence class, and thus $1/1, 2/2, 3/3, 4/4, \ldots$ all are representations of the identity for multiplication. We leave as an exercise the task of proving the multiplicative identity to be unique.

There are interesting applications of the identity element for multiplication. For example, it enables us to find a convenient way of finding other members of an equivalence class. For example, to find other members of the equivalence class of 2/3, we can multiply 2/3 by various representations of the identity element x/x;

$$\frac{2}{3} \cdot \frac{2}{2} = \frac{4}{6} \qquad \frac{2}{3} \cdot \frac{3}{3} = \frac{6}{9} \qquad \frac{2}{3} \cdot \frac{4}{4} = \frac{8}{12}$$

Many others are possible. Moreover, the process is reversible and, consequently, we can find an algorithm for reducing fractions. Suppose we have 12/36 and wish to reduce to a fractional representation in which numerator and denominator are relatively primed. If we apply the fundamental theorem of arithmetic (chapter 4) to both the numerator and the denominator, we obtain

$$\frac{12}{36} = \frac{2 \cdot 2 \cdot 3}{2 \cdot 2 \cdot 3 \cdot 3}$$

If we then write

$$\frac{2 \cdot 2 \cdot 3}{2 \cdot 2 \cdot 3 \cdot 3} = \frac{1}{3} \cdot \frac{2 \cdot 2 \cdot 3}{2 \cdot 2 \cdot 3}$$

then the fraction

$$\frac{2 \cdot 2 \cdot 3}{2 \cdot 2 \cdot 3}$$

is the multiplicative identity and

$$\frac{12}{36} = \frac{1}{3} \cdot \frac{2 \cdot 2 \cdot 3}{2 \cdot 2 \cdot 3} = \frac{1}{3}$$

Thus we have a convenient way to reduce fractions without relying on trial and error and the definition of equality of fractions.

Another interesting and most significant application of this identity element for multiplication is to the algorithmic process for adding fractions. The definition of addition of fractions requires the same denominator for both fractions. Earlier we saw that we had to examine the equivalence class representing both fractions and find two representations with the same denominators. This, for large denominators, might require a rather lengthy search. What we propose is a shortcut to finding such a representation. Take, for example, the problem 1/6 + 1/15. If we use earlier techniques we find that we can replace 1/6 + 1/15 by 5/30 + 2/30 and then perform the addition. Moreover, 30 is the smallest denominator which could be found in the equivalence classes for 1/6 and 1/15. The key to the shortcut lies in determining this number 30. For this example, 30 is the number called the *least common multiple* (LCM) of 6 and 15. It is the smallest number which is divisible by 6 and by 15. To find the LCMs of 6 and 15, first write their prime factorizations.

$$6 = 2 \cdot 3 \quad \text{and} \quad 15 = 3 \cdot 5$$

Any number which is divisible by 6 must be divisible by 2 and by 3. (This idea is borrowed from an area of mathematics called number theory.) Since the LCM must also be divisible by 15, it must be divisible by 3 and by 5. From the two conditions just listed, the LCM must be divisible by 2, 3 and 5. Thus LCM of 6 and 15 is the product of $2 \cdot 3 \cdot 5$, or 30.

Knowing that the LCM of 6 and 15 is 30 enables us to rewrite 1/6 and 1/15 with 30 as a denominator for both by using the multiplicative identity element. Since $6 = 2 \cdot 3$ and $30 = 2 \cdot 3 \cdot 5$, multiply 1/6 by 5/5; that is,

$$\frac{1}{6} \cdot \frac{5}{5} = \frac{1 \cdot 5}{6 \cdot 5} = \frac{5}{30}$$

Since $15 = 3 \cdot 5$ and $30 = 2 \cdot 3 \cdot 5$, multiply 1/15 by 2/2; that is,

$$\frac{1}{15} \cdot \frac{2}{2} = \frac{1 \cdot 2}{15 \cdot 2} = \frac{2}{30}$$

Thus

$$\frac{1}{6} + \frac{1}{15} = \frac{1}{6} \cdot \frac{5}{5} + \frac{1}{15} \cdot \frac{2}{2} = \frac{5}{30} + \frac{2}{30} = \frac{7}{30}$$

and we have obtained a convenient way of converting 1/6 and 1/15 to the correct representations to complete the addition problem.

Application of the LCM technique to fractions is called finding the *least common denominator* (LCD). We can, of course, refine the process some by shortcutting still further, but we have saved a significant amount of time by applying the multiplicative identity element. Finding the LCM of two numbers can be formalized by saying that the LCM of p and q is the product obtained by multiplying the set of prime factors, obtained by forming the union of the sets of prime factors of p and q.

The set of prime factors of 6 is {2, 3} and the set of prime factors of 15 is {3, 5}. The union of these two sets gives {2, 3, 5} and the product of these primes is 30. Hence 30 is the LCM of 6 and 15. Then the further application of the multiplicative identity element gives us the correct representations for the two fractions. For the LCM of 8 and 12 we have the set of prime factors of 8, {2, 2, 2}, and for 12 we have {2, 2, 3}. There are more than one factor of 2 in each set. We must list all prime factors *including repeated factors*. The union of {2, 2, 2} and {2, 2, 3} is {2, 2, 2, 3} and the LCM of 8 and 12 is 2·2·2·3, or 24.

It is interesting to observe that most students are able to find LCDs but have little understanding as to why the method works. Our approaches in the teaching of modern mathematics should include detailed work as to *why* this technique works and not just *how* it is executed.

In addition to these properties for multiplication as an operation, there is the property which uses two operations, that is, the distributive property for multiplication over addition:

$$\frac{a}{b}\left(\frac{c}{d} + \frac{e}{f}\right) = \frac{a}{b} \cdot \frac{c}{d} + \frac{a}{b} \cdot \frac{e}{f}$$

To prove the distributive property we shall find the fractional expressions for both sides of the statement and compare them. Then

$$\frac{a}{b}\left(\frac{c}{d} + \frac{e}{f}\right) = \frac{a}{b}\left(\frac{cf + de}{df}\right)$$

$$= \frac{a(cf + de)}{b \cdot d \cdot f}$$

$$= \frac{acf + ade}{bdf}$$

(Note the use of the alternate definition of addition for fractions.) And

$$\frac{a}{b} \cdot \frac{c}{d} + \frac{a}{b} \cdot \frac{e}{f} = \frac{ac}{bd} + \frac{ae}{bf}$$

$$= \frac{acf}{bdf} + \frac{ade}{bdf}$$

$$= \frac{acf + ade}{bdf}$$

(Observe also the use of LCD technique.) Since the two sides yield the same expression, they are equal, and the distributive property for multiplication over addition holds for the set of fractions.

7.8   Multiplicative Inverse

In the last section we noted that the operation of multiplication is commutative and associative and that there exists an identity element. Moreover, multiplication is distributive over addition. In this section, we wish to define a new concept called an *inverse* and show that there are multiplicative inverses for nearly all members of the set of fractions.

If we have a fraction a/b with $a \neq 0$ and $b \neq 0$, is there a fraction x/y such that

$$\frac{a}{b} \cdot \frac{x}{y} = \frac{1}{1}$$

We use the representation $1/1$ for the multiplicative identity element. Multiplying a/b by x/y, we obtain

$$\frac{a \cdot x}{b \cdot y} = \frac{1}{1}$$

By the definition of equality of fractions, we have

$$ax \cdot 1 = by \cdot 1 \quad \text{or} \quad a \cdot x = b \cdot y$$

If the definition of equality of fractions is reversed,

$$ax = by \quad \text{and} \quad \frac{x}{y} = \frac{b}{a}$$

So there is a fraction which when multiplied by a/b gives the multiplicative identity element. If for any given fraction a/b there exists such a fraction (here found to be b/a) satisfying this condition, this fraction is called the *multiplicative inverse* of the fraction a/b. Thus b/a is the multiplicative inverse of a/b, and $3/2$ is the multiplicative inverse of $2/3$. We sometimes call $3/2$ the *reciprocal* of $2/3$. The term *multiplicative inverse* has some advantages in that the term *multiplicative* denotes the operation and the term *inverse* denotes a particular connection between the two functions.

Not every fraction has a multiplicative inverse. In our derivation of the value of x/y in the above, we placed restrictions on a and b in a/b. From earlier discussions we know $b \neq 0$ for any fraction. Here, we also said a must be nonzero. If $a = 0$, the supposed inverse would be $b/0$, which is undefined for our purposes. Hence $0/b$ does not have a multiplicative inverse. Moreover, it is the only fraction which does not have such a multiplicative inverse.

It is also possible to prove that this inverse, when it exists, is unique. We prove it in a manner similar to other uniqueness proofs by assuming that there are two distinct inverses and showing that this is a contradiction and that, therefore, there is only one such inverse. The student should work out the details.

Exercises

1. Find the following by the definition of multiplication:
(a) $2/3 \cdot 3/4$ (b) $4/9 \cdot 8/11$
(c) $1/1 \cdot 2/2$ (d) $5/2 \cdot 2/5$
(e) $0/7 \cdot 8/9$ (f) $0/7 \cdot 2/2$

2. Which of the following are true?
(a) $2/3 \cdot 3/4 = 1/1$ (b) $2/3 \cdot 4/4 = 1/1$
(c) $5/6 \cdot 0/4 = 0/24$ (d) $5/9 \cdot 9/5 = 2/2$
(e) $2/2 \cdot 2/2 = 1/1$ (f) $0/4 \cdot 1/1 = 0/4$
(g) $6/11 \cdot 11/6 = 0/1$

3. In which of the true statements in Exercise 2 do we find multiplication by the multiplicative identity element? In which do we find multiplication by the additive identity element? In which do we find a fraction multiplied by its multiplicative inverse?

4. What are the multiplicative inverses of the following:
(a) $2/3$ (b) $3/4$
(c) $10/10{,}001$ (d) $3/3$
(e) $0/9$

5. Reduce, if possible, by using the multiplicative identity:
(a) 2/4   (b) 3/27
(c) 12/48   (d) 102/212

6. Find the least common multiple of the following pairs:
(a) 6, 12
(b) 15, 4
(c) 30, 72
(d) 5, 11
(e) a pair of prime numbers p and q

7. Find the LCM of the following trios of numbers:
(a) 6, 15, 9   (b) 3, 7, 28

8. Use the LCM technique to add the following:
(a) 1/6 + 5/12   (b) 7/15 + 3/4
(c) 9/30 + 4/72   (d) 1/5 + 1/11

9. Prove that the multiplicative identity is unique.

10. Prove that if a fraction has a multiplicative inverse, it is unique.

7.9   Subtraction and Division

We now turn to subtraction and division for the set of fractions; first
the operation of subtraction is defined.

DEFINITION 7.5 $a/c - b/c = (a - b)/c$, if and only if
$a - b \geq 0$.

The restriction $a - b \geq 0$ must appear in Definition 7.5; subtraction on whole numbers is defined only under these circumstances. This
definition also parallels the first definition for addition of fractions and
has the same kind of interpretation. For example,

$$\frac{3}{5} - \frac{1}{5} = \frac{3 - 1}{5} = \frac{2}{5}$$

can be illustrated by a diagram as follows. Take 3/5 as the shaded
region (fig. 7.6). If we remove shading from one area, we obtain figure
7.7. Thus 2/5 of the region is left. Such illustrations serve as motivation
for the above definition of subtraction.

3/5

FIGURE 7.6

FIGURE 7.7

To show that subtraction is not commutative or associative is easy, and it is left for the student to do.

The distributive property for multiplication over subtraction does hold for the set of fractions. The property is stated as

$$\frac{a}{b}\left(\frac{d}{c} - \frac{e}{c}\right) = \frac{a}{b} \cdot \frac{d}{c} - \frac{a}{b} \cdot \frac{e}{c}$$

This definition holds if and only if $d/c - e/c$ is definable; that is, $d - e$ must be greater than or equal to zero. The expression

$$\frac{a}{b} \cdot \frac{d}{c} - \frac{a}{b} \cdot \frac{e}{c}$$

is defined when $d/c - e/c$ is defined. We will not prove that this property holds, as it is not necessary for what follows. We assume that it is true (as it is).

The operation of division on the set of fractions is also defined in a manner similar to division on whole numbers.

DEFINITION 7.6 $a/b \div c/d = e/f$, where $c \neq 0$, if and only if $a/b = c/d \cdot e/f$.

The restriction that c be nonzero will become more significant as we develop the algorithmic process for the operation of division. Since the definition says that

$$\frac{a}{b} \div \frac{c}{d} = \frac{e}{f} \quad \text{where } c \neq 0 \quad \text{if and only if } \frac{a}{b} = \frac{c}{d} \cdot \frac{e}{f}$$

we take the "if and only if" part and find e/f in terms of a, b, c and d. Since

$$\frac{a}{b} = \frac{c}{d} \cdot \frac{e}{f} \quad \text{then} \quad \frac{a}{b} = \frac{ce}{df}$$

The fractions are equal so we may write

$$a(df) = b(ce)$$

Applying the associative property on whole numbers, we write this last expression as

$$(ad) \cdot f = (bc) \cdot e$$

This is the condition for two fractions to be equal, and we write

$$\frac{e}{f} = \frac{ad}{bc}$$

but $ad/bc = a/b \cdot d/c$ and we have

$$\frac{e}{f} = \frac{a}{b} \cdot \frac{d}{c}$$

Thus we have proven that

$$\frac{a}{b} \div \frac{c}{d} = \frac{a}{b} \cdot \frac{d}{c}$$

which is the algorithmic procedure that we all use to divide one fraction by another. Since the fraction d/c must exist, we specify that c must not be zero.

We offer at this time a slightly different proof which is often used to convince elementary students that this algorithmic process is true. First we write $a/b \div c/d$ as

$$\frac{a/b}{c/d}$$

where the numerator and denominator are fractions. (Although we have not yet discussed this kind of expression, it is an important concept which we discuss later.) If we multiply this fraction by the multiplicative identity written in a certain form, we obtain

$$\frac{a/b}{c/d} \cdot \frac{d/c}{d/c}$$

The choice of the form of the identity becomes obvious as we proceed.

$$\frac{a/b}{c/d} \cdot \frac{d/c}{d/c} = \frac{a/b \cdot d/c}{c/d \cdot d/c}$$

$$= \frac{a/b \cdot d/c}{cd/dc}$$

$$= \frac{a/b \cdot d/c}{1/1}$$

Since dividing by $1/1$ gives the expression in the numerator,

$$\frac{a}{b} \div \frac{c}{d} = \frac{a}{b} \cdot \frac{d}{c}$$

Some comments are in order about this last proof. Clearly, there are some steps which would have to be justified, such as dividing by $1/1$, and, of course, the form of the fractional representation should be explained. Most youngsters can learn to apply the process, but they also should *understand* why this algorithmic process works. To develop such an understanding will require very careful treatment of this subject by the elementary teacher.

It is also possible to show by example that division is not commutative or associative. We leave the task of constructing these examples to the student.

Exercises

1.   Find the following and reduce wherever possible:
(a) $3/4 - 2/4$
(b) $5/6 - 1/6$
(c) $7/8 - 3/4$ (Hint: Apply the LCD technique first.)
(d) $5/9 - 0/7$
(e) $2/3 - 7/8$

2. Find the following by using the definition of division:
(a) $3/4 \div 5/6$ (b) $2/3 \div 2/3$
(c) $0/8 \div 1/2$

3. Find the following by using the algorithmic process for division:
(a) $3/4 \div 5/6$ (b) $2/3 \div 2/3$
(c) $0/8 \div 1/2$ (d) $10/3 \div 3/10$
(e) $1/2 \div 2/15$

4. Is the set of fractions closed for the operation of division? Why?

5. Is the following statement true?

$$\left(\frac{a}{b} + \frac{c}{d}\right) \div \frac{e}{f} = \left(\frac{a}{b} \div \frac{e}{f}\right) + \left(\frac{c}{d} \div \frac{e}{f}\right)$$

If this property is true, name it.

6. Examine an elementary textbook series in arithmetic to see how the idea of dividing one fraction by another is approached.

7.10   Is Less than and Is Greater than

In this section we define the "is less than" relation on fractions and thus show that it is possible to order fractions in a manner similar to the ordering of the whole numbers.

The fraction a/b is less than the fraction c/d if and only if the product ad is less than the product bc. Symbolically, this is written as

$$\frac{a}{b} < \frac{c}{d} \text{ if and only if } ad < bc$$

Thus, $2/3 < 3/4$ because $2 \cdot 4 < 3 \cdot 3$. The products must be in the right order or the results will be wrong. Is $1/2 < 12/24$? Obviously not, but we experiment by applying the definition of "is less than."

$$\frac{1}{2} < \frac{12}{24} \text{ if and only if } 1 \cdot 24 < 2 \cdot 12$$

However, $1 \cdot 24 < 2 \cdot 12$ is not true, so $1/2 < 12/24$ also is not true.

We could also compare the two fractions of an inequality by comparing numerators *if* the denominators are the same. For example, to find if $4/7 < 10/14$ is true, first use the LCM technique and rewrite the fractions with the LCD:

$$\frac{8}{14} < \frac{10}{14}$$

This is obviously a true statement, for $8 \cdot 14$ is clearly less than $10 \cdot 14$. Or, since 8 is less than 10, the statement is also true. This approach enables us to use the diagram illustrations of rectangles (or pies) and lends support and motivation to the definition of "is less than."

"Is greater than" is defined in a similar manner: $a/b > c/d$ if and only if $ad > bc$. Thus $10/14 > 4/7$ because $10 \cdot 7 > 14 \cdot 4$. From these definitions and the properties of equality, we can deduce the trichotomy property for fractions, which states that

$$\frac{a}{b} = \frac{c}{d} \quad \text{or} \quad \frac{a}{b} < \frac{c}{d} \quad \text{or} \quad \frac{a}{b} > \frac{c}{d}$$

where *or* is used in the exclusive sense. Clearly, if $a/b = c/d$, we know that $ad = bc$. Hence, $ad < bc$ cannot be true if $ad = bc$ is true (from the trichotomy property for whole numbers), so $a/b < c/d$ cannot be true. We follow a similar line of reasoning to deduce that $a/b > c/d$ also cannot be true. Thus, if $a/b = c/d$, the other two, $a/b < c/d$ and $a/b > c/d$, are false. In a similar fashion, we can show that if $a/b < c/d$, then $a/b = c/c$ and $a/b > c/d$ are both false. Also we can show that if $a/b > c/d$, then $a/b = c/d$ and $a/b < c/d$ are both false.

By trichotomy property, one and only one of the following can be true for two given fractions, a/b and c/d.

$$\frac{a}{b} = \frac{c}{d} \tag{1}$$

$$\frac{a}{b} < \frac{c}{d} \tag{2}$$

$$\frac{a}{b} > \frac{c}{d} \tag{3}$$

It is easy to show that "is less than" defined on the set of fractions satisfies only the transitive property, not the reflexive or symmetric properties. For "is less than" to be reflexive we must have $a/b < a/b$, but this is false because $ab < ab$ is false. Hence "is less than" is not reflexive.

"Is less than" is not symmetric because the following would have to be true: If $a/b < c/d$, then $c/d < a/b$. However, this is not true, because if $a/b < c/d$, then $ad < bc$, and for $c/d < a/b$ to be true, we must have $cb < ad$. But this cannot happen if $ad < bc$, so "is less than" is not symmetric. However, it is transitive; that is, if $a/b < c/d$ and $c/d < e/f$, then $a/b < e/f$. To prove this, consider the following: If $a/b < c/e$, then, by definition, $ad < bc$, and if $c/d < c/f$, then $cf < de$. Multiply $ad < bc$ by f, to obtain $adf < bcf$. Multiply $cf < de$ by b, to obtain $bcf < bde$. By the transitive property of "is less than" on whole numbers, if $adf < bcf$ and $bcf < bde$, then $adf < bde$. By one of the cancellation properties on "is less than," if $adf < bde$, then $af < be$. But $af < be$ is, by definition, the condition that $a/b < e/f$, which is what we wanted. Thus, "is greater than" is transitive, and it behaves in precisely the same fashion on fractions as on whole numbers.

Knowing the properties of "is less than" we can now order the set of fractions in the same manner that we ordered the set of whole numbers. For example, given $1/2$, $2/3$ and $3/4$, we can establish the following true statements:

$$\frac{1}{2} < \frac{2}{3} \qquad \frac{2}{3} < \frac{3}{4} \quad \text{and} \quad \frac{1}{2} < \frac{3}{4}$$

which can be put in the following order:

$$\frac{1}{2} < \frac{2}{3} < \frac{3}{4}$$

All fractions can be done in a similar fashion. Consequently, we could put the fractions on a number line, for example,

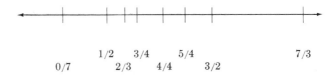

Moreover, there are so many fractions to be placed that we can only indicate a sample of them on the number line.

7.11 Cancellation Properties

In chapter 4 on whole numbers we discussed the following cancellation properties:

1. If $a = b$, then $a + c = b + c$.
2. If $a + c = b + c$, then $a = b$.
3. If $a \cdot c = b \cdot c$, $c \neq 0$, then $a = b$.
4. If $a = b$, then $a \cdot c = b \cdot c$.
5. If $a + c < b + c$, then $a < b$.
6. If $a < b$, then $a + c < b + c$.
7. If $a \cdot c < b \cdot c$, $c \neq 0$, then $a < b$.
8. If $a < b$, then $ac < bc$, if $c \neq 0$.

We will show that these are also true statements if a, b and c are fractions and not whole numbers; we will prove some statements and leave the rest for exercises.

Statement (1), if $a/b = c/d$, then $a/b + e/f = c/d + e/f$, is the first we choose to prove; we start by finding $a/b + e/f$.

$$\frac{a}{b} + \frac{e}{f} = \frac{af + be}{bf}$$

Multiplying by d/d, we obtain

$$\frac{af + be}{bf} \cdot \frac{d}{d} = \frac{adf + bde}{bdf}$$

From the hypothesis (if $a/b = c/d$) we obtain $ad = bc$, and if we replace ad by bc, we have

$$\frac{adf + bde}{bdf} = \frac{bcf + bde}{bdf}$$

$$= \frac{b(cf + de)}{b(df)}$$

$$= \frac{b}{b} \cdot \frac{cf + de}{df}$$

$$= \frac{cf + de}{df}$$

$$= \frac{c}{d} + \frac{e}{f}$$

and the proof is complete.

The second statement is the converse of the first: If $a/b + e/f = c/d + e/f$, then $a/b = c/d$. The proof is as follows:

$$\frac{a}{b} + \frac{e}{f} = \frac{af + eb}{bf} \quad \text{and} \quad \frac{c}{d} + \frac{e}{f} = \frac{cf + de}{df}$$

By the definition of equal fractions,

$$(af + eb)df = bf(cf + de) \quad \text{or} \quad afdf + bdef = bfcf + bdef$$

Since this equation refers to whole numbers, we may apply the cancellation property (2) for whole numbers,

$$afdf = bfcf$$

Applying (3), we obtain

$$ad = bc$$

which is the defining statement for $a/b = c/d$, and the proof is complete. We have already proved Statements (1) and (2):

1. If $\dfrac{a}{b} = \dfrac{c}{d}$, then $\dfrac{a}{b} + \dfrac{e}{f} = \dfrac{c}{d} + \dfrac{e}{f}$.

2. If $\dfrac{a}{b} + \dfrac{e}{f} = \dfrac{c}{d} + \dfrac{e}{f}$, then $\dfrac{a}{b} = \dfrac{c}{d}$.

Statements (3) through (8) can be written in fractional form:

3. If $\dfrac{a}{b}\cdot\dfrac{e}{f} = \dfrac{c}{d}\cdot\dfrac{e}{f}$, and $\dfrac{e}{f} \neq \dfrac{0}{f}$, then $\dfrac{a}{b} = \dfrac{c}{d}$.

4. If $\dfrac{a}{b} = \dfrac{c}{d}$, then $\dfrac{a}{b}\cdot\dfrac{e}{f} = \dfrac{c}{d}\cdot\dfrac{e}{f}$.

5. If $\dfrac{a}{b} + \dfrac{e}{f} < \dfrac{c}{d} + \dfrac{e}{f}$, then $\dfrac{a}{b} < \dfrac{c}{d}$.

6. If $\dfrac{a}{b} < \dfrac{c}{d}$, then $\dfrac{a}{b} + \dfrac{e}{f} < \dfrac{c}{d} + \dfrac{e}{f}$.

7. If $\dfrac{a}{b}\cdot\dfrac{e}{f} < \dfrac{c}{d}\cdot\dfrac{e}{f}$, and $\dfrac{e}{f} \neq \dfrac{0}{f}$, then $\dfrac{a}{b} < \dfrac{c}{d}$.

8. If $\dfrac{a}{b} < \dfrac{e}{f}$, then $\dfrac{a}{b}\cdot\dfrac{c}{d} < \dfrac{e}{f}\cdot\dfrac{c}{d}$, when $\dfrac{c}{d} \neq \dfrac{0}{d}$.

By definition of equality of fractions, we have, for the proof of Statement (3),

$$(a \cdot c)\,(fd) = (ec)\,(bd)$$

Reassociating terms on both sides of the equal sign, we can write

$$(af)\,(cd) = (eb)\,(cd)$$

Since this is a statement on whole numbers, we can apply a cancellation property. If $(af)(cd) = (eb)(cd)$, then $af = eb$. But this defines the equality of two fractions, namely,

$$\frac{a}{b} = \frac{e}{f}$$

and the proof is complete.

We next prove (8). If $a/b < e/f$, then by the definition of "is less than," $af < be$. Multiply both sides (remember this is a statement on whole numbers) by cd. Thus, if $af < be$, then $(af)(cd) < (be)(cd)$. Rearrange terms:

$$(ac)(fd) < (bd)(ec)$$

But this is the condition for $ac/bd < ec/fd$ to be true. Consequently,

$$\frac{a}{b} \cdot \frac{c}{d} < \frac{e}{f} \cdot \frac{c}{d}$$

and Property (8) is identified.

The two proofs just given are very similar. Both essentially use the corresponding property on the set of whole numbers as a basis for proving the corresponding statement about fractions. Such a technique was used consistently throughout this chapter; some kind of relationship between the two sets of numbers and their respective operations clearly has been established. In the next section we shall formalize this relationship into a very significant mathematical statement.

Exercises

1.   Which of the following statements are true?
(a) $1/2 < 5/9$
(b) $3/4 < 7/8$
(c) $1/10 < 0/3$
(d) $1/1 < 2/2$
(e) $7/9 > 101/887$
(f) $11/13 > 52/62$
(g) If $1/2 < 2/3$ and $2/3 < 4/5$, then $1/2 < 4/5$.

2.   Given two fractions, find a fraction which is less than one fraction and greater than the other.
(a) $1/2$, $3/4$ (Hint: Find $x/y : 1/2 < x/y < 3/4$.)
(b) $7/8$, $9/10$

(c) If the fractions are a/b and c/d, show that $(a + c)/(b + d)$ satisfies the requirement of this exercise.

3. If between any two fractions there is another fraction (as described in Exercise 2), then the fractions are *dense*. Given any two fractions (for example, 1/2 and 3/4), how many fractions x/y satisfy $1/2 < x/y < 3/4$?

4. In the cancellation property, if $a \cdot c = b \cdot c$, $c \neq 0$, then $a = b$. Give an example which shows this to be a false statement when $c = 0$. Do the same for Properties (7) and (8) in the preceding section.

5. In the cancellation property, if $a/b \cdot e/f = c/d \cdot e/f$, $e/f \neq 0/f$, then $a/b = c/d$, give an example which shows this to be a false statement when $e/f = 0/f$.

6. Repeat Exercise 5 for Properties (7) and (8).

7.12   Other Representations for Fractions

In all of our discussions of fractions we have not once suggested that some of the fractions which we have been dealing with might also be describing whole numbers. We have not said, for example, that 8/4 and 2 are the same. We now wish to formalize this idea by giving an intuitive reason in the following illustration. Consider $1/4 + 3/4$. By the definition of addition, $1/4 + 3/4 = (1 + 3)/4 = 4/4$. Returning to our illustration, we have figure 7.8. The sum can be illustrated as in figure 7.9. But (4/4)'s of a rectangle can also be represented as in figure 7.10 or

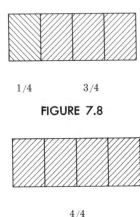

1/4   3/4

FIGURE 7.8

4/4

FIGURE 7.9

as a single rectangle (one piece of the rectangle which has been divided into one part). But this last interpretation represents one rectangle. Hence, we see that (4/4)'s of a rectangle and one rectangle represent the same thing. (Consequently, we have a plausible reason for saying 4/4 = 1.) This leads us to Definition 7.7.

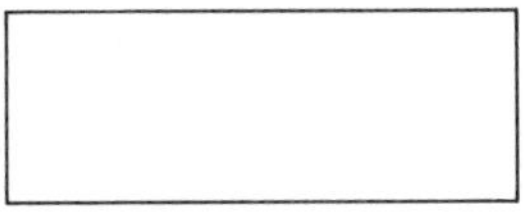

1/1

FIGURE 7.10

DEFINITION 7.7 $n/1 = n$.

Although Definition 7.7 does not apply directly to 4/4, 4/4 = 1/1 and, by the definition,

$$\frac{1}{1} = 1 \quad \text{when } n = 1$$

Moreover, 8/2 = 4/1 = 4 or 12/3 = 4/1 = 4. Thus there is an equivalence class of fractions which also represents the same number represented by a whole number. However, there are fractions which do not represent whole numbers. For example, 2/3 can never be written in the form $n/1$.

As a consequence of Definition 7.7 we can write some new interesting notations. For example, if we write 3 + 4/5, we really mean 3/1 + 4/5, as we have no definition of addition which describes how to add a whole number and a fraction. The 3 in 3 + 4/5 means that 3 represents an equivalence class of fractions to which 3/1 belongs. Hence, to find 3 + 4/5, we work 3/1 + 4/5. Moreover, 3/1 + 4/5 = 15/5 + 4/5 = 19/5. This last form, 19/5, is sometimes called an *improper* fraction where the word *improper* means that the numerator is a whole number greater than the denominator. In the past, this was not considered to be a proper way to write a fraction, hence the name *improper*. Actually there is nothing wrong with this form mathematically, and quite often it is the best form to use in a problem.

We also may adopt another form of writing 3 + 4/5 as a direct consequence of the above definition, the mixed number form, for example,

$$3\frac{4}{5} = 3 + \frac{4}{5}$$

In practice, $3\frac{4}{5}$ (read "three and four-fifths") is only a shortened form for $3 + 4/5$, and we often use it instead of $3 + 4/5$ or $19/5$. In fact, we spend some time in elementary school arithmetic showing how to get from $3\frac{4}{5}$ to $19/5$ or from $19/5$ to $3\frac{4}{5}$. To write $3\frac{4}{5}$ as a fraction we first write

$$3\frac{4}{5} = 3 + \frac{4}{5}$$

By definition

$$3 + \frac{4}{5} = \frac{3}{1} + \frac{4}{5} \quad \text{and} \quad \frac{3}{1} + \frac{4}{5} = \frac{15}{5} + \frac{4}{5} = \frac{19}{5}$$

We could reverse the process since the equality is symmetric, but instead we use an algorithmic process developed especially for this. To convert $19/5$ to a mixed number, we divide 19 by 5 and write 3; the remainder 4 becomes $4/5$ when written in fraction form. This, however, requires the use of another idea (division) which we will discuss in a moment. We also spend some time in arithmetic instruction teaching youngsters how to add, subtract, multiply and divide mixed numbers. We can develop some shortcuts, but most of the algorithmic processes require us to convert back to fractional form, work the problem and then write the answer as a mixed number. For example, multiply $2\frac{1}{3}$ and $3\frac{4}{5}$.

$$\left(2\frac{1}{3}\right)\left(3\frac{4}{5}\right) = \frac{7}{3} \cdot \frac{19}{5} \qquad \text{Converting to Fractional Form}$$

$$= \frac{133}{15} \qquad \text{Multiplying}$$

$$= 8\frac{13}{15} \qquad \text{Converting to Mixed Number Form}$$

From the mathematical point of view, there is no reason for the use of the mixed number form; it is simply another representation for a fraction. It is, however, more convenient to speak of $3\frac{4}{5}$ apples (of which we have some physical notion) than to speak of $19/5$ apples.

We have suggested that 19/5 might be converted to $3\frac{4}{5}$ by using division. This would require the establishment of some connection between division of whole numbers (the answer for a division) and fractions. If we return to the definition where $n/1$ was defined to be n, we can begin such a connection. Consider the problem $n \div 1$. By definition of division on whole numbers, $n \div 1 = n$. Thus $n/1 = n = n \div 1$, and we have still another interpretation for the fractional symbol $n/1$. Also, 4/4 when written as $4 \div 4$ gives us 1, and 8/2 when written as $8 \div 2$ gives us 4. We would obtain both answers by using the definition of $n/1 = n$. Thus we can write

$$\frac{n}{1} = n \div 1$$

and we have a partial connection between division of whole numbers and fractions.

Can 2/3 be written as $2 \div 3$? Our definition of division of whole numbers did not define expressions such as $2 \div 3$ because the answer is not a whole number. If it were true that $2/3 = 2 \div 3$, all fractions could be written as division problems. Consider the following argument. Suppose we say that $2 \div 3$ is some number (not a whole number), for example, the fraction x/y. If we broaden somewhat the definition of division of whole numbers, we could write

$$2 \div 3 = \frac{x}{y} \text{ if and only if } 2 = 3 \cdot \frac{x}{y}$$

But since x/y is a fraction, then we ought to use the fractional form for 2 and for 3. Thus $2 = 3 \cdot x/y$ becomes $2/1 = 3/1 \cdot x/y$ and

$$\frac{2}{1} = \frac{3x}{y} \quad \text{or} \quad 2y = 3x$$

By definition of equality of fractions,

$$\frac{2}{3} = \frac{x}{y}$$

So, if $2 \div 3$ is to have meaning in division of whole numbers, then $2 \div 3$ must be 2/3.

Another way of looking at this is to consider $2 \div 3$ as a division problem of fractions.

$$2 \div 3 = \frac{2}{1} \div \frac{3}{1} = \frac{2}{1} \cdot \frac{1}{3} = \frac{2}{3}$$

and we have obtained the same results. Therefore, we define

$$p \div q = \frac{p}{q} \qquad q \neq 0$$

where p and q are whole numbers.

In our discussion we excluded fractions with zero denominators because we wanted the equality of fractions to be an equivalence relation. Earlier we said that division by zero (in whole numbers) was undefined. These ideas agree because $p \div 0$ is undefined, so we must also leave $p/0$ undefined.

Thus, we have observed several alternate forms for writing fractions and have defined (after considering plausible reasons) connections between fractions and whole numbers. We also noted the use of improper fractions and mixed number forms. Although we have not spent much time in dealing with the algorithmic processes for mixed numbers, it is suggested that a prospective elementary teacher examine it carefully from a teaching point of view. It is easy to justify the use of mixed numbers from a mathematical point of view but perhaps not so easy to develop from a teaching point of view. However the notion of mixed numbers is developed, care should be taken to insure that *understanding* is achieved and not just rote manipulation of the procedures.

Exercises

1.   Prove the four cancellation properties not proven in Section 7.11.

2.   Convert to mixed number representation:
(a) 10/3   (b) 7/2
(c) 110/15   (d) 110/5
(e) 2/3   (f) 0/7

3.   Convert to fractional form:

(a) $4\frac{2}{3}$ (b) $7\frac{1}{9}$

(c) $2\frac{3}{5}$ (d) $0\frac{4}{9}$

(e) $5\frac{0}{3}$

4.   If $a/b \cdot c/d = e/f \cdot c/d$, show that if we multiply both by the multiplicative inverse of c/d, we have $a/b = e/f$.

5.   What is Webster's definition of *improper*? What is the mathematical definition of *improper* in an improper fraction?

6.   Develop a rule for adding two mixed numbers *without* converting to fractions. Apply it to $2\frac{1}{3} + 3\frac{4}{5}$.

7.   What is the procedure for dividing one mixed number by another mixed number? Try it on $2\frac{1}{3} \div 3\frac{4}{5}$.

8.   What kind of number do we obtain if we divide a whole number a by a whole number b ($b \neq 0$)? Is division of whole numbers a closed operation?

9.   Is division of fractions a closed operation on the set of fractions? Why?

10.   Since we defined $p \div q = p/q$, give a reason why $0/0$ is not used as a fraction.

7.13   Summary

In this chapter we have defined the set of fractions and defined operations of addition, subtraction, multiplication and division. We found the following to be true:

1. Addition is a closed operation.
2. Multiplication is a closed operation.

3. $\dfrac{a}{b} + \dfrac{c}{d} = \dfrac{c}{d} + \dfrac{a}{b}$.

4. $\left(\dfrac{a}{b} + \dfrac{c}{d}\right) + \dfrac{e}{f} = \dfrac{a}{b} + \left(\dfrac{c}{d} + \dfrac{e}{f}\right)$.

5. There exists $\dfrac{0}{n}$ such that $\dfrac{a}{b} + \dfrac{0}{n} = \dfrac{a}{b}$.

6. $\dfrac{a}{b} \cdot \dfrac{c}{d} = \dfrac{c}{d} \cdot \dfrac{a}{b}$

7. $\left(\dfrac{a}{b} \cdot \dfrac{c}{d}\right) \cdot \dfrac{e}{f} = \dfrac{a}{b} \cdot \left(\dfrac{c}{d} \cdot \dfrac{e}{f}\right)$.

8. There exists $\dfrac{x}{x}$ such that $\dfrac{a}{b} \cdot \dfrac{x}{x} = \dfrac{a}{b}$.

9. For each $\frac{a}{b}$, $a \neq 0$, there exists a fraction (called the mul-

tiplicative inverse of $\frac{a}{b}$) such that $\frac{a}{b} \cdot \frac{b}{a} = 1$.

10. $\frac{a}{b} \cdot \frac{0}{c} = \frac{0}{d}$.

11. $\frac{a}{b}\left(\frac{c}{d} + \frac{e}{f}\right) = \frac{a}{b} \cdot \frac{c}{d} + \frac{a}{b} \cdot \frac{e}{f}$.

In addition to these properties for operations, we also included the cancellation properties:

12. If $\frac{a}{b} = \frac{c}{d}$, then $\frac{a}{b} + \frac{e}{f} = \frac{c}{d} + \frac{e}{f}$.

13. If $\frac{a}{b} + \frac{e}{f} = \frac{c}{d} + \frac{e}{f}$, then $\frac{a}{a} = \frac{c}{d}$.

14. If $\frac{a}{b} \cdot \frac{e}{f} = \frac{c}{d} \cdot \frac{e}{f}$, and $\frac{e}{f} \neq \frac{0}{f}$, then $\frac{a}{b} = \frac{c}{d}$.

15. If $\frac{a}{b} = \frac{c}{d}$, then $\frac{a}{b} \cdot \frac{e}{f} = \frac{c}{d} \cdot \frac{e}{f}$.

16. If $\frac{a}{b} + \frac{e}{f} < \frac{c}{d} + \frac{e}{f}$, then $\frac{a}{b} < \frac{c}{d}$.

17. If $\frac{a}{b} < \frac{c}{d}$, then $\frac{a}{b} + \frac{e}{f} < \frac{c}{d} + \frac{e}{f}$.

18. If $\frac{a}{b} \cdot \frac{e}{f} < \frac{c}{d} \cdot \frac{e}{f}$ and $\frac{e}{f} \neq \frac{0}{f}$, then $\frac{a}{b} < \frac{c}{d}$.

19. If $\frac{a}{b} < \frac{e}{f}$, then $\frac{a}{b} \cdot \frac{c}{d} < \frac{e}{f} \cdot \frac{c}{d}$, when $\frac{c}{d} \neq \frac{0}{d}$.

We also defined some other forms of writing numbers denoted by fractions, including improper fractions and mixed numbers, and established that certain fractions represent the same numbers as the whole numbers.

8

DECIMALS

8.1   Fractions as Decimals and Expanded Numerals

We begin our discussion of the decimal representation of fractions by showing that certain fractions are expressible as finite decimals. We shall do so by first expressing some fractions in an expanded numeral form and then extending the procedure to all fractions.

If we write out some members of the equivalence class for the fraction represented by 1/2, we note

$$\frac{1}{2} = \frac{2}{4} = \frac{3}{6} = \frac{4}{8} = \frac{5}{10} = \frac{6}{12} = \frac{7}{14} = \cdots$$

The denominator of one of these fractional forms is 10. Since ten is the base of our system of numeration, it is possible to develop an expanded numeral form for fractions as well as for whole numbers. It is obvious that those fractions which represent the same numbers as the whole numbers already have an expanded numeral form. We will confine our attention for the moment to some examples between 0 and 1.

Let us write 1/2 as 5/10 and then write

$$\frac{5}{10} = \frac{5}{1} \cdot \frac{1}{10} \quad \text{or} \quad \frac{5}{10} = 5 \cdot \frac{1}{10}$$

The fraction 1/5 can be written also as a fraction with 10 as a denominator, namely, 2/10. More specifically,

$$\frac{1}{5} = \frac{2}{1} \cdot \frac{1}{10} \quad \text{or} \quad \frac{1}{5} = 2 \cdot \frac{1}{10}$$

The fraction 1/4 can be written with a denominator which is a power of 10, for example,

$$\frac{1}{4} = \frac{25}{100}$$

$$= \frac{20 + 5}{100}$$

$$= \frac{20}{100} + \frac{5}{100}$$

$$= \frac{2}{10} + \frac{5}{100}$$

$$= 2 \cdot \frac{1}{10} + 5 \cdot \frac{1}{100}$$

We can do the same for 1/8. Since $1/8 = 125/1{,}000$, we can write

$$\frac{1}{8} = \frac{125}{1{,}000}$$

$$= \frac{100 + 20 + 5}{1{,}000}$$

$$= \frac{100}{1{,}000} + \frac{20}{1{,}000} + \frac{5}{1{,}000}$$

$$= \frac{1}{10} + \frac{2}{100} + \frac{5}{1{,}000}$$

$$= 1 \cdot \frac{1}{10} + 2 \cdot \frac{1}{100} + 5 \cdot \frac{1}{1{,}000}$$

In each of the above fractions, the denominator is a power of 10, and each fraction is expressed in tenths, hundredths or thousandths. If we adopt the correct notation for these fractions, we could consider the notation as part of the place value system. If we use a period (called a decimal point), followed by the multipliers of 1/10, 1/100 and 1/1,000, we can write a place value representation for these fractions. For example,

$$5 \cdot \frac{1}{10} \text{ can be written as } .5$$

$$2 \cdot \frac{1}{10} \text{ can be written as } .2$$

$$2 \cdot \frac{1}{10} + 5 \cdot \frac{1}{100} \text{ can be written as } .25$$

$$1 \cdot \frac{1}{10} + 2 \cdot \frac{1}{100} + 5 \cdot \frac{1}{1,000} \text{ can be written as } .125$$

and we have a place value representation for the fractions. The form $1 \cdot 1/10 + 2 \cdot 1/100 + 5 \cdot (1/1,000)$ can be considered as the expanded numeral form for the fraction and .125 as the decimal form for the same fraction.

If we examine the equivalence class of fractions represented by 1/2, we also find that $1/2 = 50/100$ or $1/2 = 500/1,000$. Writing both of these in the decimal form gives us the following:

$$\frac{1}{2} = \frac{50}{100} = .50 \quad \text{and} \quad \frac{1}{2} = \frac{500}{1,000} = .500$$

Thus, .5, .50 and .500 are all decimals which represent 1/2, as is .5000000 or any other decimal beginning with a 5 in the tenths place and followed by zeros.

We normally use .5 to represent 1/2 and frequently refer to this as a *finite decimal*. The word *finite* here means that there are a finite number of nonzero digits, after which there are only zeros for digits in the decimal representation. Actually we should consider all the zeros following the .5 in .5000 and treat all such representations with these zeros clearly indicated. Moreover, for 1/2 there are an infinite number of zeros which could be included following the .5, and this would be very difficult to write. We choose to adopt the following notation to simplify the writing problem. If we write $.500\overline{0}$, the bar over the zero means that the next digit is the same as the one under the bar, as are all others following. In the expression $.32\overline{17}$ the bar means that the next pair of digits is 17 and all subsequent pairs are 17. Thus,

$$.32\overline{17} = .3217171717, \text{ etc.}$$

This notation makes it possible to simplify the writing of decimals which have certain patterns in the digit representation.

What is the decimal representation for the fraction 1/3? If we recall some possible answers we might have learned from earlier years, we might include

$$\frac{1}{3} = .3 \quad \text{or} \quad \frac{1}{3} = .33 \quad \text{or} \quad \frac{1}{3} = .333$$

But the writing of .3, .33 or .333 suggests that these are finite decimals, and since no bar is indicated in the above forms, we probably mean

$$\frac{1}{3} = .30\overline{0} \quad \text{or} \quad \frac{1}{3} = .33\overline{0} \quad \text{or} \quad \frac{1}{3} = .333\overline{0}$$

However, $.30\overline{0}$ means $3 \cdot 1/10 + 0 \cdot 1/100 + 0 \cdot 1/1,000$, etc., or just 3/10. But $1/3 \neq 3/10$ by our definition of equal fractions, so $.30\overline{0}$ is not correct. Moreover, $.33\overline{0}$ and $.333\overline{0}$ are also not correct decimal representations for 1/3. The correct decimal representation for 1/3 is

$$.33\overline{3}$$

The process of how to arrive at this we shall explore in the next section. For the moment we wish to point out that some fractions have no finite decimal representation, and the bar notation is the only way we have of indicating the correct decimal form for fractions like 1/3, 1/7, 1/9 and many others.

8.2   Converting Fractions to Decimals

In this section we will develop a procedure to convert any fraction to decimal representation. Every fraction can be expressed as the quotient of the numerator and denominator, for example,

$$\frac{1}{3} = 1 \div 3$$

If we apply the division algorithm to this problem, we can find a procedure to give us the decimal representation for 1/3. First, 1 needs to be written as $1.00\bar{0}$. This is obvious if we write $1.00\bar{0}$ in expanded numeral form as follows:

$$1.00\bar{0} = 1 + 0\cdot\frac{1}{10} + 0\cdot\frac{1}{100} + 0\cdot\frac{1}{1,000}$$

and since all products after the 1 on the right involve a factor of zero,

$$1.00\bar{0} = 1 + 0 + 0 + 0 = 1$$

If we further assume that we know how to divide with decimals, we can actually divide 1 by 3.

```
          .33333̄
      ┌─────────
    3 │ 1.00000̄
          9
          ──
          10
           9
          ──
          10
           9
          ──
          10
           9
          ──
          10
           9
          ──
           1
```

Thus $1/3 = .3333\bar{3}$.

Two observations need to be made about this example. First, we are assuming at this point that we actually know how to perform the division involving the decimal $1.000\bar{0}$. Knowledge of this procedure would have to be developed first in the elementary school program before we could teach this process for conversion, but for the sake of time, we assume that the student does know how to perform such division. The second point involves something that happens in the actual division process itself. Each time we found a trial divisor (any one of the 3's) and proceeded to multiply by the divisor and subtract, we had repeatedly a remainder of 1; thus the next trial divisor is also 3 and so are all further divisors! Hence, we need not actually divide as far as we did before we know what to expect the remaining digits in the decimal answer to be. The repeating remainder signals the beginning of the repeat pattern of the decimal. We consider another example to further illustrate this last point.

To find the decimal representation for 1/6, we divide 1 by 6.

$$
\begin{array}{r}
.16 \\
6 \overline{\smash{\big)}\ 1.000\ \bar{0}} \\
\underline{6} \\
40 \\
\underline{36} \\
4
\end{array}
$$

The remainder, 4, has repeated, the decimal representation for 1/6 has begun to repeat and we can write

$$\frac{1}{6} = .16\bar{6}$$

We might ask if every fraction is finally expressed as a repeating decimal, as is 1/6 or 1/3. We can intuitively answer this question if we think about the division process and the remainder terms involved in this process. Suppose we are dividing some number p or q where p has been written as $p.000\bar{0}$. We know from the division process that the remainder term r satisfies the expression $0 \leq r < q$. After the first division we get some remainder, called r_1. If we divide again, we get another remainder. If this second remainder term is the same as r_1, then the quotient has already begun to repeat. If the second remainder, r_2, is different from r_1, we continue and divide again. The next remainder r_3 is the same as either r_1 or r_2, and, if $r_3 = r_1$ or $r_3 = r_2$, the decimal repeats or r_3 is different from r_1 and r_2. If the latter, we continue to divide. If we divide $q + 1$ times, we obtain $q + 1$ remainders, each of which must be less than q and greater than or equal to zero. But there are only q numbers which satisfy this condition ($0 \leq r_q < q$). Hence, one of the $q + 1$ remainders must be the same as one of the other remainders and, therefore, the decimal representation for p/q must have repeated. Thus, by this argument, *every fraction can be represented by an infinite repeating decimal*.

We are now able to convert a fraction to a decimal which will repeat (allowing us to use the bar notation).

8.3   Converting Decimals to Fractions

In this section we will develop the procedure for converting a decimal to a fraction. Suppose we have the decimal $.111\bar{1}$ and want to know what fraction is equal to it. Let the fraction be denoted by x; thus, $x = .111\overline{1}$. If we multiply both sides of this statement by 10, we have $10x = 1.111\overline{1}$. (We are assuming that we know how to multiply $1.111\overline{1}$ by 10.) This multiplication can be shown by using the expanded numeral form for $.111\overline{1}$, multiplying each term by 10 and then rewriting it in decimal form. We subtract x from $10x$ and write it vertically as follows:

$$
\begin{array}{rl}
10x = & 1.111\overline{1} \\
- \quad x = - & .111\overline{1} \\
\hline
9x = & 1.000\overline{0}
\end{array}
$$

Observe that in both numbers on the right side of the problem all digits to the right of the decimal point are the same. If we assume that these decimals subtract in the same way as finite decimals, we obtain

$$
\begin{array}{rl}
10x = & 1.111\overline{1} \\
- \quad x = - & .111\overline{1} \\
\hline
9x = & 1.000\overline{0}
\end{array}
$$

But $1.000\overline{0}$ is 1, so $9 \cdot x = 1$. Hence,

$$
x = \frac{1}{9}
$$

So $1/9 = .111\overline{1}$, and we have converted the decimal form to the corresponding fractional form for the given number.

For another example which is slightly different, we find the fraction which is equal to $.\overline{31}$. Let y be the fraction such that

$$
y = .\overline{31}
$$

Multiply by 100 to obtain

$$
100y = 31.\overline{31}
$$

Subtract $y = .\overline{31}$ to obtain

$$
\begin{array}{rl}
100y = & 31.\overline{31} \\
- \quad y = - & .\overline{31} \\
\hline
99y = & 31.\overline{00}
\end{array}
$$

or

$$
99y = 31
$$

Hence,

$$y = \frac{31}{99} \quad \text{and} \quad \frac{31}{99} = .\overline{31}$$

Some observations about this example are in order. We multiplied by 100 because we wanted to find a second decimal with a repeating part starting at the decimal point. If we had multiplied by 10, we would have obtained

$$10y = 3.1\overline{31}$$

and we could not have readily subtracted $.\overline{31}$ from $3.1\overline{31}$. Hence, the choice of 100. In fact, the choice of the multiplier is determined by the pattern of repeating digits in the decimal. In this case $.\overline{31}$ has a two-digit repeating pattern, so 100 is the number to use.

In addition, the entire objective of the procedure is to find two representations of a decimal such that the repeating portion begins at the decimal point. Consider the following example.

Example 8.1   Let $y = .4\overline{37}$. If we want two decimals for our subtraction problem, each of which has the repeating part of the decimal starting at the decimal point, then we will have to find two multipliers for this example. First, multiply by 1,000:

$$1,000y = 437.\overline{37}$$

If we also multiply $y = .4\overline{37}$ by 10, we obtain

$$10y = 4.\overline{37}$$

and we have the desired two representations for the subtraction problem. Thus

$$
\begin{array}{r}
1,000y = 437.\overline{37} \\
- \quad 10y = 4.\overline{37} \\
\hline
990y = 433.\overline{00}
\end{array}
$$

Hence,

$$y = \frac{433}{990}$$

The fraction $433/990$ may be reducible, but whether it is is immaterial because we have identified the equivalence class (containing $433/990$) which will be represented by the decimal $.4\overline{37}$. In this example, $433/990$ is not reducible because 433 is a prime number.

The procedure for converting decimals to fractions thus depends upon writing two decimals, each obtained from the given one, such that the repeating pattern begins at the decimal point. Then the subtraction step gives us an expression which we can express as a fraction with whole numbers as numerator and denominator. The procedure is not quite as straightforward as converting a fraction to a decimal, for we must first determine if we are to multiply by 10, 100, 1,000 or some other multiple of 10. However, this we determine by looking at the original decimal. From these examples, we can conclude that *every repeating decimal is expressible as a fraction.*

Exercises

1.   Convert the following fractions to decimal notation:
(a) 1/2   (b) 2/3
(c) 3/4   (d) 5/6
(e) 7/9   (f) 0/4
(g) 2/2   (h) 9/7

2.   Convert the following decimals to fractions:
(a) .111$\overline{1}$ (b) .666$\overline{6}$
(c) .3$\overline{17}$ (d) .57$\overline{23}$
(e) .4$\overline{17}$ (f) .249$\overline{9}$
(g) .9$\overline{9}$ (h) $\overline{5.62}$

3.   In Exercise 2(f) the fraction 1/4 is correct because there are two ways to represent certain fractions as decimals. We have $1/4 = .249\overline{9}$ and $1/4 = .250\overline{0}$. Therefore, $.249\overline{9} = .250\overline{00}$. Find another example of this for some other fraction. Can you state the circumstances in which this can occur?

4.   Suppose that in converting 1/4 to a decimal by the division process, we fail to choose the trial divisor to be large enough on the second division step. That is, we write

$$
\begin{array}{r}
.249 \\
4 \overline{)\ 1.0000\overline{0}} \\
8 \\
\overline{20 } \\
16 \\
\overline{40 }
\end{array}
$$

and keep repeating the same mistake. What is the decimal representation obtained for 1/4?

8.4 Operations on Decimals

Since the decimals which we have discussed thus far have been representations for fractions, and since we already have defined operations for fractions, we need not define new operations for decimals. We need only find an algorithm for use with the decimals.

We already know how to add, subtract, multiply and divide decimals. Consider the following examples.

Example 8.2 $.33\bar{3} + .500\bar{0} = ?$ Convert each decimal to fractional form:

$$.33\bar{3} + .50\bar{0} = \frac{1}{3} + \frac{1}{2}$$

Then add, obtaining 5/6; convert 5/6 back to the decimal form:

$$\frac{5}{6} = .833\bar{3}$$

Example 8.3 $(.33\bar{3})(.50\bar{0}) = ?$ Convert to fractions:

$$(.33\bar{3})(.50\bar{0}) = \frac{1}{3} \cdot \frac{1}{2}$$

which is 1/6, and converting back to decimals, we obtain

$$\frac{1}{6} = .166\bar{6}$$

Thus,

$$(.33\bar{3})(.50\bar{0}) = .166\bar{6}$$

In a similar fashion we would perform subtraction and division problems in decimals by converting to fractions, working the problems and converting the answer back to decimal form. This, however, is a rather drawn out procedure; what we would really like to do is develop an algorithm to apply directly to the decimals without converting them to fractions.

Since the decimal form was derived from the expanded numeral form, and the expanded numeral form was the basis of the column addition technique, then we should be able to apply this same technique to decimals. In fact, we could have obtained the answer to Example 8.2

by using a modified version of column addition. Writing the addition problem in vertical form, we have

$$.33\overline{3}$$
$$.50\overline{0}$$

Normally in column addition on whole numbers we start at the last right-most digit. However, there is no last digit in these infinite decimals, so we must look at the various digits to determine how to get around this difficulty. In this example we see that in the hundredths position and all others to the right, we have a 3 and a 0. The sum of these is 3, so all positions would then give a 3 in the sum. Hence, we know that after this point all digits are 3, and we have established the repeating pattern. If we add 3 and 5 in the tenths position, we obtain 8, so the answer must be $.83\overline{3}$.

Example 8.4   Find $.250\overline{0} + .1250\overline{0}$. Writing in vertical form, we have

$$.250\overline{0}$$
$$.125\overline{0}$$

Again, the digits at the right are easy to surmise since they are zeros. Beginning at the hundredths position, we can then add from right to left, and we obtain $.375\overline{0}$. Since both of these numbers are finite decimals, we can conclude that the addition algorithm for whole numbers can be applied directly by beginning at the first nonzero digit and performing normal addition. For example,

$$.34700\overline{0}$$
$$.59200\overline{0}$$

becomes

$$.347$$
$$.592$$

and the sum is .939, or $.939\overline{0}$. Carrying also applies in this example.

The technique will have to be modified slightly for examples such as the following one.

Example 8.5   Find

$$.28\overline{7}$$
$$+.3\overline{1}$$

If we write these a little further, we see that a certain pattern emerges which will aid us in finding this sum.

$$\begin{array}{cc} .\overline{287} & .287287287287\overline{287} \\ +.\overline{31} \quad \text{becomes} & +.31313131313\overline{131} \end{array}$$

Observe that a pattern is exhibited which we identify by vertical marks.

.287287	287287	$\overline{287}$
+.313131	313131	$\overline{31}$

The first six digits of both numbers correspond to the next six digits, and if we were to continue to write digits, we would find the same pattern repeating by groups of six, as we have indicated here. If we add from right to left beginning with the twelfth digits, we obtain

.287287	287287	$\overline{287}$
+.313131	313131	$\overline{31}$
.600418	600418	

And we can observe the six-digit pattern also repeats in the sum. Hence,

$$.\overline{287} + .\overline{31} = .\overline{600418}$$

In nearly all elementary school arithmetic programs in existence, only finite decimals are studied. The first reason is probably that youngsters may have some difficulty with problems like Example 8.5. Moreover, most physical problems which give rise to decimals are best described by finite decimals because we cannot measure beyond a certain degree of accuracy (we will say more about this later in this chapter when we discuss approximations). Therefore. the reader will probably be limited to discussion of the addition of finite decimals in elementary school. We use the broader scope here to show that addition can be done for any of the repeating decimals.

The subtraction of repeating decimals follows closely the above pattern, except that it is column subtraction, not addition, which is done. We offer only one example to illustrate the general form. Again the comments in the last paragraph are appropriate for the operation of subtraction.

Example 8.6   Find $.\overline{516} - .\overline{31}$.

.516516	516516	$\overline{516}$
−.313131	313131	$\overline{31}$

We observe the same kind of six-digit pattern as in addition, so we proceed and obtain

$$.516516516516\overline{516}$$
$$.31313131313\overline{131}$$
$$\overline{203385203385\overline{203385}}$$

Thus

$$\overline{.516} - \overline{.31} = \overline{203385}$$

The operation of multiplication of decimals is somewhat different from that of fractions. First, the algorithm for multiplication cannot be slightly modified to fit all products, and second, the case of products of finite decimals requires more than multiplication of whole numbers. We shall examine both major types of products, taking the finite decimals case first. Again, we do this by example.

Example 8.7   Find $(.15)(.5)$. Written in expanded numeral form, .15 is

$$1 \cdot \frac{1}{10} + 5 \cdot \frac{1}{100}$$

and .5 is

$$5 \cdot \frac{1}{10}$$

Now multiplying these, we obtain

$$\left(1 \cdot \frac{1}{10} + 5 \cdot \frac{1}{100}\right) \cdot 5 \cdot \frac{1}{10} = \left(1 \cdot \frac{1}{10}\right)\left(5 \cdot \frac{1}{10}\right) + \left(5 \cdot \frac{1}{100}\right) \cdot \left(5 \cdot \frac{1}{10}\right)$$

$$= 5 \cdot \frac{1}{100} + 25 \cdot \frac{1}{1,000}$$

$$= 5 \cdot \frac{1}{100} + 20 \cdot \frac{1}{1,000} + 5 \cdot \frac{1}{1,000}$$

$$= 5 \cdot \frac{1}{100} + 2 \cdot \frac{1}{100} + 5 \cdot \frac{1}{1,000}$$

$$= 7 \cdot \frac{1}{100} + 5 \cdot \frac{1}{1,000}$$

Writing this as a decimal, we have

$$7 \cdot \frac{1}{100} + 5 \cdot \frac{1}{1,000} = .075$$

Since both decimals in Example 8.7 are finite, the added zeros have no effect upon the above process. Moreover, we can devise an algorithm for multiplying finite decimals without completing all of the above steps.

First, the digits in the answer, 75, can be obtained by multiplying 15 by 5 in the whole number sense of multiplication. We accomplish this by merely ignoring the decimal points and treating the product as if it were the product of two whole numbers. (This we already know how to do.) Second, we need only to find a way to identify where the decimal point must go in the product which we obtained in the first step. In the two factors .15 and .5, .15 has two significant digits before the zeros $(.1500\overline{0})$, and .5 has one significant digit. The answer .075 has three significant digits, including the zero. Since $2 + 1 = 3$, and since there are three digits to the right of the decimal point in the answer, we seem to have found how to identify the decimal point location in the answer. Hence, the above example serves as an illustration as to why our algorithm works for the multiplication of finite decimals. Try working through $(.24)(.3)$ by the expanded numeral form to provide another illustration of the process.

When we leave the finite decimals and turn to the product of other repeating decimals, we find the above procedure fails for two reasons. First, we do not have a right-hand digit in a number such as $.3\overline{1}$, so we cannot treat it as a whole number. Second, there are an infinite number of digits in $.3\overline{1}$, and we cannot count these out in locating a decimal point in a product. Moreover, there is no way we can overcome these difficulties for repeating decimals (except finite ones), so we reject the above algorithmic process. We shall see later in this chapter how we can find an approximate answer to such problems, but that is another concept and does not provide us with the algorithm we want here.

For the operation of division we have a similar situation in that we can find a way to divide one finite decimal by another finite decimal, but there is no algorithmic way to divide one repeating decimal (not finite) by another. We will develop the first of these two situations by example.

Example 8.8   Find the quotient of .625 and .5. We could convert to fractions and find the quotient as a fraction and convert it back to a decimal, but we wish to find a way to do the division directly by an algorithmic process. We write these in expanded numeral form as

$$\left(6\cdot\frac{10}{10} + 2\cdot\frac{1}{100} + 5\cdot\frac{1}{1,000}\right) \div \left(5\cdot\frac{10}{10}\right)$$

Applying a property we noted earlier, we have

$$\left(6\cdot\frac{1}{10} \div 5\cdot\frac{1}{10}\right) + \left(2\cdot\frac{1}{100} \div 5\cdot\frac{1}{10}\right) + \left(5\cdot\frac{1}{1,000}\right) \div \left(5\cdot\frac{1}{10}\right)$$

$$= \frac{6}{5}\cdot\frac{10}{10} + \frac{2}{5}\cdot\frac{10}{100} + \frac{5}{5}\cdot\frac{10}{1,000}$$

$$= \left(1 + \frac{1}{5}\right)\cdot 1 + \frac{4}{10}\cdot\frac{1}{10} + 1\cdot\frac{1}{100}$$

$$= 1 + \frac{2}{10} + \frac{4}{100} + \frac{1}{100}$$

$$= 1 + \frac{2}{10} + \frac{5}{100}$$

$$= 1.25$$

Here we have used the fractional form to derive a decimal answer for the problem. Now we look at the problem and its answer and see if we can find an algorithmic process.

$$.625 \div .5 = 1.25$$

If we ignore the decimals, we can divide 625 by 5 (as whole numbers) and obtain 125. Now we need only to find a way to properly locate the decimal point. We might also observe that $6.25 \div 5$ also gives 1.25. Thus we might write

$$.625 \div .5 = 6.25 \div 5 = 1.25$$

and we have a way of locating the decimal point. Write the division problem in long division form. For example, $.625 \div .5$ may be written as

$$.5\overline{\smash{)}.625}$$

Also $6.25 \div 5$ may be written as

$$5.\overline{\smash{)}6.25}$$

Thus, to locate the decimal point, we multiply .5 and .625 by 10 to convert the problem to 6.25 ÷ 5; then we can properly divide to get 1.25.

We could formally prove that the process in Example 8.8 works for all finite decimals, but we will confine the development to the above example. Intuitively, it can be seen that the above illustration and others like it behave in precisely this way, and we will assume it as our algorithmic process for dividing one finite decimal by another.

It is also clear that the above algorithmic process cannot apply to nonfinite decimals. The placing of the decimal point in the algorithm does not work and, as in the case of multiplication, we reject the process for this type of quotient. As in the case of multiplication, we can find approximate but not exact answers. We explore this further in the next section. Also, as in the case of multiplication of nonfinite decimals, we end our discussion with no algorithmic process for division of nonfinite decimals. In both cases we will work these problems by converting the decimals to fractions, working the problems, then converting the fraction obtained to decimals.

Exercises

1. Add the following finite decimals:

(a) .217
   .346

(b) .496
   .827

(c) 6.592
   1.299

(d) 4.000
   3.75

2. Subtract the following finite decimals:

(a) .782
   .346

(b) .697
   .213

(c) 6.12
   4.675

(d) 4.00
   2.324

3. Multiply the following using the expanded numeral form, and then work by the algorithmic process:

(a) (.21)(.3)

(b) (.65)(.7)

(c) (.8)(.8)

(d) (3)(.4)

4. Divide by the algorithmic process.

(a) .652 ÷ .2

(b) .0436 ÷ .3

(c) .275 ÷ .15

(d) 2.668 ÷ 4.4

5.   Take two repeating decimals such as $.\overline{2}$ and $.\overline{3}$ and devise a way to multiply them. (Hint: Try multiplying from left to right.)

6.   Add $.\overline{89} + .\overline{532}$. Subtract $.\overline{89} - .\overline{532}$.

8.5   Approximations and Decimals

Quite often information is conveyed in a news article or other source which might say that there are 220 million people in the United States or that 354 million dollars was spent on some project. Do these statements really mean that there are precisely 200 million people or that precisely 354 million dollars was actually spent? It is usually clear from the context of the articles that the amount expressed is not exact, but that there are approximately 220 million people or that approximately 354 million was spent. These expressions are, in reality, merely approximations to the exact numbers involved and are used in precisely this sense. If, for example, the project had spent $353,987,219.67, this amount would be a little long to write out, and we conveniently write a number which is close to this one, say, within 1 million, and we then might write 354 million dollars and say we have "rounded off" the given amount to the nearest million. In a similar fashion we might actually have 223,497,123 people but write 220 million as an approximation, which is the nearest 10 million to the given number.

We present an example to further illustrate the process of rounding off.

Example 8.9   The number 4,862.3549 when rounded off to thousands is 5,000; when rounded off to hundreds it is 4,900; when rounded off to tens it is 4,860; and when rounded off to ones it is 4,862.

When we round off a number to a given position, we write the nearest number with a number in that position and zeros following. For example, 5,000 is nearer to 4,862.3549 than 4,000 is. Likewise, 4,860 is nearer to 4,862.3549 than 4,870 is. Thus, rounding off is determining which of two choices, one higher and one lower, is nearer to the given number.

If we round 4,862.3549 off to tenths, we could consider the possible answers to be 4,862.3000 or 4,862.4000. We see that the latter is closer, but we need to look beyond the hundredths digit to determine the answer. Thus, we cannot look only at the hundredths to determine which to use. If we round this number off to hundredths, we see that 4,862.35 is as close to 4,862.355 as 4,862.36 is, and both could be equally correct approximations. Often if the next digit is a 5, we round off the number in the place in question up one digit, that is, 4,862.355 rounded off to the hundredths place is 4,862.36.

In addition to conveying approximate information, there is another useful purpose for approximations. In the last section we noted that we could not conveniently multiply two infinite, repeating decimals such as $.\overline{317}$ and $.\overline{21}$. We can, however, find a number reasonably close to their product by rounding both off to some position and then multiplying the finite decimals thus obtained.

Example 8.10   Round $.\overline{317}$ and $.\overline{21}$ to tenths. We have .3 and .2, which when multiplied gives .06. Thus

$$(.\overline{317})(.\overline{21}) \approx .06$$

where the $\approx$ is read "is approximately equal to." If we round to hundredths, we have

$$(.\overline{317})(.\overline{21}) \approx (.32)(.21) = .0672$$

which is an even better approximation to the exact answer. If we round off to thousands, we have

$$(.\overline{317})(.\overline{21}) \approx (.317)(.212) = .067204$$

Thus, the more digits in the rounding off process, the more precise is the answer.

If we look at the first step in Example 8.10, where we rounded off to tenths, we note that the answer .06 is not very close. .07 would have been closer, yet we had no way of knowing this by using these rounded off values. We should not expect more accuracy than that which we started with; that is, if we use .3 and .2, their product .06 best approximates the correct value if rounded off to tenths also. Thus .1 would have been a better answer to write out. We need to be extremely careful in writing these answers when using rounded off factors in the products.

In a similar fashion, we can find quotients, or really approximations to quotients, by using rounded off values. For example,

$$.\overline{843} \div .\overline{214}$$

can be approximated by $.8 \div .2$ when the given values are rounded off to tenths. Thus

$$.\overline{843} \div .\overline{214} \approx .8 \div .2 = 4$$

Rounding to hundredths, we have

$$.\overline{843} \div .\overline{214} \approx .84 \div .21 = 4.0$$

or rounding to thousandths, we have

$$\overline{.843} \div \overline{214} \approx .843 \div .214 = 3.9392$$

If we round off further in the place value sequence, we get a still better approximation to the precise value for the given product.

We have just shown how to round off a given decimal to a given place value position. This process gives us a finite decimal which is an approximation to the given decimal. An immediate application of this procedure is to work multiplication or division problems for which we have no known convenient algorithmic process in decimals. There we approximate by rounding off the numbers involved and then apply the algorithmic procedure of finite decimals. The result obtained by this procedure is an approximation of the actual product or quotient of the given decimals.

Two other facts should be noted about rounding off decimals. First, we can round off finite decimals as well as infinite, repeating ones. An example is the 354 million dollars illustration given at the beginning of this section. Second, we can approximate an infinite repeating decimal by another infinite repeating decimal, and this type of approximation has nothing to do with rounding off decimals. For example, $.31\overline{752}$ can be approximated by $.31\overline{8}$. The application of this kind of approximation is mostly beyond the scope of the elementary school mathematics.

Exercises

1.   Round off the following decimals to tens, units, tenths and hundredths:
(a) 465.327   (b) 29.982
(c) $7.3255\overline{5}$ (d) $.3\overline{167}$
(e) $0.00\overline{0}$

2.   Find an approximation for the answer to the following problems by rounding off the given numbers to hundredths:
(a) $.4\overline{13} + .62\overline{73}$ (b) $.798\overline{36} - .055\overline{0}$
(c) $(.63\overline{75})(.39\overline{41})$ (d) $(.50\overline{0}) \div (.249\overline{9})$

8.6   Nonrepeating Decimals

In the early sections of this chapter we found that every fraction could be expressed as an infinite, repeating decimal and every infinite, repeating decimal could be expressed as a fraction. We found ways to make these conversions and performed other algorithms with this type of decimal. Now we wish to show that the infinite, repeating decimal (we include the finite decimals as infinite, repeating) is not the only kind of decimal. There are infinite decimals which do not repeat. For example, let $x = .0101101110111110111110111111\ldots$ where the three dots mean that the decimal continues in a like fashion. This is not a repeating decimal because there is no place to put the bar. It is, however, a decimal which has an easily describable pattern for the digits. It is neither a repeating decimal nor a whole number and, hence, cannot be expressed as a fraction. The number x which we have just described is not a type which we already have studied; hence, it must be some new kind of number.

A fraction is called a *rational number*. Since the number x in the above example is not a rational number, we call it an *irrational number*. It is fairly easy to construct other examples which are irrational numbers. For example,

$$p = .04044044404444\ldots$$
$$q = .82882288822288882222\ldots$$
$$r = .01230123400123001234\ldots$$

There are more irrationals than rationals. The union of the set of rationals and the set of irrationals is the set of *real numbers*. We will give some examples of irrational numbers and develop a few ideas about them.

Numbers such as $\sqrt{2}$, $\sqrt{3}$, π, $\sqrt[3]{19}$ and other similar ones are irrational numbers. At first we might be inclined to doubt some of this for we have probably seen

$$\pi = \frac{22}{7} \quad \text{or} \quad \pi = 3.14$$

In reality, these should have been written as

$$\pi \approx \frac{22}{7} \quad \text{and} \quad \pi \approx 3.14$$

since 22/7 and 3.14 are approximations for π.

If we cannot develop a set of operations on the set of irrationals, then if we wish to compute using π or some other irrational number, we shall have to round off and use a rational approximation of it. Some other approximations we might use are

$$\sqrt{2} \approx 1.414$$
$$\sqrt{3} \approx 1.732$$

and if we look in some mathematical table we can find other approximations by finite decimals for other square roots. In such a table we could find that

$$\sqrt{4} = 2$$
$$\sqrt{9} = 3$$
$$\sqrt{16} = 4$$

and, consequently, not all square roots are irrational numbers. The definition of square root says that $y = \sqrt{x}$ if and only if $y^2 = x$. Thus y is the square root of x, and x must be y times y. For the last three examples, this is true because

$$2 = \sqrt{4} \quad \text{if and only if } 2\cdot2 = 4$$
$$3 = \sqrt{9} \quad \text{if and only if } 3\cdot3 = 9$$
$$4 = \sqrt{16} \quad \text{if and only if } 4\cdot4 = 16$$

Since $2\cdot2 = 4$, then 2 is the square root of 4.

We indicated that

$$\sqrt{2} \approx 1.414$$

and $\sqrt{2} \neq 1.414$ because $(1.414)^2 = 1.999396$. However, 1.414 is a pretty good approximation for $\sqrt{2}$. In fact, we could use this technique to find an approximation for some square root which we did not know. For example, find $\sqrt{19}$. Since $\sqrt{16} = 4$ and $\sqrt{25} = 5$, then $\sqrt{19}$ is between 4 and 5. If we try 4.3, we have $(4.3)^2 = 18.49$, which is fairly close to $\sqrt{19}$. If we try 4.35, we have $(4.35)^2 = 18.9225$, which is closer to $\sqrt{19}$ than $(4.3)^2$ is. If we try 4.354, we find $(4.354)^2 = 18.947316$ and we are still closer to $\sqrt{19}$. By applying the definition to the $\sqrt{19}$ we are able to get a fairly good approximation rather quickly. If we had tried 4.36, we would have found that $(4.36)^2 = 19.0096$, which is too large, but not much. Thus we know from these calculations that

$$(4.35)^2 < (4.354)^2 < 19 < (4.36)^2$$

So $\sqrt{19}$ lies between 4.354 and 4.360. According to a table of square roots $\sqrt{19} \approx 4.358899$; we found a fairly good approximation for this decimal by guessing and using the definition of square roots.

There is an algorithmic process for finding the square root of a number. It is sometimes included in seventh and eighth grade mathematics courses. The student might want to review the process at this point. However, our approximations are what we actually use in the calculations, so it is a convenient way of finding a square root.

We will not pursue the development of the real number system, as a major portion of the ideas are found in the beginning algebra course which many ninth graders take. There we discuss the real number system and define operations on rationals and irrationals. For rationals we use the previously established operations. For the irrationals, we develop some ideas such as

$$2\sqrt{2} + 5\sqrt{2} = 7\sqrt{2}$$
$$\sqrt{3} \cdot \sqrt{7} = \sqrt{21}$$

and others dealing with square roots, cube roots and irrationals in general. This is usually done in chapters on exponents and radicals.

Exercises

1. Look up a proof that $\sqrt{2}$ is not a rational number. (Euclid proved this about 300 B.C.)

2. Find an approximation for $\sqrt{39}$.

3. If $\sqrt{2} \approx 1.414$ and $\sqrt{3} \approx 1.732$, find $\sqrt{2} \cdot \sqrt{3}$ by an approximation. Is it $\sqrt{6}$?

4. Is $3\sqrt{2} + 5\sqrt{2} = 8\sqrt{2}$? Use an approximation for $\sqrt{2}$.

5. How would you define "is less than" on decimals? Is there a convenient way to look at two decimals and tell which is the larger? Which is larger, $.417\overline{95}$ or $.4179\overline{49}$?

9

GEOMETRY

9.1   What Is Geometry?

As primitive man began his extended stay on this earth, he formed
concepts of the world and universe around him. Primitive art reflects
his awareness of many things, and the mythology of various sections of
the world reveals his serious attempt to explain his world. As civilizations developed and the art of writing became a part of each center of
civilization, man left a better and more detailed impression of his
fundamental concepts.

The evidence left by several ancient civilizations reveals an interest
in certain aspects of mathematics, namely, arithmetic and geometry.
Most of the geometric concepts were primitive in nature and were
obtained, as far as we can determine, by observation and limited ex-
perimentation. These notions were empirical in nature. For example,

the Egyptians of 3000 B.C. were aware that a triangle with sides of 3, 4 and 5 units had a right angle and that this angle was located between the sides with measures of 3 and 4. They were not aware, as far as we can determine, that the same condition existed for a triangle with sides of 5, 12 and 13 units. This fact was known only for the one limited instance and was probably discovered by accident or by some particular observation in some unknown circumstance. The Egyptians did not, at this time, recognize the generalization which the Greeks were later to make and establish—the Pythagorean theorem. The Egyptians were acquainted with many geometric facts (usually somewhat isolated from others) and were quite competent in solving certain problems of a geometric nature, in land surveying and in constructing geometric forms such as pyramids. Nearly all of their ideas and pieces of information were the result of observation and practical experience.

In contrast to the Egyptians, the Greeks pursued the ideas of geometry from a mathematical point of view and eventually developed a systematic, axiomatic geometry, which took several centuries to complete. The writings of Euclid around 300 B.C. represent a highly polished edition of this mathematical subject. Axiomatic geometry as considered by the Greeks was quite an advancement over the earlier practical kind of geometry. It was, in fact, an achievement of significant value to mathematics, for it established the experimental or observed facts by showing them to be examples of some theoretical proposition. Thus the 3, 4, 5 triangle became only one of many triangles with right angles, all of them being examples satisfying the Pythagorean theorem.

Like the Egyptians, the Greeks were interested in trying to describe the geometric world in which they lived, but they were much more theoretical in their attempt. However, the notions of geometry, while more abstract than previously, were still attempts to explain the world as the Greeks saw it.

In the Middle Ages a great deal of information was added to geometry by the proving of new theorems. Older ideas were revised and improved, and the geometry was a better theoretical subject and better described the world. However, newer ideas began to creep in geometric considerations and, in more recent history, *different* geometries evolved. New and different directions were presented and the spaces described differed. The present concepts of geometry (in the broadest sense) are quite different now from in Euclid's time.

The original meaning of the word *geometry* was derived from *geo*, meaning earth, and *meter*, meaning to measure. This meaning reflects the original nature of geometry and the emphasis of the practical geometry of the Egyptians and the general nature of the Greek geometry (although the Greeks approached it from the axiomatic point of view). The geometry considered by both Egyptians and Greeks was intended to analyze or explain the world which surrounded them. More and more people after the Greeks considered the geometry as a model of the physical world. The Romans were very successful in adapting geometry to structures, so successful that some of these structures are still in use today. Mathematicians in these civilizations further believed that the geometry adequately described the world in which they lived.

In more recent times, mathematicians began to try to find "geometries" which were quite different from the Euclidean geometry. We now have many geometric systems which are models of some kind of space—not necessarily the one in which we live. Moreover, we are not really sure as to what our space is really like. The general theory of relativity is based upon a geometry which is non-Euclidean, that is, a geometry different in some respects from the geometry of Euclid. It may be true that we actually live in a space in which parallel lines really intersect or that there is more than one line parallel to another and passing through a given point. However, for most purposes the Euclidean geometry seems to satisfy our immediate needs in describing our immediately surrounding space, so it is most often used by the student of elementary mathematics.

A more modern view of geometry must include the idea of a model of some space and a set of axioms (postulates) which accurately describes the space in question. (Frequently mathematicians set up a system of axioms and then look for a space to fit them. Both tasks are equally difficult.) If the description is complete, the set of axioms (and the subsequent theorems deducible from these axioms) is a mathematical model of the space being described. We may call this model a geometry because it describes a space, just as a number system is used to describe numbers, their operations and their relations.

We shall construct geometry based upon what we see in the world around us and what we can abstract from what we see. Our geometry shall be somewhat historical and somewhat generic. We shall also take into account what research in space conception and perception tells us about what young minds see in the world around us.

9.2   Nature and Language of Geometry

Every area of study has a language of its own, and geometry is no exception. For example, the word *triangle* has a very specific meaning and yet it is used to describe a large collection of objects of varying sizes with certain common characteristics. In addition to the language, which we will say more about later, the fundamental rules of logic are also used in geometry. These rules of logic are the means by which we establish the proof that some geometric statement is the direct consequence of other statements.

Since not all statements are the consequences of other statements, some collections of statements are assumed to be true in the beginning of any geometric discussion. Such a collection of statements should be as short, yet as complete, as possible. The statements must be consistent in the sense that one does not contradict another. The assumed statements should also be independent of each other. By independent we mean that no one of the statements is logically a consequence of the others. If any statement is a consequence of the others, it should be considered as a theorem. The collection of statements which are assumed to be true have been called postulates, self-evident truths, or axioms. We will use the word *axioms* in what follows. An example of an axiom might be any of the following:

a. Two points are sufficient to determine a line.
b. There exists only one perpendicular to a given line from a point not on the given line.
c. For any three distinct points on a line one point must be between the other two.

An axiom and a definition are similar in the sense that both are assumed to be true statements. However, an axiom describes some specific characteristic or property, while a definition normally is used to define a word or a phrase. In the axiom, "Two points are sufficient to determine a line," there are several words which should be defined. For example, what does *two* mean? What is a *point*? What does *are sufficient* mean? What is a *line*? Euclid defined a point as that which has neither length nor breadth. The axiom says two points are enough to determine something else. Perhaps the definition given for a point leaves much to be desired from our point of view, but so do many formal definitions given in many places. The dictionary which defines a horse to be a four-legged animal does not really clarify the meaning of horse. Thus a definition should be as clear as possible, concise and definitive in meaning. Sometimes such clarity, conciseness and definitiveness are difficult to achieve in words, and at times we may wish to imply a meaning without actually stating one. For example, when small youngsters want to know the meaning of a word whose definition is beyond the grasp of their limited knowledge, we sometimes give the word an intuitive meaning and operate as if we know the true meaning. We may also leave a word completely undefined in mathematics and allow *any* meaning for it, although normally we have some related statements which restrict the range of possible meanings. If we have an example of something which we have left undefined and this example seems to satisfy all that we know about the undefined word, then we have a model for that word.

Many statements in geometry are of the form, "if—then." For example,

a. *If* two lines intersect, *then* they intersect in exactly one point.
b. *If* the three angles of a triangle have the same measure, *then* the triangle is an equilateral triangle.

Statements such as these may be true or false. If the "if" part of the statement is true, then the "then" part should be true also, particularly when the "then" part is related to the "if" part and is a logical consequence of it. A statement such as "If the sun comes up tomorrow, then you will get an A in this course" shows that a statement can contain unrelated parts, parts which have no logical connection with each other. The total statement may be true or false, depending upon some other conditions not included in the statement. In general, we are not interested in statements of unrelated parts, for we have no way to determine the truth value of the statement. We are interested in statements in which the "if" part is known to be true or assumed to be true, and the "then" part is also a logical consequence of the "if" part. Then these statements become the theorems of our mathematical study. Our main task as students of mathematics is to determine what statements satisfy these conditions and to establish, by logical reasoning, the logical consequence of the "then" part from the "if" part. Most, if not all, of the high school geometry course is devoted to precisely this task. Most elementary school geometry probably should not be involved in this task, and many good mathematical and psychological reasons can be given to support this position.

The rules of logic which were mentioned earlier determine the framework within which we can prove statements. The rigorous process of proving a geometric theorem is a process of listing statements in some convincing order while knowing the reason *why* the statements are true. In the next section we give an example which illustrates this process.

9.3   Difference between Intuitive and Deductive Geometry

Suppose we take a piece of paper and cut a triangular-shaped piece from it. If someone were to ask us about the angles of this triangle, particularly the sum of the measures of the angles, what would be our observation? The student probably remembers from high school geometry that the sum of the three angles in a triangle forms a straight angle. Is it possible to determine this fact from this paper triangle? Suppose we take the triangle of figure 9.1(a) and cut it up as suggested in figure 9.1(b) by wavy lines. Then we rearrange the pieces to form the shape indicated in figure 9.1(c). If we look along the top of the shape thus formed, we see a straight line or a straight angle. Thus we have some basis for making the observation that the sum of the angles of a triangle is a straight angle.

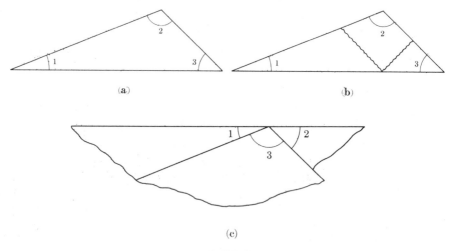

(a)

(b)

(c)

FIGURE 9.1

However, we do not really know that the line across the top is *really* a straight line; it just *looks* that way. We suspect that it is, but this is only a strong suspicion on our part. It seems to be intuitively obvious, yet we really do not know for sure until we are able to prove it logically. A proof would depend upon what axioms were assumed and what definitions had previously been given. We give a proof which is similar to many found in high school geometry texts. For the proof we refer to figure 9.2.

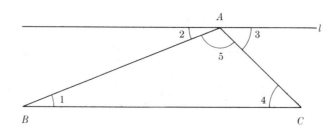

FIGURE 9.2

Proof   Through vertex A, construct a line l parallel to side BC of the triangle. (This construction would be dependent upon our knowledge of how to draw parallels.) The line AB is a transversal to the parallel lines, and alternate interior angles are of the same measure. Thus angles 1 and 2 are the same size, as are angles 3 and 4. Since angle 5 is the same as angle 5, then the sum of the measures of angles 1, 4 and 5 equals the sum of the measures of angles 2, 3 and 5. The sum of angles 2, 3 and 5 is the measure of a straight angle and, therefore, the sum of the measures of the angles of triangle ABC is the measure of a straight angle. The proof is completed.

There is a striking similarity between the proof and the experimental determination of this fact. By experimenting we frequently get an idea as to how the proof can be constructed. Many of the geometric concepts are first intuitive, and proofs are constructed later. In the elementary school, geometry is treated first intuitively, and proof is supplied later in the high school geometry course. In the geometry which follows, we shall be much more intuitive by discussing geometric statements than we will be deductive by actually proving them. We will, however, present only geometric statements which could be proved if we wished to construct the corresponding axiomatic structure. The student should make an effort to determine the plausibility of each assertion.

9.4   Points and Lines

If we are to have a geometry which we believe describes the space in which we live, we must begin with some primary building blocks to construct a model. The first primary building block is a *point*. In abstract mathematics, we would normally leave *point* undefined and place no interpretation upon it. However, from an intuitive point we find several illustrations to give a point some meaning. A point can be thought of as a location. For example, on a road map we find small towns denoted by a dot, a point on the map. The corner of the rectangular classroom where a front wall, a side wall and the floor all meet is a point; it is a location in the room. If we put a dot on the blackboard with a piece of chalk, we have an intuitive representation for a point. Such illustrations are not definitions; a dot on the blackboard might be small or large, but points are not small or large. (We noted earlier that Euclid tried to define a point as that which has neither length or breadth.) Such examples are, of course, attempts to clarify what a point is and, perhaps, add some meaning to our interpretations. We might conclude that these illustrations all say that a point is an exact location in space. We shall denote all points by a dot and a capital letter. For example, we might have points A, B and C as follows:

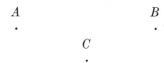

If we take a ruler and place it so that points A and B are on the edge of the ruler and, with a pencil, draw along the edge of the ruler, we are generating what we call a *line*. By illustration, we have figure 9.3. The drawing could be continued in the two directions indicated by the ruler. If the ruler were of infinite length we would have more nearly the correct drawing for a line. This illustration demonstrates that a line is a set of points, including points A and B, and has a particular characteristic of being straight. Moreover, if we try to put the ruler on points A and B again and draw along the edge with a pencil, we get precisely the same set of points that we did the first time. This intuitively suggests that two points determine a line and do so uniquely. We formalize this by Postulate 9.1.

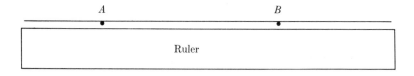

FIGURE 9.3

POSTULATE 9.1   If A and B are two distinct points, then there is one and only one line that contains both points A and B.

Note the requirement of two distinct points in Postulate 9.1. One point labeled twice, once A and once B, will not determine a unique line.

We might also observe that on a given line determined by A and B, there are other points; for example, see figure 9.4. Points C, D and E also are on the line determined by the points A and B. We also use the arrow points on each end of the line to identify the notion that the line can be extended infinitely.

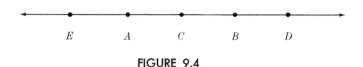

$$E \qquad A \qquad C \qquad B \qquad D$$

FIGURE 9.4

From this last drawing we can also identify another geometric characteristic called *betweenness*. Point C is on the line AB such that if we move along the line from A toward B we will pass through point C before getting to B; thus point C is *between* points A and B. Also, neither E nor D is between A and B. However, A is between E and C, and B is between C and D. B is also between A and D. A, C, B are also between E and D. In betweenness, there is an ordering of points along the line. It makes no difference which way we move along the line, C is still between A and B. As the result of describing betweenness we can now define a line segment.

DEFINITION 9.1 If A and B are any two distinct points on line AB, then a line segment is the set of points containing A, B and all points which lie between A and B.

Figure 9.5 is a drawing of a line segment where X is any point between A and B. On a given line (fig. 9.6) we can describe many line segments. For example, given line AB and points C, D and E, we can write the following line segments: AB, AC, AD, EA, EC, EB, ED, CD, CB and BD. If we go the other way, we can write DB, DC, DA, DE, BC, BA, BE, CA, CE and AE. However, line segments AB and BA describe the same set of points and are thus not different line segments but merely different descriptions of the same set.

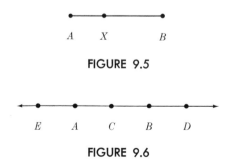

$$A \qquad X \qquad B$$

FIGURE 9.5

$$E \qquad A \qquad C \qquad B \qquad D$$

FIGURE 9.6

It also is obvious from the last paragraph that if we write AD we do not know if we mean the line AD or the line segment AD. Therefore, we adopt the following notation. By $\overleftrightarrow{AD}$ we shall mean the line AD, and by $\overline{AD}$ we shall mean the line segment. This should help us clarify the meaning of what we write and should clearly distinguish between the two ideas.

The drawings which we have made of the lines intuitively suggest that there are an infinite number of points on the line. We see that if $\overline{AB}$ is a line segment on $\overleftrightarrow{AB}$, then X is a point between A and B (fig. 9.7). Furthermore, since $\overline{AX}$ is a line segment, there is some point Y which is between X and A. Between A and Y there is another point, Z, and we can continue this process indefinitely. Hence, we conclude that there are an infinite number of points on a line.

$$A \qquad Y \qquad X \qquad\qquad B$$

FIGURE 9.7

We are also able to define another type of geometric term by looking at the line. Take a line l with a point A on it, as in figure 9.8. The point A separates the set of points of the line into three disjoint sets containing (1) the point A; (2) those points of l to the right of A; and (3) those points of l to the left of A. The sets of points on either side of A are called *half-lines*. We may also consider these half-lines as open, since the separation point A is not unioned with either set. To identify precisely each open half-line, label two points B and C such that A is between B and C; for example, see figure 9.9. The open half-line to the right of A may be named as $\overset{\circ}{\overrightarrow{AB}}$ where the small circle on the arrow means that A is not included and the arrow means that portion of the line containing B. Likewise, we write $\overset{\circ}{\overrightarrow{AC}}$ for the other open half-line.

$$A$$

FIGURE 9.8

If we take the set of points $\overset{\circ}{\overrightarrow{AB}}$ and union it with $\{A\}$, we now have a *ray*, denoted by $\overrightarrow{AB}$ with the small circle missing from the arrow over AB. Also, we might have $\overrightarrow{AC}$. Rays $\overrightarrow{AB}$ and $\overrightarrow{AC}$ on some

C   A   B

FIGURE 9.9

line l are called opposite rays. Opposite rays of a line must have a common end point. For example, on the line in figure 9.10, rays $\overrightarrow{CB}$ and $\overrightarrow{AC}$ are not opposite rays. Neither are $\overrightarrow{AB}$ and $\overrightarrow{BA}$. Note that here the order of writing $\overrightarrow{AB}$ and $\overrightarrow{BA}$ identifies different rays. Some opposite rays on this line are $\overrightarrow{CD}$ and $\overrightarrow{CA}$, $\overrightarrow{AC}$ and $\overrightarrow{AB}$ and $\overrightarrow{BA}$ and $\overrightarrow{BE}$.

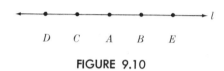

D   C   A   B   E

FIGURE 9.10

We might also note that $\overrightarrow{CA}$, $\overrightarrow{CB}$ and $\overrightarrow{CE}$ all describe the same set of points and, therefore, are all names for the same ray. We need to denote the separation point C and some other point in the open half-line set of points. Here, A, B and E all belong to the same open half-line to the right of point C, so any one of these could be used to identify the given ray.

Exercises

1.   Draw a horizontal line. Select two points on this line and label them A and B. Now label a third point C on the same line such that C is between A and B. Label another point D such that B is between C and D. One name for the given line is $\overleftrightarrow{AB}$. Give all other names possible from the above conditions for the given line.

2.   On a piece of paper, put four dots representing four points A, B, C and D such that no three of them lie on the same line. Draw all possible lines using only these four points. What is the maximum number possible?

3.   Arrange three points on a sheet of paper so that they determine only one line. Now try to arrange these three points such that they determine two and only two lines. What is true about this last request?

4. Points are *collinear* if they lie on the same line. Using this definition and other facts, complete the following table:

Number of Points	Maximum Number of Points Collinear	Maximum Number of Lines Determined by Points
2	2	1
3	3	1
3	2	3
4	4	1
4	3	4
4	2	
5	5	1
5	4	
5	3	
5	2	
6	2	
7	2	
x	2	

5. On XY below, does $\overset{\circ}{\overrightarrow{XY}}$ contain X? Does $\overline{XY}$ contain X? Locate Z such that X lies between Z and Y. Does $\overrightarrow{XY}$ contain Z? Does $\overrightarrow{YX}$ contain Z? Does $\overline{XZ}$ contain Y?

X Y

6. In Exercise 5, name two opposite rays. Name three line segments.

9.5 Distances for Lines

In chapter 5 we discussed using the number line as a teaching device to illustrate operations on certain sets of numbers. Now, we will formulate this idea in more detail and define a distance measure for lines and line segments.

We already noted that a number line had numerical values assigned to points along the line and that the numerical values were uniformly assigned on the line. We had, for example, the line in figure 9.11. We shall ignore for the present the points on the line to the left of zero, as these have negative integers assigned and we have not yet discussed the integers.

To label the points to which we assigned some of the whole numbers, we might have, for example, the line in figure 9.12. In this sense, the letters are names for the points and the numbers are the values assigned for the location of the points. In fact, we might be tempted to consider the numbers as other names for the points. There are some difficulties with notation and meaning if we do this. We shall see why in a little while.

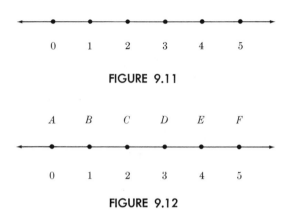

FIGURE 9.11

FIGURE 9.12

The assigning of numbers in an order to points on a line generates what is called a *coordinate system*. With each point is associated a number and with each number is associated a point. In fact, we have a one-to-one correspondence established between the two sets where one set is the set of whole numbers and the other is the points to the right of zero (a half-line).

In the last illustration of a number line there are 2 units (0 to 1 and 1 to 2) between the points A and C and between C and E. Between B and F, there are 4 units. If we adopt the notation that $m(\overline{AB})$ denotes the measure of line segment AB, then

$$m(\overline{AB}) = 1$$

$$m(\overline{AC}) = 2$$

$$m(\overline{BD}) = 2$$

$$m(\overline{BF}) = 4$$

$$m(\overline{AF}) = 5$$

$$m(\overline{DE}) = 1$$

First, the distance between two points on this line is always greater than or equal to zero, for example, $m(\overline{AA})$ is zero. Nowhere do we find a negative distance in this example. But find $m(\overline{EB})$. There are 3 units between E and B, just as there are 3 units between B and E. So $m(\overline{EB}) = m(\overline{BE}) = 3$. Thus, the direction is unimportant; only the number of units between the points is significant. Hence, there are no distances less than zero.

Second, observe that

$$m(\overline{AC}) + m(\overline{CF}) = 2 + 3 = 5$$

which is also the measure of $\overline{AF}$. This holds only if A, C and F are collinear. We may write this as

$$m(\overline{AC}) + m(\overline{CF}) = m(AF)$$

and this is a valid statement for any three collinear points A, C and F of our illustration, where C is between A and F. Also, $m(\overline{AA})$ is zero. Thus, the distance between points on a line has the following properties which we describe as a postulate (note, no proofs!).

POSTULATE 9.2   The distance between two points X and Y satisfies the following three conditions:

a. $m(X, X) = 0$.

b. $m(X, Y) = m(Y, X) > 0$, $X \neq Y$.

c. $m(X, Y) + m(Y, Z) = m(X, Z)$ if and only if X, Y and Z are collinear and Y is between X and Z.

Two further observations are in order about distance measures. We noted earlier that we might be tempted to say that point C could be called 2. However,

$$m(\overline{AC}) = 2 \qquad m(\overline{BD}) = 2$$

and

$$m(\overline{CE}) = 2 \qquad m(\overline{DF}) = 2$$

If 2 were the name for a point, we might be confused and write

$$m(\overline{AC}) = C \quad \text{and} \quad m(\overline{BD}) = C$$

or other misleading, false statements. The distance measure is always a number, not a point. Thus, we do not refer to point C as point 2.

We also might have selected a different unit of measure and had 3 units between A and C. Thus C would not be the same as 2 because the scale had changed. In fact, it makes no difference which standard unit we use, for the distance measure satisfies the postulate anyway.

Exercises

1.   Construct a ray AB with the end point labeled A, and B a point 6 units from A. Assign to A the value 0 on the number line. What is the coordinate of B? Locate points C, D, E and F which have coordinates 2, 3, 7 and 1 respectively.

2.   In Exercise 1, find the following:
(a) $m(\overline{AE})$
(b) $m(\overline{AF})$
(c) $m(\overline{BD})$
(d) $m(\overline{DA})$
(e) $m(\overline{FE})$
(f) Is $m(\overline{AE}) + m(\overline{ED}) = m(\overline{AD})$?
(g) Is $m(\overline{AE}) + m(\overline{EF}) = m(\overline{AF})$? Why?

3.   Assume for a moment that we know about negative numbers and put them on a number line, too. We might have the following line where certain points have been labeled.

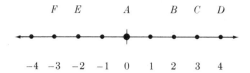

Find the following:
(a) $m(\overline{AE})$ (b) $m(\overline{EB})$
(c) $m(\overline{FC})$ (d) $m(\overline{EA})$
(e) $m(\overline{BF})$

4.   Suppose we further define $|a - b|$ to be $a - b$ if $a > b$, and $|a - b|$ to be $b - a$ if $a < b$. Further define $m(X, Y) = |y - x|$

where y is the coordinate of Y and x is the coordinate of X. Find the following:

(a) $m(\overline{AE})$ (b) $m(\overline{EB})$

(c) $m(\overline{FC})$ (d) $m(\overline{EA})$

(e) $m(\overline{BF})$

Are these the same answers as in Exercise 3?

5.   On the following number line, locate $\overrightarrow{CD}$. What are the coordinate values assigned to the points of $\overrightarrow{CD}$? (Hint: Let x be the coordinate of a point of $\overrightarrow{CD}$.)

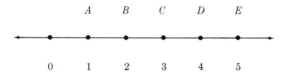

9.6   Planes and Properties of Lines in a Plane

We cannot, in general, get a cardboard piece to balance on the tip of a pencil when we hold the pencil vertically. Theoretically, we could balance the cardboard if we found the center of gravity and put the pencil point there. However, we cannot balance it on just any point on the cardboard. If we try to balance the cardboard on the side of the pencil while holding it horizontal, we again find it will not stay unless we balance it carefully through the center of gravity. However, if we take a horizontal pencil and a second pencil point and fix them some place, the cardboard will stay in precisely one place. Thus, to locate exactly a plane (a piece of cardboard), a line (a horizontal pencil) and a point (another pencil point) not on the line is needed. If we think of a plane as a flat, smooth surface which extends in all directions, we can leave it undefined (as are *point* and *line*). Our piece of cardboard was merely a finite portion of the plane. Formulating this into a statement, we have the following postulate.

POSTULATE 9.3   Through a line and a point not on the line, there is exactly one plane.

Since every line is determined by two points, three points, not all collinear, are also enough to determine exactly one plane. This is a second condition for determining a plane, an example of which is the question, How many legs are absolutely necessary for a chair to have if it is to remain standing in one position?

If we look at the plane resting on a horizontal pencil and another pencil point, we also may observe that the cardboard is touching the pencil at every point along its side. We formulate this as follows.

POSTULATE 9.4 If a plane contains two points of a line, it contains the entire line.

In the preceding example when a second pencil was added, the plane contained only one point of that line, which we call a point of intersection. Suppose we have a plane with a single point A lying in the plane. How many lines are there which pass through point A and lie entirely in the plane? Assume that this page is a representation of the plane and let A be the point:

$$A$$

$$\cdot$$

By choosing other points in the plane, we can locate lines passing through point A. We might have figure 9.13, and it is intuitively obvious that there are an infinite number of lines in the plane passing through point A.

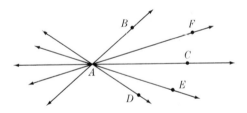

FIGURE 9.13

If there are two distinct lines which lie in the same plane, then there are two possibilities: they either intersect or they do not. If the two lines intersect, they have at least one point in common. If the two lines have two or more points in common, then by Postulate 9.3, these two lines must be the same. However, this contradicts our assumption that the lines are distinct. Hence, if two distinct lines intersect, they intersect in a maximum of one point.

When two distinct lines belong to the same plane and do not intersect, the two lines are parallel. Thus, the two lines either intersect in at most one point, or they are parallel.

We are given a line l and a point A not on line l, and we wish to determine how many lines in the plane which contain point A are parallel to line l. Since there are an infinite number of lines in the plane passing through point A, we might have figure 9.14.

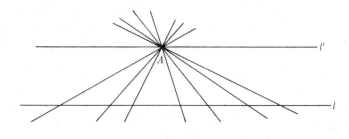

FIGURE 9.14

Now, if we keep selecting points on to the right of A, we will continue to determine lines passing through A and intersection l. Thus, it would appear that all lines intersect l. However, there is one which when drawn through A, call it l', does not appear to intersect line l. We formalize this by the following postulate.

POSTULATE 9.5   Given a line and a point A which is not on l, there is one and only one line l' containing A and parallel to line l.

Historically, the attempts to justify Postulate 9.5 led to the development of a pair of geometries in which it is not true. Lobachevski and Riemann gave axiomatic mathematical systems in which this statement was not true. It is beyond our scope to pursue these in this text, but there are several good books which describe models of these geometries. In fact, our presentation does not come close to justifying the existence of a single parallel to line l. Nor is any really good intuitive argument available for this. We must assume the existence of a unique parallel to l as we have stated in the Postulate 9.5.

If we have a plane which contains line l, we may observe a situation similar to a line with a point on it. We noted earlier that when a line had some point P on it, the point P separated the line into two half-lines or opposite rays. In a similar fashion a line separates a plane into three parts: the line l and a set of points on either side of the line. Each set of points is called a half-plane. These three sets are disjoint. By illustration let the rectangle in figure 9.15 represent a portion of the plane and l be the line. Point A is in one half-plane and point B is in the other half-plane. It is also clear that if we draw line AB, it will intersect line l.

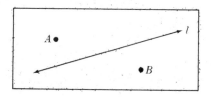

FIGURE 9.15

Exercises

1. Describe the intersection of two planes.

2. Do two parallel lines determine a plane?

3. Pick any four points in the room which do not lie in the same plane. Call them A, B, C and D. Now describe each plane by the set notation $\{X, Y, Z\}$ where X, Y and Z are three points in the plane. List all planes. Now form the intersection of pairs of planes and describe their intersections.

4. In a cube, how many planes are there which contain four vertices of the cube?

5. Skew lines are lines in space which do not lie in the same plane. Find a pair of skew lines in your room.

9.7   Angles and Triangles

We now turn to another of the elementary geometric ideas, the angle. There are several examples of angles around us, for example, the corner of a desk (fig. 9.16). The corner is the edge of the desk where it changes from one direction to another. We normally do not think of the corner, but rather the edges together, as the desk itself. More formally the angle of the corner is the union of the two edges with a common end point.

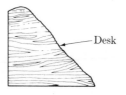

FIGURE 9.16

Of the four figures in figure 9.17, only (a) is an angle. Figures (b) and (c) have no common points, and the lines in (d) fail to satisfy the requirement of having a common end point. Later, we shall see that the two line segments of (d) do generate angles called vertical angles, but they do not satisfy the above definition for an angle. Since a line segment can also identify a portion of a ray, it is possible to rephrase the definition in terms of rays rather than line segments.

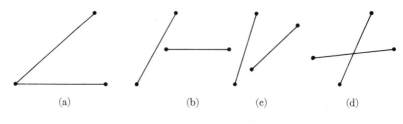

(a) (b) (c) (d)

FIGURE 9.17

DEFINITION 9.2 An angle is the set of points formed from the union of two noncollinear rays which have a common endpoint.

Noncollinear means that the rays cannot be in the same line. From Definition 9.2 we have figure 9.18(a) as an example using line segments AB and AC; figure 9.18(b) is the angle using rays AB and AC. The two sets of points are not the same because there are points in (b) which are not in (a). We would like to be able to use either definition at different times, so we choose Definition 9.2 as our operating definition. Note that the set of points in figure 9.18(a) is also "visible" in the picture and we have lost nothing by taking the ray definition.

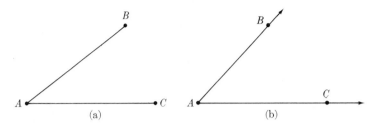

(a)   (b)

FIGURE 9.18

The definition of an angle excludes the case where the rays are collinear. This removes the so-called straight angle where the rays are opposite rays; for example, see figure 9.19. At the same time the definition says that no angle is defined if the rays are collinear as in figure 9.20. These two cases already have identifications, the first as a line and the second as a ray. This probably differs from our concepts from high school geometry, but these special cases are not really necessary for our further discussions.

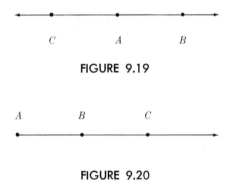

FIGURE 9.19

FIGURE 9.20

We need to adopt a notation to use as a name for an angle. If we have an angle defined by the union of $\overrightarrow{AC}$ and $\overrightarrow{AB}$, we denote the angle by $\angle BAC$ (fig. 9.21). The points B and C, one on each ray, are used to identify the ray with point A as the common point. This common point of the two rays is also called the *vertex* of the angle. We could also have used $\angle CAB$ as the name of this angle because it also describes the same set of points.

A common misconception is that an angle includes that region of the plane between its two rays. The definition of the angle says nothing about this region and, in fact, this region is called the interior of an angle. We formulate this definition more precisely by the following discussion.

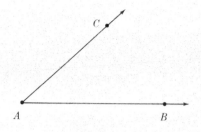

FIGURE 9.21

Take $\angle BAC$ and draw it on a plane (fig. 9.22). If we draw the lines AC and AB, we have figure 9.23. Observe that B is a point in one of the half-planes determined by $\overleftrightarrow{AC}$ and C is a point in a half-plane determined by $\overleftrightarrow{AB}$. Using shaded lines, we identify the half-planes shown in figure 9.24. The vertical shading represents the half-plane determined by $\overleftrightarrow{AB}$ which contains C and the horizontal shading represents the half-plane determined by $\overleftrightarrow{AC}$ which contains B. The region between the rays is double-shaded. Moreover, neither beginning ray is in the double-shaded region because of our definition of half-planes. Therefore, we refer to the double-shaded region as the interior of the angle. The remainder of the plane, except for the angle, is called the exterior of the angle. We formulate this idea of interior in Definition 9.3.

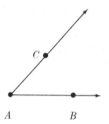

FIGURE 9.22

DEFINITION 9.3   The interior of $\angle BAC$ is the set of points obtained by intersecting two half-planes, one of them formed by $\overleftrightarrow{AC}$ and containing C and the other formed by $\overleftrightarrow{AB}$ and containing B.

In addition to angles, we also need to define a measure for angles. When we talked about line segments, we defined a distance measure

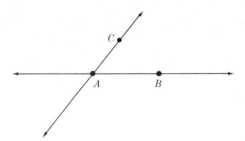

FIGURE 9.23

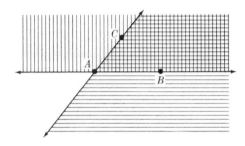

FIGURE 9.24

for the line segments. This distance measure depended upon our know-ing that we had a coordinate scale with a unit of measure and that the scale was uniformly divided or spaced along a line. We would expect to find that any angle measure would possess the same characteristics as the linear measure. If we want this to happen then we must select first some fixed angle as the standard unit. We could, of course, select any angle ABC to use, but historically the angle used most often is one related to a portion of a circle. Suppose we take a circle (to be defined later, but we assume for the moment that we know what it is) and divide the set of points which make up the circle into 360 equal sets. The equal sets are determined by dividing the circumference of the circle into 360 parts, and the length of one of these parts determines the location of two points on the circle. For example, A and B are points identified by one of these parts of the circle (see figure 9.25).

Connect these two points by line segments to the center of the circle. This then gives us angle AOB (fig. 9.26). This angle is the unit angle and we call its measure 1; the measure is said to be in degrees, to distinguish from 1 foot, etc. Thus we have a unit of measure and need only to devise an instrument which operates on degrees like a ruler

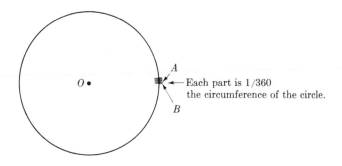

Each part is 1/360 the circumference of the circle.

FIGURE 9.25

does on linear measure. Since the circle is used to define the standard unit of the angle, it is also used to make such a measuring device, called a protractor; figure 9.27 gives its essential characteristics. We have indicated on a semicircle, with center at point O, the values 0, 45, 90, 135 and 180. If we place this over an angle with O at the vertex and the diameter of the semicircle along one side of the angle, we can read on the scale on the arc of the circle the measure of the angle. For example, $\angle AOB$ has a measure of 45, and $\angle BOQ$ has measure of 120. As with all measuring devices, we have only a good approximation of the actual size of an angle. (See figure 9.28.)

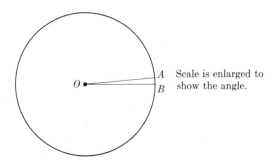
Scale is enlarged to show the angle.

FIGURE 9.26

The measure of angles is denoted by $m \angle AOB$ and is read "the measure of angle AOB." The measure is a real number greater than zero and less than 180. Thus the measure of an angle has characteristics similar to the measure of line segments.

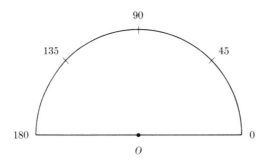

FIGURE 9.27

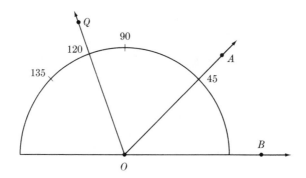

FIGURE 9.28

We are now ready to define a triangle. The word *triangle* means three angles, which every triangle has, but the definition is given in terms of the sides rather than in terms of angles. Consider three non-collinear points A, B and C and the three line segments formed by these three points, $\overline{AB}$, $\overline{AC}$ and $\overline{BC}$. This set of points is, by definition, a triangle (fig. 9.29). Other representations, depending upon the locations of A, B and C, could be those shown in figure 9.30. We might get

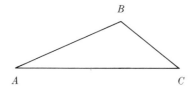

FIGURE 9.29

any configuration, for our triangle definition does not place any restrictions upon where points A, B and C are located, except that they cannot belong to the same straight line.

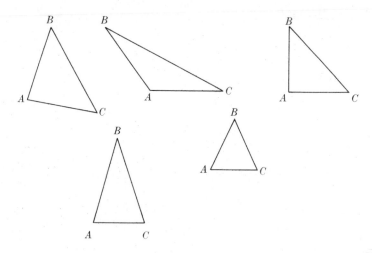

FIGURE 9.30

If we use $\overline{AB}$ and $\overline{AC}$ as parts of $\overrightarrow{AB}$ and $\overrightarrow{AC}$, we might draw figure 9.31. Thus A is the vertex of $\angle BAC$ and is a vertex of the triangle. Points B and C are also vertices of the triangle. The line segments $\overline{AB}$, $\overline{AC}$ and $\overline{BC}$ are called *sides* of the triangle. Actually $\angle BAC$ (using the ray definition) is not fully contained in triangle ABC, but we speak of $\angle BAC$ as an angle of the triangle ABC. In this sense, a triangle has three angles (a meaning for the name) as well as three sides.

We also will agree that $\triangle ABC$ will be our symbol for the expression *triangle ABC*. Actually, there are other names or symbols which

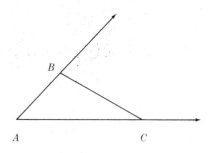

FIGURE 9.31

describe the same set of points that $\triangle ABC$ does: $\triangle BCA$, $\triangle CBA$, $\triangle CAB$, $\triangle ACB$ and $\triangle BAC$. Thus, there are six ways to identify a given triangle with vertices A, B and C.

The triangle also divides the plane into three sets of points: (1) the triangle itself; (2) the set of points in the interior of the triangle; and (3) the set of points in the exterior of the triangle obtained by the intersecting of the interiors of the three angles. The exterior is defined to be the set of points not on a triangle or not in an interior of the triangle (see figure 9.32). The rectangle is used to indicate a portion of the plane. Here the vertical shading indicates the exterior region and the horizontal shading indicates the interior region of the triangle.

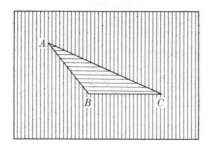

FIGURE 9.32

We can identify certain types of triangles from the placing of the vertices of the triangle in the plane. For example, if in $\triangle ABC$, $\overline{AB}$ and $\overline{AC}$ have the same measure, then the triangle is an *isosceles* triangle. If $\overline{AB}$, $\overline{AC}$ and $\overline{BC}$ all have the same measure, then the triangle is an *equilateral* triangle. If we have a triangle in which the measure of one angle is 90, then the triangle is a *right* triangle. If the measure of one angle of a triangle is greater than 90 but less than 180, then the triangle is an *obtuse* triangle. If the measures of all three angles are less than 90, then the triangle is called an *acute* triangle. It is possible for a triangle to satisfy more than one of these conditions; for example, we might have an isosceles right triangle.

From theorems from geometry, it is possible to identify some of the above triangles by another name. For example, an equilateral triangle is also an *equiangular* triangle. We sketch an intuitive argument for this statement by considering the following.

Suppose we have an isosceles triangle, $\triangle ABC$, in which $\overline{AB}$ and $\overline{AC}$ have the same measure; for example, see figure 9.33. If we cut this triangle and its interior out of a piece of paper, fold it such that point B

is placed exactly on top of C and then crease the fold we have figure 9.34. Since $\overline{AB}$ and $\overline{AC}$ are the same length and two points determine a straight line, that side of $\angle ABC$ matches the side of $\angle ACB$. Also, since CD matches DB for the same reasons, $\angle ACB$ and $\angle ABC$ actually coincide or are the same size, that is, they have the same measure. Thus, we have the following: If two sides of a triangle have the same measure, then the two angles opposite the two sides have the same measure. By *opposite* we mean that the side, except for the two end points of the line segments, lies in the interior of the angle. Thus an isosceles triangle also has two angles with the same measure. We have not proved this last fact. This is no deductive proof within the framework of axiomatic geometry. What we have offered is an intuitive discussion based upon paper folding. If we take a triangle which is not isosceles, then we cannot get the sides of two angles to match. This gives us more reason to suspect that our intuitive thoughts are correct.

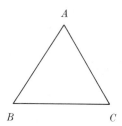

FIGURE 9.33

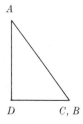

FIGURE 9.34

Now apply the above idea to an equilateral triangle. Take triangle ABC in which $\overline{AB}$, $\overline{AC}$ and $\overline{BC}$ have the same measure (fig. 9.35). We could fold the paper twice again and show all that angles are the same measure, but let us prove it, assuming that the above statement about isosceles triangles is true.

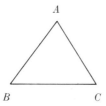

FIGURE 9.35

Proof   If $\overline{AB}$ and $\overline{AC}$ have the same measure, so do $\angle ABC$ and $\angle ACB$, i.e., $m/ABC = m \angle ACB$; and if $\overline{AB}$ and $\overline{BC}$ have the same measure, then $m \angle ACB = m \angle BAC$. Both of these statements are consequences of the isosceles triangle statement; but since the measures are real numbers, the transitive property of equality holds and if

$$m \angle ABC = m \angle ACB \quad \text{and} \quad m \angle ACB = m \angle BAC$$

then

$$m \angle ABC = m \angle BAC$$

Thus, all angles of the triangle have the same measure. Hence, if a triangle is equilateral, it is also equiangular.

It is also interesting to note that if a triangle has two angles with the same measure, it also has two sides with the same measure, i.e., the triangle is isosceles. In addition, if a triangle is equiangular, it is also equilateral. These two statements are converses of the preceding statements and can also be proved.

In Section 9.3, we used the example of a triangle and its three angles to illustrate the difference between the intuitive and the deductive approaches. We wish to repeat an intuitive argument here to determine the sums of the measures of the angles of a triangle. Cut a triangle ABC out of a piece of paper, along with the interior of the triangle (fig. 9.36).

Cut the corners off along the dotted lines indicated, then rearrange the pieces as in figure 9.37. The segments DB and CE seem to fall on the same line, but if we place our protractor on the figure with the zero mark along BD with the zero of the protractor at A, we find that the segment CE falls on 180. Since the angles have been put together to form this configuration, we think the sums of the measures of the angles is 180. This is the intuitive conclusion and it does agree with a theorem from geometry. Hence, we know that *the sum of the measures of the angles of a triangle is 180.*

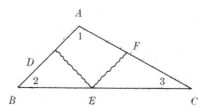

FIGURE 9.36

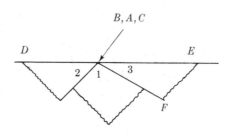

FIGURE 9.37

Exercises

1. Is it possible for a right triangle to be an acute triangle or an obtuse triangle?

2. Is it possible for an obtuse triangle to be an isosceles triangle? If so, describe the triangle as to where specific sides and angles are located.

3. Is it possible for an isosceles triangle to be an acute triangle? If so, give an example.

4. (a) Name all the triangles in the following figure:

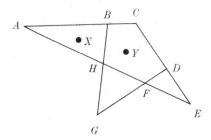

(b) For which triangles is X an interior point? (c) For which triangles is Y an exterior point? (d) Is A an exterior point of $\triangle ABH$?

5. Suppose that in the definition of an angle we had omitted the condition that the two rays were not to lie on the same line.
(a) If we had the following line segment, what would be the measure of $\angle ABC$?

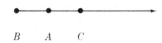

B   A   C

(b) If we had the following line segment, what would be the measure of $\angle ABC$?

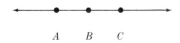

A   B   C

6. Draw (a) an isosceles triangle, (b) an obtuse triangle, (c) an isosceles right triangle and (d) an equilateral triangle.

7. Suppose that we define two angles to be supplementary angles if the sum of their measure is 180. Given the following angles and their measures, find the measure of the supplement of each.
(a) $m \angle ABC = 45$ (b) $m \angle CDE = 85$
(c) $m \angle DEF = 90$ (d) $m \angle EFG = 125$

8. We define two angles to be complementary angles if the sum of their measures is 90. Given the following angles and their measures, find the measure of the complement of each.
(a) $m \angle ABC = 45$ (b) $m \angle BCD = 85$
(c) $m \angle CDE = 5$ (d) $m \angle DEF = 125$

9.8   Curves

As we did with the word *line*, we properly leave the word *curve* undefined. However, we need some intuition to enable us to think intelligently about a curve. If we take a pencil and start right here at point A and move the pencil over this page in some manner, we generate a curve. Some examples which might have been created are shown in figure 9.38. We probably would have expected figure (a) or (b), but we would not normally think of (c) and (d) as curves. However, if we think of a curve as the path the pencil point made, then (c) and (d) do qualify. In fact, we may think of a curve as a line which does not bend. Note that each of these curves was drawn without lifting the pencil.

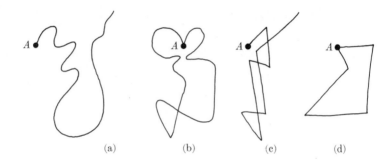

(a)   (b)   (c)   (d)

FIGURE 9.38

The curves (a) and (c) above are called open curves, as they do not return to their respective points. On the other hand, curves (b) and (d) do return to their starting points and, therefore, are called closed curves. Moreover, curve (b) differs from curve (d) in that it crosses itself while (d) does not. We call curves such as (d) simple, closed curves. In figure 9.39, (b), (c) and (d) are simple, closed curves, while (a) and

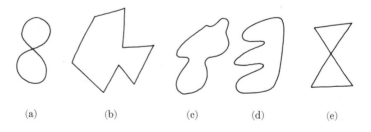

(a)   (b)   (c)   (d)   (e)

FIGURE 9.39

(e) are closed curves but not simple, closed curves. Other examples of simple, closed curves are triangles, squares and circles.

A simple, closed curve in a plane divides the plane into three sets: the curve, an inside and an outside. (We already noted this about the triangle.) If we know the shape of the curve we can also describe the shape of the interior. For example, a triangular region might be the interior of a triangle. Since every simple, closed curve has an interior, it is possible to describe something about the curve by looking at the interior of that curve. One such way of describing the character of the boundary is by defining those interior sets which are convex. A set is convex if for every pair of points A and B in the set, the line segment lies entirely in the set. Figure 9.40 shows examples of curves which define interiors which are convex. Figure 9.41 gives examples of curves which define interiors which are not convex.

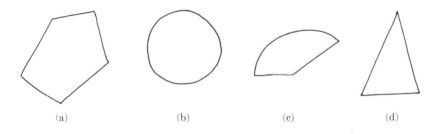

(a) (b) (c) (d)

FIGURE 9.40

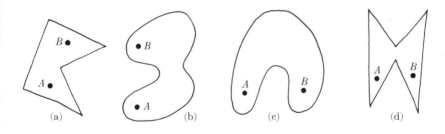

(a) (b) (c) (d)

FIGURE 9.41

In each of the examples in figure 9.40 it is possible to find points A and B such that the line segment AB contains points in the exterior region. Thus each fails to satisfy the definition of convex. By comparing the two sets of examples, we can see that the convexity of the interior region does affect the shape of the curve which defines that interior region. In fact, we can also test the convexity of the set formed by the union of the curve and its interior. Each of four examples in figure 9.39 which had convex interiors is still convex when we union the curve and its interior. Each of the four examples in figure 9.40 is still not convex, and it is clear that the exterior of all eight examples is also not convex.

Certain other sets are also convex, for example, a triangle unioned with its interior, the interior of an angle, a line segment, a ray, a line and a half-plane. The shape of these sets is influenced by their boundaries (if they have one) and the boundaries possess properties similar to those of our other examples of convex sets. One last example of convex sets which we can add to this list is the plane itself.

Exercises

1.   Which of the following are simple, closed curves?

(a)   (b)   (c)   (d)

2.   Which of the following curves with their interiors (if any) are convex sets?

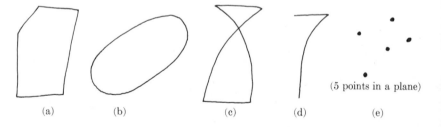

(5 points in a plane)

(a)   (b)   (c)   (d)   (e)

3.   Suppose we have two convex sets (defined by a curve and its interior), and from the intersection of these sets we get a set. Is this set convex? Give an example to support your answer.

4.   Take the same two sets of Exercise 3 and form the union of the sets. Is this set convex? Give an example to support your answer.

9.9   Polygons

Probably the most important group of geometric figures which we use consistently is the class of polygons, which includes such shapes as triangles, squares, rectangles, pentagons, etc. All have boundaries or curves composed of line segments, each of which is a simple, closed curve. Hence we define a polygon as follows.

DEFINITION 9.4   A polygon is a simple, closed curve which is made up as the union of line segments with common end points.

Figure 9.42 shows examples of polygons. Obviously, not all polygons are convex sets but most that we find useful are.

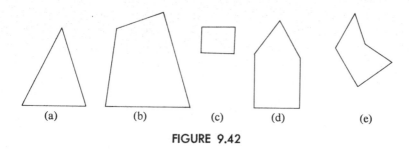

(a)   (b)   (c)   (d)   (e)

FIGURE 9.42

The name *polygon* means many sides. Thus a pentagon is a five-sided figure; a hexagon is a six-sided figure. These names allow us to classify polygons by the number of sides first and by other characteristics second. For example, we have already seen that there are several types of triangles. They are first triangles and secondly isosceles, right or obtuse triangles. We will extend this type of classification to other polygons.

By definition a quadrilateral is a four-sided polygon. In general, it may take any shape, convex or not; for example, see figure 9.43. These figures in 9.43 are all quadrilaterals, and all except (e) are convex. If we wish to be more specific, we will have to impose additional conditions on the four-sided figure and use different names for different types. We first impose a condition that two of the sides of the quadrilateral be parallel. (More precisely we mean that lines determined by the two sides are parallel.) We then have examples such as those in figure 9.44, where sides $\overline{AB}$ and $\overline{CD}$ are parallel. The collection of quadrilaterals with one pair of sides parallel is called *trapezoids*. Two of the four examples look like other quadrilaterals familiar to us. These trapezoids are all simple, convex, closed curves.

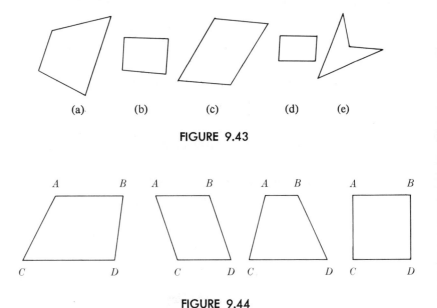

FIGURE 9.43

FIGURE 9.44

We next impose the condition that the second pair of sides also be parallel; for example, see figure 9.45. This collection of quadrilaterals is called parallelograms. Again we note that some resemble other familiar quadrilaterals, but they are still parallelograms. We also note that they are convex. In comparing the parallelograms with the trapezoids, we see that the parallelograms are all trapezoids but not all trapezoids are parallelograms.

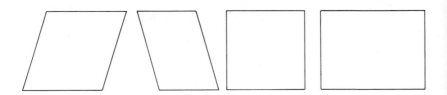

FIGURE 9.45

If we impose still another condition upon these quadrilaterals, we have two choices. We can say something either about the angles or about the length of the sides. We choose the angles first and return to the length of sides later. The only really special angle which distinguishes one particular type of parallelogram from the rest is the right angle; a parallelogram with four right angles, is called a *rectangle*; for example, see figure 9.46. Notice that the variety of examples continually diminishes as we impose more conditions.

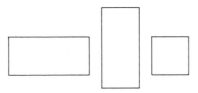

FIGURE 9.46

If we further require that adjacent sides have the same measure, we obtain a quadrilateral which we call a square (fig. 9.47).

FIGURE 9.47

If we require that our parallelogram have adjacent sides with the same measure, we obtain a *rhombus* (fig. 9.48). If we further require that the rhombus have right angles, we obtain a square.

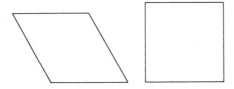

FIGURE 9.48

Thus, the classification of quadrilaterals goes through the following sequence of conditions:

1. With four sides, we obtain, in general, a quadrilateral.
2. A quadrilateral with a pair of sides parallel is a trapezoid.
3. A trapezoid with a second pair of sides parallel is a parallelogram.
4. (a) A parallelogram with right angles is a rectangle.
   (b) A parallelogram with adjacent sides of the same measure is a rhombus.
5. A rectangle with adjacent sides of the same measure is a square, or a rhombus with right angles is a square.

Figure 9.49 shows the relationships between these types of quadrilaterals.

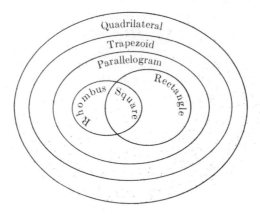

FIGURE 9.49

It is interesting to note that the square is most special, satisfying all the following conditions. A square is all of the following:

a. curve
b. closed curve
c. simple, closed curve
d. simple, convex, closed curve
e. polygon
f. quadrilateral
g. trapezoid (one pair of sides parallel)
h. parallelogram (second pair of sides parallel)
i. rectangle (four right angles)
j. rectangle (adjacent sides of the same measure)

A total of ten conditions totally define a square. For most elementary students, we usually use fewer than ten in our definition; we normally ignore the first five of these conditions. We also do not necessarily relate these classifications as we have done here. We define a rectangle, parallelogram, square, etc., on their own set of conditions and treat them separately. This may be the proper way to do this from a pedagogical point of view, but the way just completed has a mathematical advantage (as we shall see in the next chapter).

Our definitions specified that rectangles and squares have four right angles. Actually, in practice, we need to require that only one angle be a right angle and the remaining three will also be right angles. What is more important is that the requirement of four right angles means that the sum of the measures of the angles of a quadrilateral must be 360, as illustrated by figure 9.50. Here we have a quadrilateral *ABCD* with line segment *DB*. Note that the line segment divides the quadrilateral into two triangles, namely, triangles *ABD* and *BCD*. Since the sum of the measures of the angles of a triangle is 180, the angles of two triangles total 360. Furthermore, ∠*ABD* and ∠*CBD* together form ∠*ABC*; ∠*ADB* and ∠*BDC* also form ∠*ADC*. Hence, these pairs of angles form angles in the quadrilateral. More importantly,

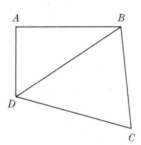

FIGURE 9.50

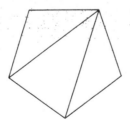

FIGURE 9.51

the sum of the measures of the angles of a quadrilateral is 360. What is equally significant is that this argument applies to any convex polygon. For example, draw line segments through a pentagon to divide it into triangles and repeat the above process (fig. 9.51). We conclude that the sum of the measures of the angles of a pentagon is $3 \cdot 180$, or 540.

Exercises

1.   What is the name of an eight-sided figure? Give an example of one you probably see every day. What is the name of a nine-sided figure? An n-sided figure? A two-sided figure?

2.   What is the sum of the measures of the angles of a triangle? A square? A rectangle? A hexagon? An octogon? By induction, find a formula which gives the sum for any polygon with n sides.

3.   A diagonal of a convex polygon is the line segment joining two vertices such that the interior points of the segment are in the interior of the polygon. How many diagonals does a triangle have? A quadrilateral? A pentagon? A hexagon? An n-gon?

9.10   Circles

In addition to the polygons there are other types of curves which are identified and named, the most common of which is the circle.

DEFINITION 9.5   A circle is a set of points in a plane such that the distance of each point of the set from a fixed point called the center is the same.

Note that the center is not a part of the set of points of a circle. It is merely used to locate the points which are on the circle.

A line segment from one point on the circle to the center of the circle is called a *radius*. From Definition 9.5 it is easy to see that all radii have the same measure. A line segment from one point of the circle to another point of the circle and passing through the center is called a *diameter*. If such a line segment does not pass through the center, it is called a *chord*. For example, in the circle of figure 9.52, $\overline{AB}$ is a diameter, $\overline{OC}$ is a radius and $\overline{AC}$ is a chord. We denote a circle by $\odot$.

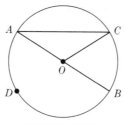

FIGURE 9.52

A circle is a simple, closed curve. The interior of the circle is a convex set. In the figure 9.52, $\angle AOC$ is called a *central angle* and $\angle CAB$ is called an *inscribed angle*. We may also have a semicircle, the set of points denoted by the diameter AB and the portion of the circle from A to B containing point C. There is, of course, another semicircle, which contains point D. The region bounded by a semicircle is convex.

Exercises

1. Draw a circle with a radius of 5. Identify on this circle a radius, a diameter, a central angle and an inscribed angle.

2. On a circle, draw two diameters such that an angle of intersection at the point measures 90. Put this circle on a piece of paper and cut out the circle and its interior. Fold the circle along one diameter and fold a second time along the other diameter. What do you observe about the lengths of the curves of the circle between ends of the diameters? Are they the same lengths? Compose a statement which describes this conclusion.

9.11 More about Right Triangles

A right triangle is a triangle with one right angle. Since the sum of the measures of the angles is 180 and one of the angles is a right angle with measure 90, then the two remaining angles are complementary, i.e., their measures total 90. There are additional properties of right triangles. For example, let $\triangle ABC$ be a right triangle with ABC a right angle (fig. 9.53). We call sides $\overline{AB}$ and $\overline{BC}$ the legs of the triangle and side $\overline{AC}$ the hypotenuse. A famous theorem called the Pythagorean theorem relates the lengths of the three sides of a right triangle. It states that the sum of the squares of the measures of the legs is equal to the square of the measure of the hypotenuse. For example, suppose $\triangle ABC$ is the triangle where $m(\overline{AB}) = 3$, $m(\overline{BC}) = 4$ and $m(\overline{AC}) = 5$ (fig. 9.54). By the Pythagorean theorem,

$$3^2 + 4^2 = 5^2$$

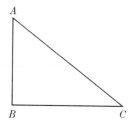

FIGURE 9.53

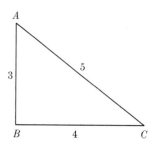

FIGURE 9.54

The converse of the Pythagorean theorem is also true: If the sum of the squares of the measures of two sides of a triangle is equal to the square of the measure of the third side, then the triangle is a right triangle. For example, if a triangle has sides of 5, 12 and 13 units the triangle is a right triangle, for example,

$$5^2 + 12^2 = 13^2$$

In such a triangle, the sides of the right angle always are always the smallest in the triangle.

One of the important concepts related to the Pythagorean theorem is perpendicularity. Two lines are perpendicular if the angles formed at their point of intersection are right angles. Also, from a point A not on line l there is one and only one line l' which is perpendicular to line l. We will not prove these statements but shall assume them to be true.

Exercises

1. Given a right triangle ABC, find the missing information in each part listed below.
    (a) If $\angle ABC$ is the right angle, $m(\overline{AB}) = 46$ and $m(\overline{BC}) = 8$, what is $m(\overline{AC})$?
    (b) If $m\angle ABC = 90$, $m(\overline{AC}) = 13$ and $m(\overline{AB}) = 5$, what is $m(\overline{BC})$?
    (c) If $m\angle BCA = 90$, $m(\overline{AC}) = 10$, $m(\overline{AB}) = 15$, what is $m(\overline{BC})$?

2. If triangle ABC is an isosceles right triangle with two legs having measure of 6, what is the length of the hypotenuse?

3. If we lean a ladder which is 26 feet long against a vertical building such that its base is resting 10 feet from the building, how far up the building is the top of the ladder?

10

MORE ABOUT GEOMETRY

10.1   Area

As with the case of linear measure, in order to measure area we need to select first a standard unit of area. The choice of the unit of area depends upon several factors. First, the unit of area must be easy to apply to any region bounded by a simple, closed curve. This requirement eliminates some units, such as a circular unit. To cover the interior of a rectangle with circles is impossible because portions cannot be covered; for example, see figure 10.1.

A triangular region as a unit of area satisfies more closely the criterion of covering a whole region. However, with the triangular unit area, we are not able to effectively compute areas when we are given linear measures of the sides of any polygon—the second major requirement which a unit of area must meet.

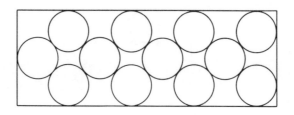

FIGURE 10.1

If we examine the various geometric figures which might be used as a unit of area for measuring, we find that the square best satisfies the requirement of covering given regions of areas and, at the same time, lends itself to the problem of computing areas; therefore, the standard unit of area is a square. Moreover, the sides of the square are 1 unit in length, for example, 1 inch, 1 yard, 1 foot, 1 centimeter or whatever else we might choose as a linear unit of measure. However, the unit of area thus defined is 1 *square* unit.

Take a square whose sides measure 5 and begin to cover the square with a square unit of area; for example, see figure 10.2. Start in the lower left-hand corner and put down a unit square. Place others adjacent to this unit across the bottom of the square to be measured for area (fig. 10.3). If we continue to put unit squares inside the large square, we eventually have figure 10.4, and find that 25 square units of area are necessary to cover the given square region. We should perhaps note that we are not really measuring the area of the square itself but are measuring its interior, or the region bounded by the square. We also can see that the number 25 can be obtained by multiplying a 5 on one side of the square by a 5 on an adjacent side. Thus we could compute the area to be 25 by multiplying 5 times 5. This fact is extremely important to us, as it greatly simplifies the process of finding the area of a region. To use the covering process to measure the area of a region bounded by a large square would be quite a task. This example is a good intuitive device to show that there is a shorter way of finding the area, that is, by computing it. Moreover, the example suggests the following formula which can always be used in computing area:

$$A = x^2$$

where A is the area bounded by a square with sides which are x in length.

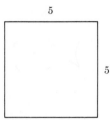

FIGURE 10.2

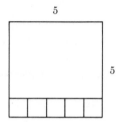

FIGURE 10.3

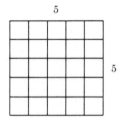

FIGURE 10.4

To see how the covering process works for regions other than squares, we take a rectangle with one pair of sides 6 units in length and the other pair of sides 2 units in length. If we were to cover the interior region by unit squares, we would have figure 10.5. There are 12 unit squares needed to cover the rectangle; hence, its area is 12. We could calculate this area if we multiplied 6 by 2. We can generalize further by the following formula:

$$A = L \cdot W$$

where A is the area of the region bounded by a rectangle with one pair of sides L in length and the other pair of sides W in width.

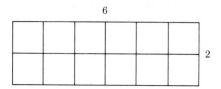

FIGURE 10.5

It is also easy to show that the covering process works if the square or rectangle has fractional lengths on a side. For example, cover the interior of a rectangle which is 5 units on one side and 3/2 on the other with unit squares (fig. 10.6). Here we have actually put down 10 unit squares to cover the given region, but in one row 1/2 of each square lies outside the rectangle. (See the shaded area.) So the region is actually covered by 5 unit squares and 5 pieces of unit squares, each being 1/2 of a unit square. The sum of all these parts totals $7\frac{1}{2}$ unit squares. If we compute the area by the formula just given, we find

$$A = L \cdot W = 5 \cdot \frac{3}{2} = \frac{15}{2} = 7\frac{1}{2}$$

and the formula still works.

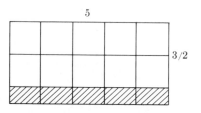

FIGURE 10.6

If we try to cover a parallelogram with squares, we find two places in which the squares extend beyond the parallelogram. Figure 10.7 is an example. The total count for the squares covering the region is 21; the shaded portions were not counted. Moreover, the top and bottom sides of the parallelogram are 7 units in length, and the vertical height of the parallelogram is 3. Thus the area of the region bounded by a parallelogram can be computed if we know the length of one pair of sides and the distance between two sides. The formula is

$$A = B \cdot h$$

where A is the area of the region bounded by a parallelogram with one pair of sides B in length and these sides h length apart. (We sometimes refer to the sides B in length as bases and the distance between these as height. The choice of the letters B and h helps identify the parts to be measured.)

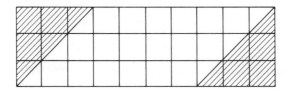

FIGURE 10.7

There is a second way to arrive intuitively at the same formula. Given the parallelogram in figure 10.8 with the measures B and h, we cut the parallelogram out of a piece of paper and cut off one end along AC. Now move this piece to the other end (fig. 10.9). We have formed a rectangle with sides B and h, and the area is

$$A = B \cdot h$$

which is precisely our formula for the area of the parallelogram. (Such an illustration proves nothing, but it does serve as a good intuitive way of finding the formula. Elementary school students should be able to appreciate this.)

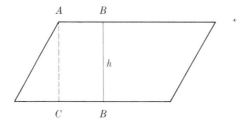

FIGURE 10.8

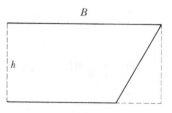

B

FIGURE 10.9

For the area of the region bounded by a trapezoid we consider the following paper-folding problem. Cut out a trapezoid and its interior, such as trapezoid $ABCD$ (fig. 10.10). Fold so that line segment AB lies on line CD (fig. 10.11). The dotted line indicates the creased fold in the paper. Now if we look at $\triangle DFE$, we find that it is an isosceles triangle because the fold FG is halfway between $\overline{AB}$ and $\overline{CD}$. Fold the end over so that point D coincides with point E, and do the same for the other end (fig. 10.12). The shape is a rectangle, and the area of the rectangle $FGHJ$ is

$$A = m(\overline{FG}) \cdot \frac{1}{2} h$$

We know intuitively from the first fold that its height or side is $(1/2)h$. We must find $m(\overline{FG})$. Since this is a rectangle,

$$m(\overline{FG}) = m(\overline{JH})$$

and $m(\overline{JH}) = m(\overline{AB}) + m(\overline{DJ}) + m(\overline{CH})$. But $m(\overline{DJ}) = (1/2)m(\overline{DE})$ and $m(\overline{CH}) = (1/2)m(\overline{BC})$ where $m(\overline{DE})$ and $m(\overline{BC})$ were obtained after the first fold. So,

$$m(\overline{FG}) = m(\overline{AB}) + \frac{1}{2}m(\overline{DE}) + \frac{1}{2}m(\overline{BC})$$

We also know from the first folding that

$$m(DC) = m(\overline{AB}) + m(\overline{DE}) + m(\overline{BC})$$

So $m(\overline{DE}) + m(\overline{BC}) = m(\overline{DC}) - m(\overline{BA})$ and

$$\frac{1}{2}m(\overline{DE}) + \frac{1}{2}m(\overline{BC}) = \frac{1}{2}m(\overline{DC}) - \frac{1}{2}m(\overline{AB})$$

Putting this in the statement for $m(\overline{FG})$, we have

$$m(\overline{FG}) = m(\overline{AB}) + \frac{1}{2}m(\overline{DC}) - \frac{1}{2}m(\overline{AB})$$

$$= \frac{1}{2}m(\overline{AB}) + \frac{1}{2}m(\overline{DC})$$

$$= \frac{1}{2}(b_1 + b_2)$$

Thus the area of the trapezoid is

$$A = \frac{1}{2}(b_1 + b_2) \cdot h$$

We have derived the formula from a paper-folding device, but we have used many real number operations, too.

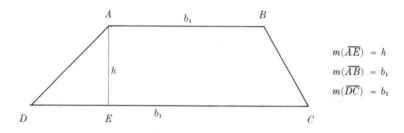

$$m(\overline{AE}) = h$$
$$m(\overline{AB}) = b_1$$
$$m(\overline{DC}) = b_2$$

FIGURE 10.10

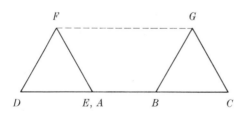

FIGURE 10.11

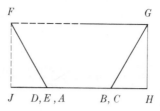

FIGURE 10.12

We have found formulas for all of the quadrilaterals for which we have special names. We now turn to the triangle, considering first a right triangle. Suppose we have $\triangle ABC$ where ABC is a right angle (fig. 10.13). If we take a rectangle which has sides $\overline{AB}$ and $\overline{AC}$, we have figure 10.14. If we draw $\overline{AC}$ we have our right triangle. Moreover, $\overline{AC}$ divides the rectangle into two triangles with the same area. Hence, the area of our triangle is 1/2 the area of the rectangle. So

$$\text{Area of triangle} = \frac{1}{2} L \cdot W \quad \text{where } L = m(\overline{AB}) \quad \text{and} \quad W = m(\overline{BC})$$

We normally write this as

$$A = \frac{1}{2} b \cdot h$$

where b is a base of the triangle, i.e., $b = m(\overline{BC})$, and $h = m(\overline{AB})$, and h is called the altitude, or height.

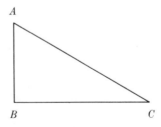

FIGURE 10.13

Suppose we have triangle ABC which is not a right triangle. We might have the two possibilities in figure 10.15. Consider 10.15(a) first. We construct the addition of figure 10.16 to the triangle ABC, where ADB is a right angle and D is on $\overleftrightarrow{BC}$. Let $b = m(\overline{BC})$, $e = m(\overline{DB})$

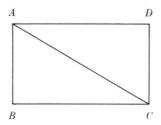

FIGURE 10.14

and $h = m(\overline{AD})$. We can write

$$\text{Area of } \triangle ABC = \text{Area of } \triangle ADC - \text{Area of } \triangle ADB$$

$$= \frac{1}{2} h(e + b) - \frac{1}{2} h(e)$$

$$= \frac{1}{2} h[e + b - e]$$

$$= \frac{1}{2} h \cdot b$$

For case (b) we do the same by dividing the triangle internally into two right triangles and following a similar set of steps. We would obtain

$$\text{Area of } \triangle ABC = \frac{1}{2} bh$$

where $b = m(\overline{BC})$ and $h = m(\overline{AD})$ when D is on $\overline{BC}$ such that $\angle ADC$ is a right angle.

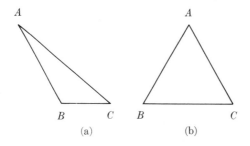

FIGURE 10.15

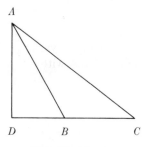

FIGURE 10.16

There is no easy, intuitive way to develop a formula for the area of a circular region. If we knew some calculus, we could devise a way to get the formula, but this is beyond the scope of this text and certainly beyond the scope of the elementary school program of mathematics. We would probably find that the formula will have to be given without an intuitive introduction of any kind. This is not always bad pedagogy, provided the whole framework of elementary mathematics is not done that way. We simply say that the formula for the area of a circular region is

$$A = \pi \cdot r^2$$

where r is the length of a radius. Note that here is a case in which we must use some approximation for π, such as 22/7 or 3.14, and the area is, consequently, only an approximation.

Exercises

1. Find the area of the following squares. What is the unit of area used in each and in what units is the area expressed?
(a) with a side of 4 inches
(b) with a side of 2.5 centimeters
(c) with a side of .8 mile
(d) with a side of 1.1 gobs

2. Find the area of the following:
(a) a rectangle with two adjacent sides of 10 inches and 12 inches
(b) a parallelogram with a side of 6 inches and 8 inches between the sides of 6 inches
(c) a trapezoid with bases of 8 and 12 feet and an altitude of 4 feet
(d) a right triangle with both legs of 6 feet
(e) a triangle with a base of 8 yards and an altitude of 4 yards

3.   Find the area of the following. What unit of area did you use?
(a) a rectangle which is 6 inches by 1 foot
(b) a triangle with an altitude of 1.5 yards and a base of 2 feet
Can we work these two problems without first converting all linear measures to the same units?

4.   What is the area of a circle with (a) radius of 4 inches, (b) diameter of 8 feet. Use π = 3.14 to find the areas.

5.   If the formula for the circumference of a circle is $C = 2\pi r$, where r is the radius, find the circumferences of the circles in Exercise 4.

6.   Take a round tin can or other circular object. Measure the diameter of the circular shape. Use a scale which has 1/16 inch or a centimeter scale. Take a string and wrap around the circle. Do not stretch the string. Mark it where it comes together and then measure this length of string on a ruler. Now divide the circumference (the length of the string) by the length of the diameter. The value which you obtain is a measured approximation for π. How close to the value of 3.14 did you come?

7.   Suppose we have a right triangle ABC such that $m\angle ABC = 90$, $m(AB) = 3$, $m(BC) = 4$ and $m(AC) = 5$. Construct the following diagram where each side of the triangle is the side of a square. Count up the squares in the square on AB; add to these the number of squares on BC. Is the same number of squares on side AC? If so, is this then an illustration of the Pythagorean theorem?

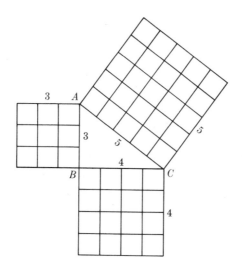

8.   (a) If we increase the sides of a square by doubling the length, what happens to the area? (b) If we double the radius of a circle, what happens to the area?

10.2   Volume

To develop the measurement of volume we need to select a standard unit of measure which works conveniently and, at the same time, allows us to calculate volumes. Using our experience with areas as a guide, we select as a unit of volume a *cube*, with each edge 1 unit in length. A cube surrounds its interior with six sides, all of which are squares; for example, see figure 10.17. We call the volume of this unit cube 1 cubic unit. With this cube, we can count the number of cubes necessary to fill up the inside of a rectangular region. For example, take a rectangular solid with edges of 2, 3 and 4 (fig. 10.18). Cover the bottom with unit cubes (figure 10.19). There are 12 cubes on this layer. If we put another layer in the region, we will have 24 unit cubes. Hence, the volume of the rectangular solid is 24 cubic units. Observe also that we can compute the volume by multiplying the three given dimensions (such as we did for areas). Thus

$$V = 2 \cdot 3 \cdot 4$$

$$= 24$$

If the three edges for any rectangular solid are L, W and H, then the volume V is

$$V = L \cdot W \cdot H$$

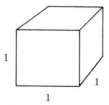

FIGURE 10.17

The sides of a rectangular solid are rectangles, so the formula works nicely. If the solid has a rectangular top and base and other sides are parallelograms, then the H becomes the shortest distance between the top and bottom; for example, see figure 10.20. The volume is still $L \cdot W \cdot H$.

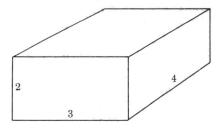

FIGURE 10.18

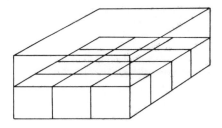

FIGURE 10.19

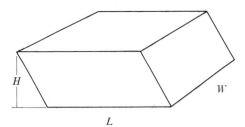

FIGURE 10.20

The volume of a pyramid is related to the above formula, but is 1/3 as large; for example, see figure 10.21. The volume is

$$V = \frac{1}{3} L \cdot W \cdot H$$

If the base is not a rectangle, then the $L \cdot W$ part of the formula becomes the area of the base, whatever the shape of the base. If the base is circular, then the area of the base is πr^2 and the volume of the circular pyramid, which is called a cone, is

$$V_{\text{cone}} = \frac{1}{3}\pi r^2 \cdot H$$

where H is still the shortest measure from the peak to the plane containing the base.

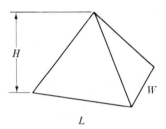

FIGURE 10.21

In a similar fashion the rectangular solid formula can be extended to the cylinder. This is a solid which has a circle for a base; for example, see figure 10.22. Its volume is

$$V_{\text{cylinder}} = \pi r^2 \cdot h$$

where r is the radius of the base and h is the shortest distance between two bases. A typical example is a tin can. A good intuitive example is to take a tin can and a tin cone with bases of the same size and the same height. We must fill the cone with water three times to provide enough water to fill the cylindrical can. The same comparison can be made for a rectangular box and pyramid with the same base and height.

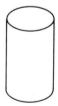

FIGURE 10.22

To establish the volume of a sphere is difficult. If we look at the formula we can see why. The volume of a sphere is

$$V_{\text{sphere}} = \frac{4}{3} \cdot \pi \cdot r^3$$

The 4/3 and the π factors make it difficult to find intuitive examples for this formula. For our purposes, we simply give the above formula and let it suffice for our discussion.

Exercises

1. Find the volume of the following rectangular solids:

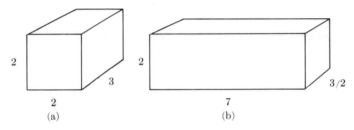

2   (a)   7   (b)

2. Find the volume of the following:

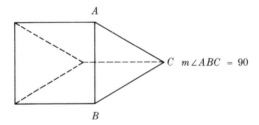

$C \quad m \angle ABC = 90$

3. Find the volume of the following:

(a)

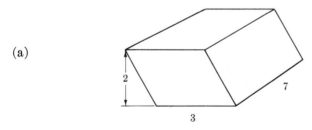

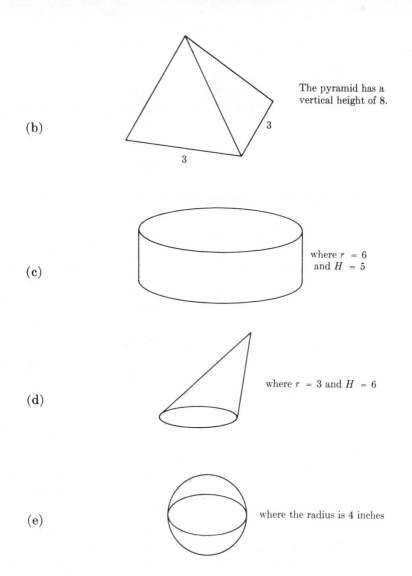

(b)

The pyramid has a
vertical height of 8.

3

3

(c)

where $r = 6$
and $H = 5$

(d)

where $r = 3$ and $H = 6$

(e)

where the radius is 4 inches

(f) Suppose we wish to put a sphere of radius 3 inside a cylinder such
that the cylinder is touching the sphere on the top and bottom as
well on as the sides. What is the volume of the space inside the
cylinder which is not inside the sphere? What relation does this
volume have to the volume of the sphere?

4.   If we double the radius of a sphere, what happens to the volume?

5.   (a) Is the interior of a cube a convex set? (b) Is the interior of
a pyramid a convex set? (c) Is the interior of a sphere a convex set?

10.3   Lateral Area

Each of the solids in the preceding sections also has a surface, or *lateral*, area; for example, the lateral area of the cube is the six squares which comprise the faces of the cube. Each face of the rectangular solid is a rectangle; thus its lateral area is the sum of the areas of each face. The lateral area of the cube is

$$LA = 6 \cdot x^2$$

where x is the length of one side of a square. To obtain the lateral area of the rectangular solid, find the area of each face (the faces of the rectangular solid come in pairs) and then add these areas. The same may be used when the sides are parallelograms rather than rectangles.

For the pyramid, the process is similar. Find the area of each side and the area of the base and add them. The cone is treated in a similar fashion, but the faces have an irregular shape. However, for a right circular cone it is possible to give the lateral area as

$$LA = \pi r \sqrt{r^2 + h^2}$$

where r is the radius of the base and h is the altitude of the cone. The total surface area is obtained by adding πr^2 to the above.

Another ordinary solid which has a surface area given by formula is the sphere:

$$A = 4\pi r^2$$

where r is the radius of the sphere.

Most of the more complicated solids are not included in elementary school mathematics. It is possible to identify by intuitive example these solids, since most of them exist in the world around us, but the development of certain volumes and surface areas is best left to more advanced classes in mathematics. One way of developing some surface areas is by paper folding. For example, a cube can be made by cutting a pattern from paper and folding it along the lines. Figure 10.23 is but one example. Try to find other ways to arrange the six squares so that they fold into a cubic shape.

The total surface of the cylinder can be illustrated in a like manner. Take a tin can and cut off the two circular ends. Cut the side from top to bottom and lay it out flat (fig. 10.24). The areas of the top and bottom of the can are circular areas, each of which can be computed by $A = \pi r^2$, where r is the radius. The rectangular piece is h high by the circumference of the circle wide. The circumference is $2\pi r$ where the r is the

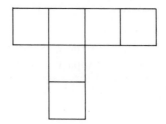

FIGURE 10.23

radius of the circle. Thus the total surface area is

$$\text{Area} = 2 \cdot \pi r^2 + 2\pi r \cdot h$$

Other geometric surfaces can be treated in a similar manner. Try constructing a surface which has a face in the shape of a regular pentagon. How many faces will the surface have? Is there a use for such a surface?

FIGURE 10.24

Exercises

1.   Find the areas of the following:
(a) a rectangle with length of 7 and width of 4
(b) a square with sides of 3
(c) a square with a diagonal of $5\sqrt{2}$
(d) a parallelogram with a height of 8 and a base of 4
(e) the following trapezoid:

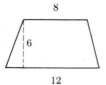

2.   Is a square a rectangle? Is a rectangle a parallelogram? Is a parallelogram a trapezoid? Is this concept different from your previous concept of these words? Look up the definitions of these words in an elementary textbook series and compare.

3.   Cut out a parallelogram and its interior from a piece of paper. Draw a diagonal, and cut along it. What two figures did you obtain? Are they precisely the same size and shape? Give a statement of the area of one of these shapes in terms of the area of a parallelogram.

4.   What is the volume of a rectangular box which is 12 units long, 3 wide and 4 deep? Since we did not specify the dimensions in feet, inches or miles, what is the unit of the volume?

5.   Find the volumes of the following:
(a) a sphere of radius 4 inches and one of 8 inches. Did the volume increase twice as much when we doubled the radius?
(b) a pyramid with a square base, 300 feet on a side, and with a height of 250 feet. If the pyramid is made of stone which weighs 60 lb per cubic foot, what does it weigh?
(c) a cylinder with a height of 12 inches and a base with a radius of 3 inches. If it were made of stone weighing 60 lb per cubic foot, what would it weigh?

6.   Find the lateral area of the following:
(a) a sphere with radius of 4 and one with radius of 8. Did the lateral area double when the radius was doubled?
(b) the cylinder of Exercise 5(c)
(c) the rectangular box of Exercise 4

11

OTHER SETS
OF NUMBERS

11.1　Introduction

When we developed the whole numbers and fractions in earlier chapters, we dealt with only the nonnegatives. We purposely neglected negatives to parallel the development of arithmetic concepts in the elementary school. Now we are ready to extend our previously developed concepts in other directions. The projected use of the negatives in elementary school is not an impossibility. Although it is doubtful that the concepts of negatives will be developed as far as they are by algebra, it is important for the elementary teacher to know how his work in mathematics is related to what the students will study in years to follow.

In this chapter we shall be somewhat more mathematical and will formally define portions of our presentations; we will devote a little less of our discussions to the intuitive development of concepts.

11.2   Integers

In developing the operations for the set of whole numbers, we found that we had to make certain restrictions on the operations of subtraction and division. For division, we defined $a \div b$, $b \neq 0$, to be c if and only if $a = b \cdot c$ and c is a whole number. In chapter 7 on fractions, we discovered that

$$a \div b = \frac{a}{b} \qquad b \neq 0$$

We noted that division of whole numbers sometimes produced fractions and that the above definition could be extended beyond the original intent. We defined the operation of subtraction:

$$a - b = c \quad \text{if and only if } a = b + c$$

where a, b and c are whole numbers. We subsequently noted that this definition has meaning if and only if $a - b \geq 0$; that is, the subtraction was limited to only those problems which produced whole numbers for answers.

We now wish to pursue the definition of subtraction in these cases which were not considered previously, that is, when $a - b$ is not greater than or equal to zero, then $a - b$ must be less than zero.

Consider the following example. If we have eight candy bars and give away five, we would have three candy bars left. We can represent this transaction by the following mathematical statement:

$$8 - 5 = 3 \quad \text{because } 8 = 5 + 3$$

Now suppose that we have five candy bars and we wish to give them away to eight people. If this is all that is required, we could give each person a portion of a bar and come out with equal portions for all eight people. Suppose that we want each person to get a whole bar. This does not appear to be possible unless we round up some more candy bars; moreover, if we try to write this as a corresponding subtraction problem, we have

$$5 - 8 = ?$$

If we borrow three candy bars from a neighbor, we would have enough to make a statement like

$$8 - 8 = 0$$

but then we owe our neighbor three candy bars. This is different from having three left from the first example; we need to identify the three in each case differently.

A bookkeeper would write the numeral 3, representing the candy bars left, in black ink and the 3, representing the candy bars owed, in red ink. By doing so, he would identify both the number of the bars and their status, i.e., whether they are leftover or owed. Mathematically, we do precisely the same thing by "tagging" the owed 3 with a small bar, $^-3$, with the bar placed at the upper left-hand corner of 3. We place it there to prevent any confusion with the subtraction sign. Thus we might write

$$5 - 8 = {}^-3$$

Mathematically, we are creating some new numbers of the form, $^-3$, $^-5$, $^-1$, etc., which we call negative integers. Since these are created from the whole numbers, we shall call them nonzero whole numbers, or positive integers. (We could call them red integers and black integers, but there are obvious difficulties about this.) The set of negative integers, positive integers and zero is called the set of integers.

One quick observation can be made as the result of the above definition of negative integers. The subtraction of whole numbers can be extended to include cases such as $5 - 8$, $10 - 17$, $3 - 19$, etc., for we have defined a new number to represent each case. We have

$$5 - 8 = {}^-3 \qquad 10 - 17 = {}^-7 \quad \text{and} \quad 3 - 19 = {}^-16$$

or

$$5 - 8 = {}^-(8 - 5) \qquad 10 - 17 = {}^-(17 - 10)$$

and

$$3 - 19 = {}^-(19 - 3)$$

Secondly, zero is not identified in our definition as either positive or negative. Intuitively, $^-0$ means "owes someone zero candy bars," a situation no different from having zero left. Hence, $^-0 = 0$ in our symbolism, and we categorize it as neither positive nor negative.

We could also adopt the notation of $^+3$ for a positive 3, which is another symbol for the whole number 3. Most of the time we will not use the $+$ in identifying the positive 3 in what follows. If a number does not have a $+$ or a $-$ preceding it, it is assumed to be positive.

We now turn to the task of developing the operations on the set of integers. We start with the operation of addition. It is clear that the sum of two positive integers is a positive integer because we have already defined addition for problems such as $3 + 5$, $7 + 9$, $10 + 34$. For the sums of two negative integers, consider the following problem:

$$^-3 + {}^-4 = ?$$

If we return to our interpretation of owing three candy bars and also owing four candy bars, we see that we owe a total of seven candy bars. Hence,

$$^-3 + {}^-4 = {}^-(3 + 4) = {}^-7$$

This meaning is consistent with our interpretation and gives an intuitive example, formalized as

$$^-a + {}^-b = {}^-(a + b)$$

Given the problem $^-3 + 4$, we can also apply our interpretation to find an answer. If we owe three and have four, then we will end up with one left. So

$$^-3 + 4 = 1$$

On the other hand, if we have $^-4 + 3$, we see we still owe one so

$$^-4 + 3 = {}^-1$$

Both of these cases can be formalized as follows:

$$^-a + b = (b - a) \quad \text{if } b > a$$

and

$$^-a + b = {}^-(a - b) \quad \text{if } a > b$$

If we have $^-3 + 3$, our interpretation leaves us with 0. Thus,

$$^-3 + 3 = 0$$

and, formally,

$$^-a + a = 0$$

This statement is parallel to one that we found about fractions, i.e., the concept of an inverse. When dealing with negatives, we call the inverse the additive inverse; we call ^-a the additive inverse of a because

$$^-a + a = 0$$

and zero is the additive identity element of the set of integers. Each positive integer thus has an additive inverse and each negative integer has an additive inverse. Since $0 + 0 = 0$, zero has an additive inverse, namely zero. Moreover, each integer has a unique inverse.

We summarize the addition of integers in the following definitions.

1. $a + b = a + b$, if a and b are positive integers.
2. $^-a + {}^-b = {}^-(a + b)$, if ^-a and ^-b are negative integers.
3. $^-a + b = (b - a)$, if $b > a$.
4. $^-a + b = {}^-(a - b)$, if $a > b$.
5. $^-a + a = 0$.

It is easy to see from the definitions above that the operation of addition on negatives is commutative. Also, the operation is associative, but we will not prove it here. We have already indicated that there is an additive identity.

We now turn to the multiplication of integers. We again consider the definition of the operation by cases.

1. $a \cdot b = a \cdot b$, if a and b are positive integers. (This definition is the same as that for the products of whole numbers.)
2. $^-a \cdot b = {}^-(a \cdot b)$, if b is a positive integer.

We can justify the above definitions if we think of ^-a as a debt of a units and there being b such debts. The total debt becomes $^-(a \cdot b)$. For example, $^-3 \cdot 2 = {}^-3 + {}^-3 = {}^-6 = {}^-(3 \cdot 2)$.

3. $(^-a)(^-b) = a \cdot b$.

Case (3) is harder to justify by our debt interpretation because it is difficult to think of ^-b such debts. Consider the following problem:

$$(^-a)(^-b) + {}^-(a \cdot b) = \text{?}$$

We know

$$^-(a \cdot b) = (^-a)(b)$$

so

$$^-(a)(^-b) + {}^-(a \cdot b) = (^-a)(^-b) + (^-a)(b)$$

If we assume that the distributive property holds for integers, we can write

$$(^-a)(^-b) + (^-a)(b) = (^-a)[^-b + b]$$

But $[^-b + b] = 0$, so, summarizing, we have

$$(^-a)(^-b) + {}^-(a \cdot b) = (^-a)(^-b) + (^-a)(b)$$
$$= (^-a)[^-b + b]$$
$$= (^-a) \cdot 0$$

If we know that $(^-a) \cdot 0 = 0$, we finally have

$$(^-a)(^-b) + {}^-(a \cdot b) = 0$$

Hence, by the definition of additive inverse, we know that $(-a)(-b)$ is the additive inverse of $^-(a \cdot b)$. But since $^-(a \cdot b)$ is a negative integer and its additive inverse must be positive, $(-a)(-b)$ is a positive integer. In particular, $(-a)(-b) = a \cdot b$.

The definition of multiplication of integers is summarized as follows:

1. $a \cdot b = a \cdot b$, if a and b are positive integers.
2. $(^-a) \cdot b = {}^-(a \cdot b)$ and $(a) \cdot (^-b) = {}^-(a \cdot b)$.
3. $(^-a)(^-b) = (a \cdot b)$.

We can show that the following statements are true for multiplication of integers. We shall assume that

1. $a \cdot 0 = 0$ for a being any integer.
2. multiplication is commutative.
3. multiplication is associative.
4. the distributive property for multiplication over addition holds for integers.
5. there is a multiplicative identity element, namely, 1, such that $a \cdot 1 = a$ for all integers a.
6. $^-a = {}^-1 \cdot a$.
7. If $a \cdot b = 0$, then $a = 0$ or $b = 0$, a, b being integers.

We now consider the operation of subtraction on integers. We borrow the definition for subtraction from whole numbers and omit the restrictions.

DEFINITION 11.1 $a - b = c$, if and only if $a = b + c$, where a, b and c are integers.

We noted earlier in this chapter that if $a - b \geq 0$, we have the whole number definition, where a and b are positive integers. If $a - b < 0$ and a and b are positive integers, $a - b = ^-(b - a)$. We need to consider only the following three cases:

1. $(^-a) - (b)$,
2. $(^-a) - (^-b)$,
3. $(a) - (^-b)$,

where a, b are symbols for positive integers.

For Case (1), by definition, there is a c such that

$$(^-a) - (b) = c \quad \text{if and only if} \quad (-a) = b + c$$

Since b is positive, and $b + c$ is negative, then c must be negative. It must be large enough to offset b and at the same time yield ^-a. It is not too difficult to see that c must be equal to $^-b + ^-a$:

$$(^-a) = b + c$$

We can check this by letting $c = ^-(b + a)$:

$$b + c = b + ^-(b + a)$$
$$= b + (^-b + ^-a)$$
$$= (b + ^-b) + ^-a$$
$$= 0 + ^-a$$
$$= ^-a$$

and we have determined that

$$(^-a) - (b) = ^-(b + a) \quad \text{or} \quad (^-a) - (b) = ^-(a) + (^-b)$$

For Case (2), we follow the above procedure and determine the value of c.

$$(^-a) - (^-b) = c \quad \text{if and only if} \quad (^-a) = (^-b) + c$$

It is easy to see that c must be $(^-a + b)$. Therefore

$$(^-a) - (^-b) = ^-a + b$$

For Case (3), we again find c.

$$a - (^-b) = c \quad \text{if and only if } a = (^-b) + c$$

The value for c must be $(b + a)$. Therefore

$$a - (^-b) = a + b$$

If a or b or both are zero, the same cases hold and our values for c are simplified; and we obtain corresponding values.

It is also possible to use a shortcut in the operation of subtraction. In every case, (1)-(3), the original subtraction problem was converted to an addition problem, one involving the additive inverse of one of the numbers. For example,

$$(^-a) - (b) = ^-a + ^-b$$

$$(^-a) - (^-b) = ^-a + b$$

$$a - (^-b) = a + b$$

This is, of course, due to our definition of subtraction. The student should attempt to formulate a statement which describes the algorithm for these cases.

For the operation of division, we have a situation quite similar to division on whole numbers. First, not all division problems of integers will produce an integer, so we will have to limit division to the problems which do produce integers. We borrow the definition from the whole numbers.

DEFINITION 11.2 $a \div b = c$, if and only if $a = b \cdot c$, where a, b and c are integers and $b \neq 0$.

Definition 11.2 clearly applies to the positive integers. We need only to consider the following cases:

1. $^-a \div b$,

2. $a \div ^-b$,

3. $^-a \div ^-b$.

In the first two cases, it is easy to see that the c which fits the definition must be a negative integer, for

$$^-a \div b = c \quad \text{if and only if } ^-a = b \cdot c$$

Since the product is negative and b is positive, then c must be a negative integer. Moreover, c must be the same as $a \div b$. Hence,

$$^-a \div b = {}^-(a \div b)$$

Similarly,

$$a \div {}^-b = {}^-(a \div b)$$

In the third case,

$$(^-a) \div (^-b) = c$$
$$(^-a) = (^-b) \cdot c$$

Since the product $(^-b) \cdot c$ is negative, and ^-b is a negative integer, c must be a positive integer. Moreover,

$$c = a \div b$$

Therefore,

$$(^-a) \div (^-b) = (a \div b)$$

We also observe that every division problem involving integers is expressible as a problem involving the positive integers or whole numbers and the additive inverses of these numbers.

Exercises

1. Find the following:
(a) $2 + (^-3)$
(b) $(^-3) + (^-7)$
(c) $(^-5) + (2)$
(d) $(^-7) - (2)$
(e) $(7) - (^-2)$
(f) $8 - 3$
(g) $(^-8) - (^-10)$
(h) $(^-2)(3)$
(i) $(^-3)(^-7)$
(j) $(4)(9)$
(k) $(3)(^-8)$
(l) $(^-3) \div (3)$
(m) $(^-9) \div (^-3)$
(n) $28 \div (^-4)$

2. Find the following:
(a) ^-a if a is a positive integer
(b) $^-(^-a)$ if a is a positive integer
(c) ^-a if a is a negative integer
(d) $^-(^-a)$ if a is a negative integer
(e) ^-a if a is zero
(f) $^-(^-a)$ if a is zero

3.   If we put the integers on a number line, we might have the following figure:

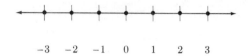

$$-3 \quad -2 \quad -1 \quad 0 \quad 1 \quad 2 \quad 3$$

Find a way to work addition and subtraction problems of positive and negative integers on this number line.

4.   Suppose we define "is less than" on integers as follows: $a < b$, if and only if there exists a positive integer c such that $a + c = b$. Put the following numbers in order using this definition: $^-3, 7, 4, 1, {}^-5, 0, {}^-1$.

5.   In the summary at the end of chapter 9, there are eight statements under the category of cancellation properties. Which of these statements are also true for the set of integers? Can those statements which are not true be restated in some manner which would make true corresponding statements?

11.3   Rational Numbers

We have extended the whole numbers to include the integers by defining negative integers, and we have developed some of the properties on this set of integers. Now we will extend the set of fractions and develop the set of rational numbers. We shall refer to the fractions, except zero, as the positive rationals and define the set of all rationals to be of the form

$$\frac{a}{b} \qquad b \neq 0$$

where a and b can be positive or negative integers. If a and b are positive integers or if $a = 0$, we have the set of fractions previously defined in chapter 7.

Following the development in that chapter we define the equality of two rational numbers as follows:

$$\frac{a}{b} = \frac{c}{d} \quad \text{if and only if } ad = bc$$

where a and b are integers and $b \neq 0$, $d \neq 0$. We have, as a consequence of this definition, the following properties:

$$\frac{-p}{q} = \frac{p}{-q} \quad \text{because} \quad (-p)(-q) = p \cdot q$$

$$\frac{-p}{-q} = \frac{p}{q} \quad \text{because} \quad (-p)(q) = (p)(-q)$$

These two properties, along with the definition of equality of rationals, enable us to establish equivalence classes. For example, we have for the rational number 1/2 the following set of symbols:

$$\left\{ \cdots \frac{-4}{-8}, \frac{-3}{-6}, \frac{-2}{-4}, \frac{-1}{-2}, \frac{1}{2}, \frac{2}{4}, \frac{3}{6}, \frac{4}{8}, \cdots \right\}$$

For $-1/2$ we have

$$\left\{ \cdots \frac{-4}{8}, \frac{-3}{6}, \frac{-2}{4}, \frac{-1}{2}, \frac{1}{-2}, \frac{2}{-4}, \frac{3}{-6}, \frac{4}{-8}, \cdots \right\}$$

Moreover, we could prove that the equality for rational numbers is an equivalence relation; that is, equality is reflexive, symmetric and transitive. We leave this for the student to do as an exercise.

We define addition on rational numbers by using the common denominator definition.

DEFINITION 11.3 $a/b + c/b = (a + c)/b$, where $b \neq 0$ and a, b, c are integers.

For example,

$$\frac{2}{3} + \frac{-4}{3} = \frac{2 + (-4)}{3} = \frac{-2}{3}$$

or

$$\frac{-7}{-5} + \frac{-3}{-5} = \frac{(-7) + (-3)}{-5} = \frac{-10}{-5}$$

or

$$\frac{4}{-7} + \frac{0}{-7} = \frac{4 + 0}{-7} = \frac{4}{-7}$$

In the last example, $0/-7$ serves as an additive identity. For the positive rationals we noted earlier that the fraction $0/7$ was the additive identity. This means $0/-7$ and $0/7$ belong to the same equivalence class because

$$\frac{0}{-7} = \frac{0}{7}$$

Since the set of rationals has an additive identity, it is possible to define the additive inverse for rationals.

DEFINITION 11.4   If for each rational number a/b, $b \neq 0$, a and b are integers, there exists a rational number $^-(a/b)$ such that

$$\frac{a}{b} + {}^-\!\left(\frac{a}{b}\right) = \frac{0}{b}$$

then the rational number $^-(a/b)$ is called the additive inverse of a/b.

From Definition 11.4 we see that the notation $^-(a/b)$ must mean $-a/b$ or else we would not be able to add the rationals. Hence, we define the notation

$$^-\!\left(\frac{a}{b}\right) = \frac{-a}{b}$$

and the additive inverse of a/b is $-a/b$. Although we could also prove that this inverse is unique, for the sake of convenience, we assume that it is.

It is not difficult to prove that addition of rationals is commutative and associative. We assume that the associative property is true; the proof of the commutative property, $a/b + c/b = c/b + a/b$, follows.

Proof   We know that

$$\frac{a}{b} + \frac{c}{b} = \frac{a+c}{b}$$

$$= \frac{c+a}{b}$$

By definition,

$$\frac{a}{b} + \frac{c}{b} = \frac{c}{b} + \frac{a}{b}$$

and the proof is completed.

We define subtraction as we defined it for the fractions (nonnegative rationals).

DEFINITION 11.5 $a/b - c/b = (a - c)/b$,   where $b \neq 0$, and a, b and c are integers.

Note that Definition 11.5 does not require (as in chapter 7) that $a - c > 0$, because we can determine $a - c$ regardless of the size of a and c, since we are dealing with integers. We cite two examples:

$$\frac{4}{3} - \frac{8}{3} = \frac{4 - 8}{3} = \frac{-4}{3}$$

or

$$\frac{-9}{5} - \frac{-12}{5} = \frac{(-9) - (-12)}{5} = \frac{(-9) + (12)}{5} = \frac{3}{5}$$

It is also clear that subtraction is not commutative. For example,

$$\frac{4}{3} - \frac{8}{3} = \frac{-4}{3} \qquad \frac{8}{3} - \frac{4}{3} = \frac{4}{3} \quad \text{and} \quad \frac{-4}{3} \neq \frac{4}{3}$$

For the operation of multiplication, we use the same definition for rationals as we did for fractions (see chapter 7).

DEFINITION 11.6 $a/b \cdot c/d = ac/bd$,   where a, b, c, d are integers and $b \neq 0$, $d \neq 0$.

For example,

$$\frac{-2}{-3} \cdot \frac{-4}{7} = \frac{(-2)(-4)}{(-3)(7)} = \frac{8}{-21}$$

or

$$\frac{2}{5}\cdot\frac{7}{-10} = \frac{2\cdot 7}{5(-10)} = \frac{14}{-50}$$

or

$$\frac{-4}{9}\cdot\frac{-3}{-3} = \frac{(-4)(-3)}{(9)(-3)} = \frac{12}{-27}$$

In the last example, note that

$$\frac{-4}{9} = \frac{12}{-27} \quad \text{because } (-4)(-27) = (12)(9)$$

Hence, the fraction $-3/-3$ must be the representation for the multiplicative identity element, just as $3/3$ was in the set of fractions. Moreover, since $-3/-3 = 3/3$ we have the same multiplicative identity for rational numbers as we have for fractions; it is also unique.

We could make all the comments here about reducing rationals as we did in chapter 7 about reducing fractions. In addition, the entire development of the least common denominator approach is appropriate for rationals. The one step which may be needed first is illustrated by the following example.

$$\frac{3}{-4} + \frac{-7}{-5} = ?$$

We first rewrite the fractions with positive integers as denominators:

$$\frac{3}{-4} + \frac{-7}{-5} = \frac{-3}{4} + \frac{7}{5}$$

Now we apply the common denominator technique and proceed with the problem.

For the operation of division for rationals, we simply extend the fraction definition in chapter 7. Moreover, it is possible to apply the algorithm process to rationals as well as to positive fractions.

THEOREM 11.1 $a/b \div c/d = a/b \cdot d/c$, if $b \neq 0,\, d \neq 0,\, c \neq 0$ and a, b, c and d are integers.

Theorem 11.1 also suggests multiplicative inverses, that is, the multiplicative inverse of c/d, $c \neq 0$, $d \neq 0$, is d/c.

The properties for multiplication and division of rationals are the same as those for the positive rationals. They are (a) multiplication is associative, and (b) multiplication is commutative. It is also possible to prove that the distributive property for multiplication over addition holds for the rationals. In fact, the listing of properties in the summary of chapter 7 can be the listing of properties for operation on rationals. The cancellation properties hold, and if we define "is less than" as we did in chapter 7, these properties also hold with a slight change in number 19. What must that change be?

The one concept that we discussed in chapter 7 which is rarely applied to negative rationals is the mixed number notation. For example, how would $-7/3$ be written as a mixed number? It could not be written as $2 - 1/3$; $^{-}2 - 1/3$ is possible, but not $-2\frac{1}{3}$ which would be read as $^{-}2 + 1/3$. Other possibilities are $^{-}(2\frac{1}{3})$ and $^{-}(2 + 1/3)$.

Exercises

1. Find the following:
(a) $-2/3 + 3/-4$
(b) $-2/-5 + -3/7$
(c) $5/-2 - 3/2$
(d) $4/5 - (-7/4)$
(e) $3/4 \cdot -7/-3$
(f) $(-2/-5)(-3/-4)$
(g) $3/4 \div -3/5$
(h) $(-3/-5) \div (-2/-3)$
(i) $(-2/-7) \cdot (-3/-3)$
(j) $(4/-9) \cdot (0/-2)$

2. Is it possible to define $p \div q$, $q \neq 0$, where p and q are integers, to be the rational number p/q?

3. Draw a number line and locate the following rational numbers on it: $-3/2$, $2/3$, 1, $-6/-3$, $3/-4$, $-1/1$. Is $-3/2 < 3/-4$? Is $-6/-3 < 1$?

4. What is the additive inverse of each of the following:

(a) $\dfrac{2}{3}$

(b) $\dfrac{-2}{3}$

(c) $\dfrac{2}{-3}$

(d) $\dfrac{-2}{-3}$

5. What is the multiplicative inverse of each of the following:

(a) $\dfrac{-2}{3}$

(b) $\dfrac{-4}{-7}$

(c) $\dfrac{5}{-9}$

(d) $\dfrac{0}{-7}$

12

THE METRIC SYSTEM

12.1 The Metric System as an Extension of the Place Value System

The following are typical units in the metric system:

$$1 \text{ centimeter} = 10 \text{ millimeters}$$

$$1 \text{ decimeter} = 10 \text{ centimeters}$$

$$1 \text{ meter} = 10 \text{ decimeters}$$

In the various relations among these given units, the multiples are multiples of 10. This suggests that the various units in the metric system exhibit behavior similar to that of the place value system. For example, in place value language, we can write

$$1 \text{ ten } = \text{ ten } 1\text{'s}$$

$$1 \text{ hundred } = \text{ ten } 10\text{'s}$$

$$1 \text{ thousand } = \text{ ten } 100\text{'s}$$

In comparing the two tables given here, we note the suggested similarity. Replace *1's* by *millimeters* and *ten* by *centimeters*, and the first line of the place value becomes the first line of the metric measurement. Thus, the metric system of linear measure is a type of place value system representation.

12.2   Units of Metric Measure

As with any system of measure, we must select a standard unit of measure. In the metric system, the standard unit for linear measure is a meter. It was first believed that the meter was one ten-millionth of the distance from the equator to the North Pole, but as better methods of measuring the earth were developed, it became evident that the above description of a meter was not accurate. The exact description of a meter is the distance between two marks on a certain bar of platinum iridium kept at the temperature of melting ice. The standard bar is kept at the International Bureau of Weights and Measures in France. The Bureau of Standards in the United States has a similar bar which is a copy of the original. With the meter as a starting unit, other units of length in the metric system are defined as multiples of the meter or as fractional parts of the meter. The multiples and fractional parts are determined by powers of 10. For example,

$$1 \text{ dekameter } = 10 \text{ meters}$$

$$1 \text{ hectometer } = 10 \text{ dekameters}$$

$$1 \text{ kilometer } = 10 \text{ hectometers}$$

Thus, if we take 10 meters of length, a new unit of measure can be defined, called a dekameter. In the word *dekameter, deka* means ten; hence, dekameter means 10 meters. The reluctance of most people to convert from our system of measure to the metric system is based, in part, on the necessity of learning a new vocabulary. However, the words, when analyzed, help clarify the meaning. Similarly, 1 hectometer means 10 dekameters. We might have chosen to call a hectometer a deka-dekameter, for that is its literal meaning. Thus, a hectometer is 10 dekameters, or more specifically, expressed in terms of a meter, 100 meters. In the same fashion, a kilometer means 1,000 meters, *kilo* meaning 1,000 and meter being 1 meter in length.

This may be summarized in the following table:

$$1 \text{ dekameter} = 10 \text{ meters}$$

$$1 \text{ hectometer} = 10 \text{ dekameters} = 100 \text{ meters}$$

$$1 \text{ kilometer} = 10 \text{ hectometers} = 1,000 \text{ meters}$$

For units of measure smaller than a meter in length, we have the following:

$$1 \text{ decimeter} = \frac{1}{10} \text{ meter}$$

$$1 \text{ centimeter} = \frac{1}{10} \text{ decimeter}$$

$$1 \text{ millimeter} = \frac{1}{10} \text{ centimeter}$$

The word *decimeter* is made up of *deci*, meaning 1/10, and *meter*, meaning 1 meter in length. Hence, decimeter means 1/10 meter. Since a centimeter is equal to 1/10 decimeter and a decimeter is 1/10 meter, a centimeter means 1/100 meter. Similarly a millimeter means 1/1,000 meter. (We could not use *kilo* again because we would have one word meaning two different things, so the word *milli* is used here.)

These relations may also be put in the following form:

$$1 \text{ decimeter} = \frac{1}{10} \text{ meter, or .1 meter}$$

$$1 \text{ centimeter} = \frac{1}{10} \text{ decimeter, or .01 meter}$$

$$1 \text{ millimeter} = \frac{1}{10} \text{ centimeter, or .001 meter}$$

Here we have used the decimal form for 1/10 meter, 1/100 meter and 1/1,000 meter. Note the usefulness of the place value system in base ten in expressing these relations.

In general, these seven units of linear measure are sufficient for most uses by most people in the world. Larger and smaller units are possible and can be found in tables of metric measure in science books. However, they are not necessary for our purposes, so we omit them.

If we wish to weigh objects in the metric system, we must start with a standard unit of weight. The unit in the metric system is the gram. As we will see later, the gram is approximately .035 ounce, a small unit of measure. In exactly the same fashion as in linear measure, we describe other units in terms of the gram. Hence,

$$1 \text{ dekagram} = 10 \text{ grams}$$

$$1 \text{ hectogram} = 10 \text{ dekagrams} = 100 \text{ grams}$$

$$1 \text{ kilogram} = 10 \text{ hectograms} = 1,000 \text{ grams}$$

One of the positive factors of using a metric system of measure is that the words chosen have continuity with each type of measurement. For example, dekagram means 10 grams and dekameter means 10 meters. If we had a deka-gob, it would mean 10 gobs. Thus, while in weights (mass) we are dealing with grams, the creation of additional units is accomplished in the same verbal fashion as in the lengths—by use of Latin prefixes, which carry the same meaning, i.e., dekameter and dekagrams.

Smaller units of weight can be identified in a corresponding fashion:

$$1 \text{ decigram} = \frac{1}{10} \text{ gram} = .1 \text{ gram}$$

$$1 \text{ centigram} = \frac{1}{10} \text{ decigram} = .01 \text{ gram}$$

$$1 \text{ milligram} = \frac{1}{10} \text{ centigrams} = .001 \text{ gram}$$

Note again the use of the Latin prefixes in the same context. One decimeter is .1 meter, and 1 decigram is .1 gram.

In the metric system the standard unit of capacity is the liter. A liter is 1.0567 liquid quarts or .9081 dry quart. Other units we generate in the same manner as linear measure, for example,

$$1 \text{ dekaliter} = 10 \text{ liters}$$

$$1 \text{ hectoliter} = 10 \text{ dekaliters} = 100 \text{ liters}$$

$$1 \text{ kiloliter} = 10 \text{ hectoliters} = 1,000 \text{ liters}$$

Again observe the use of the same prefixes that we used in linear and weight measure. For smaller capacities than a liter, we again use prefixes.

$$1 \text{ deciliter} = \frac{1}{10} \text{ liter} = .1 \text{ liter}$$

$$1 \text{ centiliter} = \frac{1}{10} \text{ deciliter} = .01 \text{ liter}$$

$$1 \text{ milliliter} = \frac{1}{10} \text{ centiliter} = .001 \text{ liter}$$

The use of the prefixes certainly simplifies the task of remembering what size unit we are using, whether it be linear weight or capacity. This is one of the advantages of using the metric system of measure. It probably does not appear to be an advantage, since we already know a given system, but we will find that a little effort will make this system as easy to handle as the one we now use. For the time being, the student should memorize these prefixes and their meanings.

Exercises

1. How many liters is 18.5 deciliters?

2. How many meters is 18.5 decimeters?

3. How many grams is 18.5 decigrams?

4. How many centimeters is 7.6 hectometers?

5. How many dekaliters is 127 centiliters?

6. Convert to decimeters:
(a) 39 millimeters   (b) 4,956 millimeters
(c) 39 centimeters   (d) 86 meters
(e) 1.76 hectometers   ·(f) .06 kilometer

7. If a rectangle is 8 centimeters long and 6 centimeters wide, what is its area? What is the unit of area?

8. If a cube is 2 meters on an edge, what is its volume? What is the unit of volume?

9. If the area of a region is 4,625 square centimeters, what is its area when expressed in square decimeters? How many square centimeters is 1 square decimeter?

12.3   Conversion between Systems of Measure

In order to make a comparison between the two systems of measure, we must know a conversion factor from one system to the other. For example, from the definitions of the units of measure we know that 1 meter is 39.3700 inches. This piece of knowledge is all we need to compute several conversions for length:

Metric Unit	English Unit
1 meter	39.3700 inches
1 centimeter	.393700 inch
1 kilometer	.621372 mile
1 dekameter	10.9361 yards

Note that all of the conversions are from metric to some unit in the English system. It is also possible to convert the other way. For example, 1 inch is approximately 2.54 centimeters. It is not necessary to remember all conversions, but it is necessary to remember one conversion and know how to get the others. Consider this question: How many feet are in 10 meters? If we start with 10 meters and know that each meter is 39.37 inches, then 10 meters is 39,317 inches. Since it takes 12 inches to make a foot, then there are 393.7 ÷ 12 feet in 10 meters. If we know the one conversion fact and the relations between units within each system, it is possible to make the change from one system to another.

A word about the importance of converting from one system to another is in order. If or when the United States Congress passes a law putting the United States on the metric system of measure, then it will be extremely important to know how to convert from English to metric. In reality this is not too difficult if we remember three facts:

$$1 \text{ quart} = .9463 \text{ liter}$$
$$1 \text{ inch} = 2.54 \text{ centimeters}$$
$$1 \text{ ounce} = 28.349 \text{ grams}$$

These facts will make it easy to compare measure given in both systems. Changing from the English to the metric system will cause those of us who have used the English system for some time a little difficulty, and a period of adjustment will be necessary. For the new school youngster, conversion will not be needed. He will learn the metric system and no other!

All conversion problems are similar to the 10-meters-to-feet example. We do another involving weight.

Example 12.1   How many grams is 3.79 pounds? Since each pound contains 16 oz, 3.79 pounds would contain 2.79×16 or 60.64 ounces. Each ounce is equivalent to 28.35 grams, so $(60.64) \cdot (28.35)$ is the desired number of grams. Thus 3.79 pounds equals 1,719.144 grams.

Exercises

1.   Convert the following to the given metric units:
(a) 14 feet = _____ centimeters
(b) 3 rods = _____ kilometers (1 rod = 16.5 ft)
(c) 3 inches = _____ millimeters
(d) 14 pounds = _____ dekagrams
(e) 132 ounces = _____ hectograms
(f) 3.5 gallons = _____ liters

2.   Convert to the given English measure:
(a) 14 kilometers = _____ feet
(b) 1,295 millimeters = _____ inches
(c) 4,622 grams = _____ pounds
(d) 29 liters = _____ gallons
(e) 16 hectoliters = _____ pints
(f) 124 square centimeters = _____ square inches

13

THE LANGUAGE OF
INFORMATION

13.1   Introduction

The art of communication includes the passing of factual information
from one person to another. However, in ordinary language we are
frequently guilty of using imprecise words. For example, to say that
an elephant is big attempts to impart the notion of size by comparing
the elephant with other objects. An elephant is big in comparison to a
dime but small in comparison to the moon. In order to convey factual
information, we must be more precise than we were in the elephant
example. For this reason we try to formulate a precise definition of the
terms we use. For example, if we say the height of an average U.S. male
citizen is 5 feet 10 inches, we are incorrect in our choice of words. There
is no average U.S. male citizen. Such a creature does not exist. On the
other hand, if we take the heights of all U.S. male citizens, add them

together and divide by the number of U.S. male citizens we might very well obtain 5 feet, 10 inches. To be correct, we really should say the following: The average height of all U.S. male citizens is 5 feet, 10 inches.

There are certain words which appear frequently in print, and especially in educational literature, which are capable of being given precise mathematical definitions. In what follows we give a few examples.

13.2 The Average

We have already seen the word *average* used in the illustration of the preceding section. We now define it.

> **DEFINITION 13.1** The mathematical average of a set of numbers is obtained by finding the sum of the numbers and dividing this sum by the number of numbers. The quotient obtained is said to be the average of the numbers.

Example 13.1 Find the average of 6, 7, 8, 5, 4. The sum is 30, and if we divide 30 by 5, we obtain, as the average, 6. Note that the number which is the average is a member of the set. This need not be the case for other sets of numbers. The average of 7, 8, 9, 4 and 2 is also 6, and 6 is not a member of this set of numbers. In each case, 6 represents the number which indicates a central tendency of the set of numbers and little more. That the average height of U.S. male citizens is 5 feet 10 inches does not tell us what the range (tallest to shortest) of heights is or if more men are taller than this or not. It gives us a tendency trend of heights. If we know that the average heights of U.S. female citizens is 5 feet, 5 inches, we can make some comparisons. On the average, U.S. males are taller than U.S. females. However, a given male may be taller or shorter than, or the same height as, a given female. The average is a piece of data that conveys an overall picture.

Example 13.2 If John made test scores on examinations of 39, 72, 88, 91 and 66, what is his average test score? The sum of the scores is 356 and if we divide this sum by 5 (the number of test scores), we obtain the average of 71.2. An interesting application of this information is found when the passing average score would 70. John would pass even though he failed two of the tests.

Exercises

1.   Find the average for the following sets of numbers:
(a) 16, 19, 12, 10, 23, 16
(b) 70, 80, 90, 60, 50
(c) 6, 6, 6, 6, 6, 6
(d) 0, 4, 8, 12, 16
(e) 1, 2, 3, 4, 5, 6, 7

13.3   The Median

Along an interstate highway a sign often is posted between the strips of road which says "Keep off the Median." The sign is obviously intended to tell drivers not to drive on the grassy portion of the roadbed that separates the two strips of pavement. This grassy portion is the middle part of the highway right-of-way, referred to as the median. Hence, *median* means middle in this context. This also is the meaning of the word *median* as applied to a set of numbers. However, the numbers are ordered from smallest to largest. For example, the set of numbers 6, 7, 8, 5 and 4 when ordered becomes 4, 5, 6, 7, 8. In this set the median is 6. It is the middle number of the set of ordered numbers.

To make the idea of a median applicable to all sets of numbers, we define it to be the value of the number which is equal to or exceeded by exactly one-half of the values in the set of ordered numbers. In the example just cited, 6 was the median. However, this number was not equal to or exceeded by exactly one-half, since there were an odd number of members in the set. In this case we chose the number which was exceeded by the same number of numbers that it exceeded.

For the set 1, 2, 3, 4, 5, 6, the median lies between 3 and 4, so we normally pick the mean of this central pair of numbers, i.e., 3.5. In the first example the median is a member of the set and in the second example it is not. In both examples the median is also the mean of the set. However, the mean and median need not be the same. Consider the following example.

Example 13.3   In the set of numbers 2, 4, 7, 8, 9, the average was determined earlier to be 6 and the median is 7.

The median and the average are both indicators of the group of numbers in the set, but one does not necessarily convey the same idea about the set as the other. For example, if a student receives test scores of 0, 0, 0, 0, 100 and 100 in a given class, the median is 0 whereas the mean is $33\frac{1}{3}$. The median would, in this case, indicate at least one-half of the scores to be zero. The average would not indicate this. On the other hand, the average suggests that the range of scores perhaps varies above and below $33\frac{1}{3}$ (except in the case when all scores were exactly $33\frac{1}{3}$) and the median would not give any indication of this at all. Both measures are indicators of central tendencies, yet are not the same indicators.

Exercises

1.   Find the median of the following sets of numbers:
(a) 6, 7, 9, 14, 32   (b) 7, 9, 11, 13, 15
(c) 2, 7, 14, 8, 32, 19, 40   (d) 0, 0, 0, 10, 10, 10.

5.   In the exercises at the end of Section 13.2, find the median of the given sets.

6.   In which of these problems are the medians and averages different?

7.   Suppose a school board wishes to prove to its public that its teachers are well paid. The salaries are as follows:

Salary	No. of Teachers
$1,200	5
1,500	10
1,600	8
1,800	2
2,100	1
2,400	2
2,600	1
5,000	1

Which figure would best support the school board's position, the mean or the median? Should the teachers use that same figure in asking for more money?

8.   Sometimes another term is used to indicate something about a set of numbers. If a number occurs more than any other, it is sometimes called a *mode*. In Exercise 7 which teacher's salary is a mode? Would the teachers have a better figure if they were to use the mode rather than the average or median in their requests for increased salaries?

13.4 Graphs

One of the convenient ways to give information is in a table such as table 13.1. These scores represent the scores of the beginning bowling class. The mode score is 130. More people bowled scores around the mode score than any other. The average and the median could also be computed from the above data. The table reveals a range of scores from 100 to 165 inclusive. It is also possible to put these data in another form which is as easy to read and, at the same time, reveals additional information. This form is called a graph. The graph might take one of three forms: a bar graph, a line graph or a point graph.

TABLE 13.1

Bowling Score	No. of People Who Made This Score
100	3
105	5
110	7
115	12
120	17
125	18
130	21
135	19
140	16
145	11
150	9
155	6
160	4
165	2

Graph A (fig. 13.1) is a point graph. The axes of the graph are the scores bowled and the number of bowlers who bowled a particular score. The two columns of the table then become the two axes of the graph. The points are located to indicate the relationship between the two numbers. For example, the dot opposite 4 and directly about 160 indicates that four bowlers made scores of 160.

Graph B (fig. 13.2) is a bar graph which represents the same data. The axes are the same, but instead of a point we use a vertical bar to represent the relationship. This bar graph has an advantage over the point graph in that it is easier to see the differences and recognize the mode as being the tallest. It is also easier to see that the median (middle score) is about 130, for the bar at 130 divides almost evenly the bars into two groups which are the same size. The median is 130.

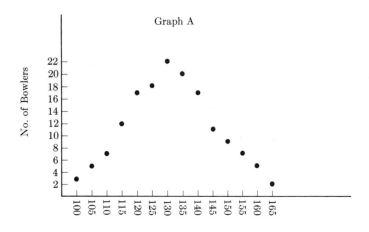

FIGURE 13.1

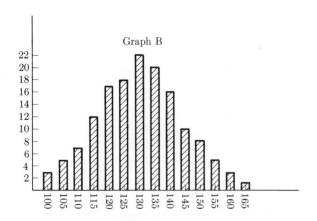

FIGURE 13.2

Graph C (fig. 13.3) is a line graph which represents the same data. It is formed by connecting the points of the point graph to make a broken line. Again observe that the graph can be used to find certain facts such as the mode.

It is not important which form of the graph one uses, as all convey the same idea. The line graph may be more pleasing to the eye in that it is easier to see a total picture at a glance; it is probably the most common one used.

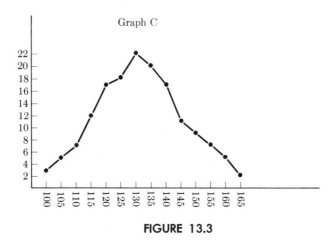

FIGURE 13.3

Since a graph is intended to tell facts about data, one should be able to glance at a line graph and see these facts without effort, for example, figure 13.4. Suppose this is the graph of the stock market averages for the twelve months of a given year. What happened to the market during the year? A first possible observation is that there were two times when the market reached a high of 950 and three months when the market reached a low of 800. The first half of the year reflects a somewhat steady increase from 800 to 950. Something drastic happened between June and July as the market dropped quite rapidly. A somewhat sharp rise took place between September and October. We could draw some other conclusions from the graph, but these are enough to see that the graph is a viable means of conveying information with a picture.

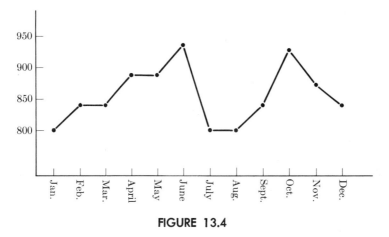

FIGURE 13.4

Exercises

1.   Given the years and the number of automobiles made by the Horseless Gang Company, put in graph form:

1910—2	1925—6	1940—60
1915—12	1930—30	1945—0
1920—40	1935—50	1950—10

Describe some trends for this company. What might be a cause for the 1945 data?

2.   Locate the following pairs on a graph: (2, 2), (3, 3), (4, 4), (5, 5), (6, 6) and (7, 7). Draw a line graph. What kind of line graph did you obtain?

3.   Look up the population figures for the United States from 1800 to 1970. What would you predict as the 1980 population? How could one arrive at this figure using the graph?

INDEX

INDEX

Associative property
  addition, 46, 149, 264, 270
  intersection of sets, 30
  multiplication, 50, 150, 264, 270
  union of sets, 30
Average, 284

Base five, 114
  addition, 121
  multiplication, 123
Base twelve, 129
  addition, 130
  multiplication, 130
Base two, 125
  addition, 128
  multiplication, 128
Betweenness, 203
Binary operation, 43
"Borrowing," 103

Cancellation property
  for addition of fractions, 162, 164
  for addition of whole numbers, 70, 71
  for multiplication of fractions, 162, 164
  for multiplication of whole numbers, 70, 71
Cardinal number, 42
"Carrying," 78
Centigram, 278
Centiliter, 279
Centimeter, 277
Circle, 234
  area, 248
Closure, 43
Collinear, 206
Commutative property
  of addition, 44, 144, 264
  intersection of sets, 29
  of multiplication, 49, 148, 263, 272
  union of sets, 29
Convexity, 227
Coordinate system, 207
Correspondence, one-to-one, 37
Counter example, 55
Cube, volume of, 250
Curves
  closed, 226
  convex, 227

Curves (*continued*)
  interior of, 227
  simple, 226
  simple closed, 226
  simple convex closed, 227
Cylinder, volume of, 252

Decigram, 278
Deciliter, 279
Decimals, 173
  converting to fractions, 178
  expanded numeral form, 175
  finite, 175
  infinite repeating, 178
  nonrepeating, 191
  operations on, 182
  rounding off, 189
Decimeter, 277
Dekagram, 278
Dekaliter, 278
Dekameter, 276
Denominator, 135
  least common, 153
Distance, 206
Distributive property
  addition over multiplication, 54
  intersection over union, 30
  multiplication over addition, 52
  multiplication over subtraction, 68
  union over intersection, 30
Division
  fractions, 157
  integers, 266
  rationals, 272
  whole numbers, 69
  by zero, 69

Element, 20
Empty set, 21
Equality
  of fractions, 136
  of rational numbers, 268
  of sets, 24
Equivalence relation, 138, 269
Expanded numeral form, 12
Exponent, 11
  properties, 13
  zero, 14
Exponential notation, 12